Java™ Studio
Creator
Field Guide

Gail Anderson • Paul Anderson

Sun Microsystems Press
A Prentice Hall Title

Prentice Hall PTR, Upper Saddle River, NJ 07458
www.phptr.com

© 2004 Gail Anderson and Paul Anderson
Published by Prentice Hall PTR
Prentice-Hall, Inc.
Upper Saddle River, NJ 07458

Prentice Hall PTR offers excellent discounts on this book when ordered in quantity for bulk purchases or special sales. For more information, please contact U.S. Corporate and Government Sales, 1-800-382-3419, corpsales@pearsontechgroup.com. For sales outside of the U.S., please contact International Sales, 1-317-581-3793, international@pearsontechgroup.com.

Acquisitions Editor: *Gregory G. Doench*
Editorial Assistant: *Raquel Kaplan*

Sun Microsystems Press Publisher: *Myrna Rivera*

ISBN: 0-13-149168-7
Text printed on recycled paper
2 3 4 5 6 7 8 9 10 11—CRS—0807060504
Second printing, July 2004

Sun Microsystems Press
A Prentice Hall Title

Contents

CHAPTER 2   CREATOR BASICS   20

CHAPTER 3   JSF STANDARD COMPONENTS 52

CHAPTER 4 PAGE NAVIGATION 96

CHAPTER 5   JAVABEANS COMPONENTS 124

CHAPTER 7   ACCESSING DATABASES 204

CHAPTER 9   DEBUGGING WITH CREATOR 302

Foreword

The developers who set out to build Java Studio Creator had a very difficult task: to make the creation of sophisticated enterprise applications easy.

The set of technologies that comprise Java2 Enterprise Edition (J2EE) is huge. The good side is that J2EE is battle hardened and field proven to be an excellent base for large scale mission critical applications. There are many excellent books that cover all of the aspects of J2EE in great detail. But all of this leads to the bad side of J2EE: it can be difficult and time-consuming to learn and use. Tremendous effort goes into making J2EE as simple as possible, but it remains daunting.

Java Studio Creator is a huge leap in the simplification of the process of developing J2EE based web applications. Developers don't need to deal with all of the gory details: Creator just handles them. Instead, developers can focus on what their application does and looks like in a very simple and straightforward way. They weave together data sources through a simple drag-and-drop interface. Very little knowledge of Java or J2EE is required to develop applications in Creator. Creator not only simplifies the process: it also accelerates it.

This book contains all that you need to know to generate enterprise applications using Creator. It doesn't require that you know anything about J2EE or even Java: there are gentle introductory chapters that lead you through what you need to know. This is a great entry point for developers from other platforms (like Visual Basic!) to enter the world of large-scale, mission-critical applications. It's fun. Take the plunge.

James Gosling
Sun Microsystems, Inc.

Preface

You're about to embark on a journey that we hope will prove both enjoyable and fruitful. Certainly the aim of any application development tool is to help developers become efficient and allow them to spend time on creative tasks while the tool silently generates the drudgery for them. To that end, we hope this book will teach you the ins and outs of Creator so that you can quickly begin to build web applications. Before you start, we'd like to take a moment to explain the organization of the book and the "method behind the madness" of our project examples.

How This Book Is Organized

Chapter 1 introduces the world of Java and its supporting technologies. Creator depends on these well-established Java technologies to do its job. With the Java programming language and XML, JavaServer Faces component system, and NetBeans tool building technology, Creator has tapped the available standards. Here we provide a gentle introduction to these topics, so you'll get the "big picture" of how Creator fits into the Java world. We also spend ample time on the Java programming language since you will use Java often with Creator. If you come from another programming environment, we want you to feel comfortable right away with the myriad of pieces that make up a Java-based web application.

Chapter 2 introduces Creator, with the aim of getting you up to speed with its various windows, the design canvas, and its editors. A good tool lets you accomplish tasks in the order that's best for the developer. Knowing how to move about within a Creator project will quickly make you productive. You'll also build your first project from scratch.

Chapter 3 is your "Components Catalog." This reference chapter lets you choose the best component for your application from Creator's store of components, validators, and data converters. All the projects that you build use these components, so as we discuss each one, we'll point you to places in the book where you can see how they work.

Chapter 4 introduces Page Navigation in Creator. You'll learn how to specify page flow in a web application and understand which components are suitable for page navigation. We'll also discuss Creator's navigation model and illustrate page navigation with several projects that you can build.

Chapter 5 explains JavaBeans components (beans). JavaBeans components provide one of the key supporting technologies that Creator uses. Developers who understand the advantages of JavaBeans components can build robust applications with reusable components for related or evolving applications.

Chapter 6 shows you how to access a web service from a Creator-built application. Creator bundles a full selection of web services, which are all readily usable once you add them to your project. In this chapter, you'll build an application that uses the Google Search Web Service.

Chapter 7 shows you how to use a database with Creator. You'll build projects with essential database operations, such as read, update, insert, and delete. Web applications that tie into databases are an important and common need for today's developer. Creator's data-aware components make linking to a database easy and straightforward.

Chapter 8 shows you how to customize a web application from Creator. You'll learn how to localize an application and how to internationalize it. We also show you how to write and install custom validation methods.

Chapter 9 shows you defensive programming techniques for web development and how to use Creator's debugger in your projects. You'll learn how to set breakpoints, look at the server log file, and respond to exceptions. Although this chapter is at the end of the book, we expect you to refer to it as soon as you start doing serious web development.

About the Examples

Java Studio Creator Field Guide is an example-driven book. You may certainly download and run all the projects in the chapters, but the real value of this book comes from doing these examples yourself, step by step. You can always check your work against our examples as you build your projects, too.

Chapter 1

Welcome to Creator! Creator is an IDE (Integrated Development Environment) that helps you build web applications. While many IDEs out in the world do that, Creator is unique in that it is built on a layered technology anchored in Java. At the core of this technology is the Java programming language. Java includes a compiler that produces portable bytecode and a Java Virtual Machine (JVM) that runs this byte code on any processor. Java is an important part of Creator because it makes your web applications portable.

But Java is more than just a programming language. It is also a *technology platform*. Many large systems have been developed that use Java as their core. These systems are highly scalable and provide services and structure that address some of the high-volume, distributed computing environments of today.

1.1 Introduction

Creator depends on multiple technologies, so it's worthwhile touching on them in this chapter. If you're new to Java, many of its parts and acronyms can be daunting. Java technologies are divided into related packages containing classes and interfaces. To build an application, you might need parts of one system and parts of another. This chapter provides you with a road map of Java technologies and documentation sources to help you design your web applications with Creator.

We'll begin with an overview of the Java programming language. This will help you get comfortable writing Java code to customize your Creator applications. But before we do that, we show you how to find the documentation for Java classes and methods. This will help you use them with confidence in your programs.

Most of the documentation for a Java Application Program Interface (API) can be found online. Sometimes all you need is the name of the package or the system to find out what API a class, interface, or method belongs to. Java consists of the basic language (all packages under `java`) and Java extensions (all packages under `javax`). Once you locate a package online, you can explore the interfaces and classes and learn about the methods they implement.

Here's a good starting point for the Java API documentation.

```
http://java.sun.com/docs/
```

This page contains links to the Java 2 Platform Standard Edition, which contains the core APIs. It also has a link to all of the other Java APIs and technologies, found at

```
http://java.sun.com/reference/docs/index.html
```

Since the APIs change with improvements, new features, and bug fixes, it's best to check these "main" pages for the most up-to-date documentation.

Creator is also built on the technology of JavaServer Faces (JSF). You can find the current JSF API documentation at

```
http://java.sun.com/j2ee/javaserverfaces/1.0/docs/api/
index.html
```

JSF is described as part of the J2EE Tutorial, which can be found at

```
http://java.sun.com/j2ee/1.4/docs/tutorial/doc/index.html
```

These are all important references for you. We've included them at the beginning of this book so it's easy to find them later (when you're deep in the challenges of web application development). For now, let's begin with Java as a programming language. Then we'll look at some of the other supporting technologies on which Creator is built.

1.2   The Java Programming Language

This cursory overview of the Java programming language is for readers who come from a non-Java programming environment. It's not meant to be an in-depth reference, but a starting point. Much of Creator involves manipulating components through the design canvas and the components' property sheets. However, there are times when you must add code to a Java page bean (the supporting Java code for your web application's page) or use a JavaBeans component in your application. You'll want a basic understanding of Java to more easily use Creator.

Object-Oriented Programming

Languages like C and Basic are procedure-oriented languages, which means data and functions are separated. To write programs, you either pass data as arguments to functions or make your data global to functions. This arrangement can be problematic when you need to hide data like passwords, customer identification codes, and network addresses. Procedure-oriented designs work fine when you write simple programs but are often not suitable to more complex tasks like distributed programming and web applications. Function libraries help, but error handling can be difficult and global variables may introduce side effects during program maintenance.

Object-oriented programming, on the other hand, combines data and functions into units called *objects*. Languages like Java hide private data (*fields*) from user programs and expose only functions (*methods*) as a public interface. This concept of *encapsulation* allows you to control how callers access your objects. It allows you to break up applications into groups of objects that behave in a similar way, a concept called *abstraction*. In Java, you implement an object with a Java class and your object's public interface becomes its *outside view*. Java has inheritance to create new data types as extensions of existing types. Java also has interfaces, which allow objects to implement required behaviors of certain classes of objects. All of these things help you separate an object's implementation (inside view) from its interface (outside view).

All objects created from the same class have the same data type. Java is a strongly typed language, and all objects are implicitly derived from type `Object` (except the built-in primitive types of `int`, `boolean`, `char`, `double`, `long`, etc.). You can convert an object from one type to another with a converter. Casting to a different type is only allowed if the conversion is known by the compiler. Creator's Java editor helps you create well-formed statements with dynamic syntax analysis and code completion choices. You'll see how this works in Chapter 2.

Error handling has always been a tough problem to solve, but with web applications error handling is even more difficult. Processing errors can occur on the server but need to propagate in a well-behaved way back to the user. Java implements exception handling to handle errors as objects and recover gracefully. The Java compiler forces programmers to use the built-in exception handling mechanism.

And, Java forbids global variables, a restriction that helps program maintenance.

Creating Objects

Operator new creates objects in Java. You don't have to worry about destroying them, because Java uses a garbage collection mechanism to automatically destroy objects which are no longer used by your program.

```
Point p = new Point();        // create a Point at (0, 0)
Point q = new Point(10, 20);  // create a Point at (10, 20)
```

Operator new creates an object at run time and returns its address in memory to the caller. In Java, you use *references* (p and q) to store the addresses of objects so that you can refer to them later. Every reference has a type (Point), and objects can be built with arguments to initialize their data. In this example, we create two Point objects with x and y coordinates, one with a default of (0, 0) and the other one with (10, 20).

Once you create an object, you can call its methods with a reference.

```
p.move(30, 30);        // move object p to (30, 30)
q.up();                // move object q up in y direction
p.right();             // move object p right in x direction

int xp = p.getX();     // get x coordinate of object p
int yp = p.getY();     // get y coordinate of object p
q.setX(5);             // change x coordinate in object q
p.setY(25);            // change y coordinate in object p
```

As you can see, you can do a lot of things with Point objects. It's possible to move a Point object to a new location, or make it go up or to the right, all of which affect one or more of a Point object's coordinates. We also have getter methods to return the x and y coordinates separately and setter methods to change them.

Why is this all this worthwhile? Because a Point object's data (x and y coordinates) are *hidden*. The only way you can manipulate a Point object is through its public methods. This makes it easier to maintain the integrity of Point objects.

Classes

Java already has a `Point` class in its API, but for the purposes of this discussion, let's roll our own. Here's our Java `Point` class, which describes the functionality we've shown you.

Listing 1.1 Point class

```java
// Point.java - Point class
class Point {
// Fields
   private double x, y;        // x and y coordinates

// Constructors
   public Point(double x, double y) { move(x, y); }
   public Point() { move(0, 0); }

// Instance Methods
   public void move(double x, double y) {
     this.x = x;   this.y = y;
   }
   public void up() { y++; }
   public void down() { y--; }
   public void right() { x++; }
   public void left() { x--; }

   // getters
   public double getX() { return x; }
   public double getY() { return y; }

   // setters
   public void setX(double x) { this.x = x; }
   public void setY(double y) { this.y = y; }
}
```

The `Point` class is divided into three sections: Fields, Constructors, and Instance Methods. Fields hold internal data, constructors initialize the fields, and instance methods are called by you with references. Note that the fields for x and y are *private*. This enforces data encapsulation in object-oriented programming, since users may not access these values directly. Everything else, however, is declared public, making it accessible to all clients.

The `Point` class has two *constructors* to build `Point` objects. The first constructor accepts two double arguments, and the second one is a default constructor with no arguments. Note that both constructors call the `move()` method to initialize the x and y fields. Method `move()` uses the Java `this` keyword to distinguish local variable names in the method from class field names in the object. The setX() and setY() methods use the same technique.[1]

Most of the Point methods use void for their return type, which means the method does not return anything. The ++ and -- operators increment or decrement their values by one, respectively. Each method has a *signature*, which is another name for a function's argument list. Note that a signature may be empty.

Packages

The Point class definition lives in a file called **Point.java**. In Java, you must name a file with the same name as your class name. This makes it convenient for the Java run-time interpreter to find class definitions when it's time to instantiate (create) objects. When all classes live in the same directory, it's easy to compile and run Java programs.

In the real world, however, classes have to live in different places, so Java has *packages* that allow you to group related classes. A package in Java is both a directory and a library. This means a one-to-one correspondence exists between a package hierarchy name and a file's pathname in a directory structure. Unique package names are typically formed by reversing Internet domain names (com.mycompany). Java also provides access to packages from class paths and JAR (Java Archive) files.

Suppose you want to store the Point class in a package called MyPackage.examples. Here's how you do it.

```
package MyPackage.examples;
class Point {
    . . .
}
```

Package names with dot (.) delimiters map directly to path names, so **Point.java** lives in the **examples** directory under the **MyPackage** directory. A Java *import* statement makes it easy to use class names without fully qualifying their package names. Import statements are also applicable to class names from any Java API.

```
// Another Java program
import java.util.Date;
import javax.faces.context.*;
import MyPackage.examples.Point;
```

---

1. The this reference is not necessary if you use different names for the arguments.

The first import statement provides the Date class name to our Java program from the java.util package. The second import uses a wildcard (*) to make *all* class definitions available from javax.faces.context. The last import brings our Point class into scope from package MyPackage.examples.

Exceptions

We mentioned earlier that one of the downfalls of procedure-oriented languages is that subroutine libraries don't handle errors well. This is because libraries can only detect problems, not fix them. Even with libraries that support elaborate error mechanisms, you cannot force someone to check a function's return value or peek at a global error flag. For these and other reasons, it has been difficult to write distributed software that gracefully recovers from errors.

Object-oriented languages like Java have a built-in exception handling mechanism that lets you handle error conditions as objects. When an error occurs inside a try block of critical code, an exception object can be thrown from a library method back to a catch handler. Inside user code, these catch handlers may call methods in the exception object to do a range of different things, like display error messages, retry, or take other actions.

The exception handling mechanism is built around three Java keywords: throw, catch, and try. Here's a simple example to show you how it works.

```
class SomeClass {
    . . .
    public void doSomething(String input) {
        int number;
        try {
            number = Integer.parseInt(input);
        }
        catch (NumberFormatException e) {
            String msg = e.getMessage();
            // do something with msg
        }
        . . .
    }
}
```

Suppose a method called doSomething() needs to convert a string of characters (input) to an integer value in memory (number). In Java, the call to Integer.parseInt() performs the necessary conversion for you, but what about malformed string arguments? Fortunately, the parseInt() method throws a NumberFormatException if the input string has illegal characters. All we do is place this call in a try block and use a catch handler to generate an error message when the exception is caught.

All that's left is to show you how the exception gets thrown. This is often called a *throw point*.

```
class Integer {
    public static int parseInt(String input)
                          throws NumberFormatException {

      . . .
      // input string has bad chars
      throw new NumberFormatException("illegal chars");
    }
      . . .
}
```

The static `parseInt()` method[2] illustrates two important points about exceptions. First, the throws clause in the method signature announces that `parseInt()` throws an exception object of type `NumberFormatException`. The throws clause allows the Java compiler to enforce error handling. To call the `parseInt()` method, you must put the call inside a try block or in a method that also has the same throws clause. Second, operator `new` calls the `Number-FormatException` constructor to build an exception object. This exception object is built with an error string argument and thrown to a catch handler whose signature *matches* the type of the exception object (`NumberFormat` Exception).[3] As you have seen, a catch handler calls `getMessage()` with the exception object to access the error message.

Why are Java exceptions important? As you develop web applications with Creator, you'll have to deal with thrown exceptions. Fortunately, Creator has a built-in debugger that helps you monitor exceptions. In the chapter on debugging, we show you how to set breakpoints to track exceptions in your web application (see "Detecting Exceptions" on page 318).

Inheritance

The concept of code reuse is a major goal of object-oriented programming. When designing a new class, you may derive it from an existing one. Inheritance, therefore, implements an "is a" relationship between classes. Inheritance also makes it easy to hook into existing frameworks so that you can take on

---

2. Inside class `Integer`, the `static` keyword means you don't have to instantiate an `Integer` object to call `parseInt()`. Instead, you call the static method with a class name rather than a reference.
3. The match doesn't have to be exact. The exception thrown can match the catch handler's object exactly or any exception object derived from it by inheritance. To catch any possible exception, you can use the superclass `Exception`. We discuss inheritance in the next section.

new functionalities. With inheritance, you can retain the existing structure and behavior of an existing class and specialize certain aspects of it to suit your needs.

In Java, inheritance is implemented by *extending* classes. When you extend one class from another, the public methods of the "parent" class become part of the public interface of the "child class." The parent class is called a *superclass* and the child class is called a *subclass*. Here are some examples.

```
class Pixel extends Point {
   . . .
}

class NumberFormatException extends IllegalArgumentException {
   . . .
}
```

In the first example, Point is a superclass and Pixel is a subclass. A Pixel "is a" Point with, say, color. Inside the Pixel class, a color field with setter and getter methods can assist in manipulating colors. Pixel objects, however, are Point objects, so you can move them up, down, left or right, and you can get or set their x and y coordinates. (You can also invoke any of Point's public methods with a reference to a Pixel object.) Note that you don't have to write any code in the Pixel class to do these things because they have been inherited from the Point class. Likewise, in NumberFormatException, you may introduce new methods but inherit the functionality of IllegalArgumentException.

Another point about inheritance. You can write your own version of a method in a subclass that has the same name and signature as the method in the superclass. Suppose, for instance, we add a clear() method in our Point class to reset Point objects back to (0, 0). In the Pixel class that extends from Point, we may *override* the clear() method.[4] This new version could move a Pixel object to (0, 0) *and* reset its color. Note that clear() in class Point is called for Point objects, but clear() in class Pixel will be called for Pixel objects. With a Point reference set to either type of object, different behaviors happen when you call this method.

It's important to understand that these kinds of method calls in Java are resolved at run time. This is called *dynamic binding*. In the object-oriented paradigm, dynamic binding means that the resolution of method calls with objects

---

4. Creator uses this same feature by providing methods that are called at different points in the JSF page request life cycle. You can override any of these methods and thus provide your own code, "hooking" into the page request life cycle. We show you how to do this in Chapter 6 (see "Life Cycle Issues" on page 183).

is delayed until you run a program. In web applications and other types of distributed software, dynamic binding plays a key role in how objects call methods from different machines across a network or from different processes in a multitasking system.

Interfaces

In Java, a method with a signature and no code body is called an *abstract* method. Abstract methods must be overridden in subclasses and help define *interfaces*. A Java interface is like a class but has no fields and only abstract public methods. Interfaces are important because they specify a *contract*. Any new class that implements an interface must provide code for the interface's methods.

Here's an example of an interface.

```
interface Encryptable {
   void encode(String key);
   String decode();
}

class Password implements Encryptable {
   . . .
   void encode(String key) { . . . }
   String decode() { . . . }
}
```

The `Encryptable` interface contains only the abstract public methods `encode()` and `decode()`. Class `Password` implements the `Encryptable` interface and must provide implementations for these methods. Remember, interfaces are types, just like classes. This means you can implement the same interface with other classes and treat them all as `Encryptable` types.

Java prohibits a class from inheriting from more than one superclass, but it does allow classes to implement multiple interfaces. Interfaces, therefore, allow arbitrary classes to "take on" the characteristics of any given interface.

One of the most common interfaces implemented by classes in Java is the `Serializable` interface. When an object implements `Serializable`, you can use it in a networked environment or make it *persistent* (this means the state of an object can be saved and restored by different clients). There are methods to serialize the object (before sending it over the network or storing it) and to deserialize it (after retrieving it from the network or reading it from storage).

1.3   JavaBeans Components

A JavaBeans component is a Java class with certain structure requirements. Javabeans components define and manipulate properties, which are objects of a certain type. A JavaBeans component must have a default constructor so that it can be instantiated when needed. Beans also have getter and setter methods that manipulate a bean property and conform to a specific naming convention. These structural requirements make it possible for development tools and other programs to create JavaBeans components and manipulate their properties.

Here's a simple example of a JavaBeans component.

```
public class Book {
   private String title;
   private String author;
   public Book() { setTitle(""); setAuthor(""); }
   public void setTitle(String t) { title = t; }
   public String getTitle() { return title; }
   public void setAuthor(String a) { author = a; }
   public String getAuthor() { return author; }
}
```

Why are JavaBeans components important? First and most important, they are accessible to Creator. When you write a JavaBeans component that conforms to the specified design convention, you may use it with Creator and bind JSF components to bean properties. Second, JavaBeans components can encapsulate business logic. This helps separate your design presentation (GUI components) from the business data model.

In subsequent chapters, we show you several examples of JavaBeans components. We'll use a LoginBean to handle users that login with names and passwords and show you a LoanBean that calculates mortgage payments for loans. The Point class in Listing 1.1 on page 7 is another example of a JavaBeans component.

1.4   NetBeans Software

NetBeans software is an open source IDE written in the Java programming language. It also includes an API that supports building any type of application. The IDE has support for Java, but its architecture is flexible and extensible, making support for other languages possible.

NetBeans is an Open Source project. You can view more information on its history, structure, and relationship with Sun Microsystems at its web site

```
http://www.netbeans.org/
```

NetBeans and Creator are related because Creator is based on the NetBeans platform. In building Creator, Sun is offering an IDE aimed specifically at creating web-based applications. Thus, the IDE integrates page design with generated JSP source and page bean components. NetBeans provides features such as source code completion, workspace manipulation of windows, expandable tree views of files and components, and debugging facilities. Because NetBeans is extensible, the Creator architects included Java language features such as inheritance to adapt components from NetBeans into Creator applications with the necessary IDE functions.

1.5   The XML Language

XML is a metalanguage that dictates how to define custom languages and describe data. The name is an acronym for Extensible Markup Language. XML is not a programming language, however. In fact, it's based on simple character text in which the data are surrounded by text markup that documents data. This means you can use XML to describe almost anything. Since XML is self-describing, it's easy to read with tools and other programs to decide what actions to take. You can transport XML documents easily between systems or across the Internet, and virtually any type of data can be expressed and validated in an XML document. Furthermore, XML is portable because it's language and system independent.

Creator uses XML to define several configuration files as well as the source for the JSP web pages. Here's an example XML file (**managed-beans.xml**) that Creator generates for managing a JavaBeans component in a web application.

```
<faces-config>
  <managed-bean>
    <managed-bean-name>LoanBean</managed-bean-name>
    <managed-bean-class>asg.bean_examples.LoanBean
        </managed-bean-class>
    <managed-bean-scope>session</managed-bean-scope>
  </managed-bean>
</faces-config>
```

Every XML file has opening tags (`<tag>`) and closing tags (`</tag>`) that define self-describing information. Here, we specify a `managed-bean` element to tell Creator what it needs to know about the LoanBean component. This includes its name (LoanBean), class name and package (`asg.bean_examples.LoanBean`), and the scope of the bean (session). When you add your own JavaBeans components to Creator as managed beans, Creator generates this configuration information for you. We show you how to add a managed session bean to your project in Chapter 5.

Creator maintains and updates its XML files for you, but it's a good idea to be familiar with XML syntax. This will allow you to customize the Creator XML files if necessary.

1.6   The J2EE Architecture

The J2EE platform gives you a multitiered application model to develop distributed components. Although any number of tiers is possible, we'll use a three-tier architecture for the applications in this book. Figure 1–1 shows the approach.

The client machine supports web browsers, applets, and stand-alone applications. A client application may be as simple as a command-line program running as an administrator client or a graphical user interface created from Java Swing or Abstract Window Toolkit (AWT) components. Regardless, the J2EE specification encourages *thin clients* in the presentation tier. A thin client is a lightweight interface that does not perform database queries, implement busi-

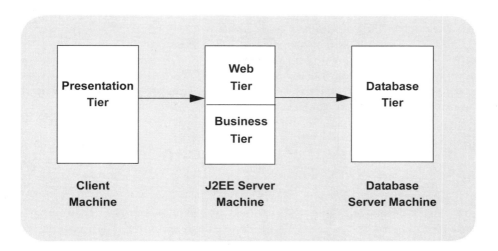

Figure 1–1 **Three-tier J2EE architecture**

ness logic, or connect to legacy code. These types of "heavyweight" operations preferably belong to other tiers.

The J2EE server machine is the center of the architecture. This middle tier contains web components and business objects managed by the application server. The web components dynamically process user requests and construct responses to client applications. The business objects implement the logic of a business domain. Both components are managed by a J2EE application server that provides these components with important system services, such as security, transaction management, naming and directory lookups, and remote connectivity. By placing these services under control of the J2EE application server, client components focus on either presentation logic or business logic. And, business objects are easier for developers to write. Furthermore, the architecture *encourages* the separation of business logic from presentation logic (or model from view).

The database server machine handles the database back end. This includes mainframe transactions, databases, Enterprise Resource Planning (ERP) systems, and legacy code. Another advantage of the three-tier architecture is that older systems can take on a whole new "look" by using the J2EE platform. This is the approach many businesses are taking as they integrate legacy systems into a modern distributed computing environment and expose application services and data to the web.

1.7   Java Servlet Technology

The Java Servlet component technology presents a request-response programming model in the middle tier. Servlets let you define HTTP-specific servlet classes that accept data from clients and pass them on to business objects for processing. Servlets run under the control of the J2EE application server and often extend applications hosted by web servers. Servlet code is written in Java and compiled. It is particularly suited to server-side processing for web applications since each Servlet session is handled in its own thread.

1.8   JavaServer Pages Technology

A JavaServer Pages (JSP) page is a text-based document interspersed with Java code. A JSP engine translates JSP text into Java Servlet code. It is then dynamically compiled and executed. This component technology lets you create dynamic web pages in the middle tier. JSP pages contain static template data (HTML, WML, and XML) and JSP elements that determine how a page constructs dynamic content. The JSP API provides an efficient, thread-based mechanism to create dynamic page content.

Creator uses JavaServer Faces (JSF), which is built on both the servlet and JSP technologies. However, by using Creator, you are shielded from much of the details of not only JSP and servlet programming, but JSF details as well.

1.9   JDBC API and JDBC RowSets

Java Data Base Connectivity (JDBC) is an API that lets you invoke SQL commands from Java methods in the middle tier. Typically, you use the JDBC API to access a database from servlets or JSP pages. The JDBC API has an application-level interface for database access and a service provider interface to attach JDBC drivers to the J2EE platform. In support of JDBC, J2EE application servers manage a pool of database connections. This pool provides business objects efficient access to database servers.

The JDBC `RowSet` API is a newer technology that makes it easier to access database information from the rows and columns in a `ResultSet` object. A JDBC `RowSet` object is a connected rowset that is an extension of a `ResultSet` object. `RowSet` objects have properties that can be manipulated, and they can participate in event notification. When you select a data source in Creator, the system generates code in the Java page bean to access the data source through `RowSet` objects.

We show you how to use databases with Creator in Chapter 7.

1.10 JavaServer Faces Technology

The JavaServer Faces (JSF) technology helps you develop web applications using a server-side user interface (UI) component framework. The JSF API gives you a rich set of UI components and lets you handle events, validate and convert user input, define page navigation, and support internationalization. JSF has custom tag libraries for connecting components to server-side objects. We show you these components and tag libraries in Chapter 3.

JSF incorporates many of the lower level tasks that JSP developers are used to doing. Unlike JSP applications, however, applications developed with JSF can map HTTP requests to component-specific event handlers and manage UI elements as stateful objects on the server. This means JSF offers a better separation of model and presentation. The JSF API is also layered directly on top of the Servlet API.

1.11 Ant Build Tool

Ant is a tool from the Apache Software Foundation (www.apache.org) that helps you manage the "build" of a software application. The name is an acronym for "Another Neat Tool" and is similar in concept to older build tools like make under Unix and gmake under Linux. However, Ant is XML-based, it's easier to use, and it's platform independent.

Ant is written in Java and accepts instructions from XML documents. Ant is well suited for performing complicated and repetitive tasks. Creator uses Ant to compile and deploy your web applications. Ant gets its instructions for building a system from the configuration file, **build.xml**. You won't have to know too much about Ant to use Creator, but you should be aware that it's behind the scenes doing a lot of work for you.

1.12 Web Services

Web services are software APIs that are accessible over a network in a heterogeneous environment. Network accessibility is achieved by means of a set of XML-based open standards such as the Web Services Description Language (WSDL), the Simple Object Access Protocol (SOAP), and Universal Description, Discovery, and Integration (UDDI). Web service providers and clients use these standards to define, publish, and access web services.

Creator's application server (J2EE 1.4) provides support for web services. In Creator, you can access methods of a web service by dragging its node onto the design canvas. We show you web services with Creator in Chapter 6.

1.13 Key Point Summary

- Creator is an IDE built on layered Java technologies that helps you build web applications.
- Procedure-oriented languages separate data and functions, whereas object-oriented languages combine them.
- Encapsulation enforces data hiding and allows you to control access to your objects.
- Java is a strongly typed object-oriented language with a large set of APIs that help you develop portable web applications.
- In Java, operator new returns a reference to a newly created object so that you can call methods with the reference.

- Java classes have fields, constructors, and instance methods. The `private` keyword is used for encapsulation, and the `public` keyword grants access to clients.
- Java packages allow you to store class files and retrieve them with `import` statements in Java programs.
- Java uses `try`, `catch`, and `throw` to handle error conditions with a built-in exception handling mechanism.
- Inheritance is a code reuse mechanism that implements an "is a" relationship between classes.
- Dynamically bound method calls are resolved at run time in Java. Dynamic binding is essential with distributed web applications.
- An interface has no fields and only abstract public methods. A class that implements an interface must provide code for the interface's methods.
- The J2EE architecture is a multitiered application model to develop distributed components.
- Java Servlets let you define HTTP-specific servlet classes that accept data from clients and pass them on to business objects for processing.
- A JSP page is a text-based document interspersed with Java code that allows you to create dynamic web pages.
- JDBC is an API for database access from servlets, JSP pages, or JSF. JDBC `RowSet` objects allow enhanced access to database sources using the JDBC API.
- JavaServer Faces (JSF) helps you develop web applications using a server-side user interface component framework.
- A JavaBeans component is a Java class with a default constructor and setter and getter methods to manipulate its properties.
- NetBeans is a standards-based IDE and platform written in the Java programming language. Java Studio Creator is based on the NetBeans platform.
- XML is a self-describing, text-based language that documents data and makes it easy to transport between systems.
- Ant is a Java build tool that helps you compile and deploy web applications.
- Web services are software APIs that are accessible over a network in a heterogeneous environment.

CREATOR BASICS

Topics in This Chapter

- Creator Window Layout
- Component Palette
- Source Editors/Code Completion
- Clips Palette
- Page Navigation Editor
- Application Outline Window
- Server Navigator Window
- Creator Help System

Chapter 2

Sun Java Studio Creator makes it easy to work with web applications from multiple points of view. This chapter explores some of Creator's basic capabilities, the different windows (views) and the way in which you use them to build your application. We show you how to manipulate your application through the drag-and-drop mechanism for placing components, setting attributes in the Properties window, controlling page flow with the Page Navigation editor, and selecting services from the Server Navigator window.

2.1 Examples Installation

We assume that you've successfully installed Creator. The best source of information on installing Creator is Sun's product information page at the following URL.

```
http://developers.sun.com/prodtech/javatools/jscreator/
```

Creator runs on a variety of platforms and can be configured with different application servers and JDBC database drivers. However, to run all our examples we've used the default application server (J2EE 1.4 Application Server) and PointBase database. Once you've configured Creator for your system, the examples you build in the text should run the same on your system.

Download Examples

You can download the examples for this book at

```
http://www.asgteach.com/download/index.htm
```

and select *Java Studio Creator Field Guide: Book Examples*. The examples are packed in a zip file. When you unzip the file, you'll see the **FieldGuide/Examples** directory and subdirectories for the various chapters and projects. As each chapter references the examples, you will be instructed on how to access the files.

You're now ready to start the tour of Creator.

2.2 Creator Views

Figure 2–1 shows Creator's initial window layout in its default configuration. When you first bring it up, no projects are open and Creator displays its Welcome window.

There are other windows besides those shown in the initial window layout. As you'll see, you can hide and display windows, as well as move them around. As we begin this tour of Creator, you'll probably want to run Creator along with the text.

Welcome

The Welcome window lets you to create new projects or work on existing ones. Figure 2–2 shows the Welcome window in more detail. It lists the projects you've worked on recently and offers selection buttons for opening existing projects or creating new projects.

To demonstrate Creator, let's use a project that we've already built with Creator. The project is in directory **FieldGuide/Examples/Projects/Login1**.

1. Select the Open an Existing Project button and browse to the **FieldGuide/ Examples/Projects** directory for Java Creator Field Guide.
2. Select **Login1** (look for the projects icon) and double click. This opens the **Login1** project and displays the design canvas for the project's first page.

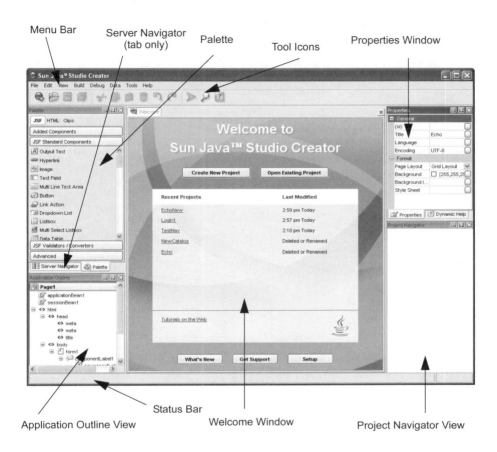

Figure 2–1 Creator's initial window layout

Design Canvas

Figure 2–3 shows a close-up of the design canvas window for project **Login1**. You see the design grid and the components we've placed on the canvas. As you select the individual components, their properties appear in the Properties window (not shown here).

Each project in Creator can have many files associated with it. Here, the design canvas window displays the design view of file **Page1.jsp**. You can have more than one of your project's files open at a time (currently, there's just one open). When you open other files, their file tab appears at the top of the editor pane. You use the File Tab to select other files.

Figure 2–2 Creator's Welcome window

The editor pane allows you to manipulate elements of your project. When the design canvas is showing, you can select components, validators, or converters from the palette. From the Server Navigator windows you can select nonvisual components, such as data sources or web services. In the design canvas, you see the components we've added to this page: a text field component, a secret field component, two component labels, two buttons, a message list component, and an output text component used as a page title.

Creator allows you to configure your display's workspace to suit the tasks you're working on. All the windows can be hidden when not needed (click the red X in a window's title bar to close it). To view the window again, select View from the menu bar and then the window name. You can dock Creator windows by selecting the pushpin in the window title bar. This action minimizes the window along the left or right side of the workspace. Make it visible again by

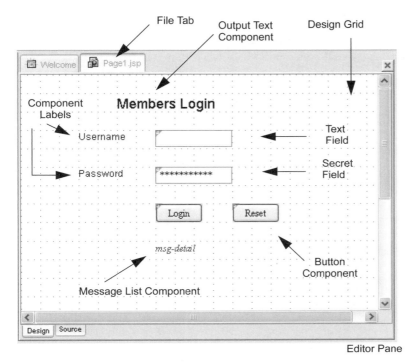

File Tab   Output Text   Design Grid
           Component

Component   **Members Login**
Labels

Username   Text
                            Field

Password   **********   Secret
                            Field

            Login   Reset

            msg-detail

                            Button
                            Component

Message List Component

Design | Source

Editor Pane

Figure 2–3 **Creator's design canvas showing project Login1**

moving the cursor over its docked position. Undock it by toggling the pushpin icon.

Select the button labeled "Login" on the design canvas. This will bring up the button component's Properties window, as shown in Figure 2–4.

Properties

Creator lets you configure the components you use by manipulating their properties. When you change a component's properties, Creator automatically updates the JSF source for you. Here are the login button's properties.

The `id` attribute uniquely identifies the component on the page. Creator generates the name for you, but you may want to change it (as we have in this example) to more easily work with the generated code. You can use the `style` attribute to change its appearance. If you click in the editing box opposite `style`, you can see what it's set to. The `position` attribute reflects the component's position on the page. When you move the button component, Creator updates this for you.

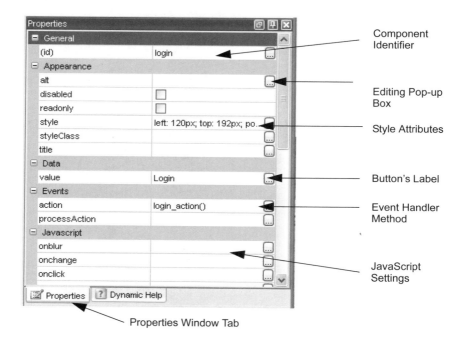

Figure 2–4 **Properties window for button component "Login"**

The `value` attribute under Data holds the button's label. Click on the Login button again in the design canvas and from the keyboard begin typing a new label. You'll see that Creator automatically selects the `value` attribute in the Properties window and enables editing as you begin typing. Finish editing with **<Enter>**.

Under Events, the `action` attribute is set to `login_action()`. This refers to an event handler method in the Java page bean that controls what happens when the user clicks the button.

Each component has a different list of attributes (although many attributes are the same). As you select other components in the design canvas, note that the list of attributes in the Properties window changes.

Palette

Figure 2–5 shows the JSF Standard Components window and JSF Validators/ Converters window. These are the palettes that let you select components and add them to your page. Page designers, for example, select a component and drag it to the design canvas, positioning it on the page. Once the component is

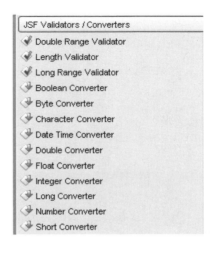

Figure 2–5 **JSF Standard Components and Validators/Converters windows**

on the page, you can configure it by changing the attributes in its Properties window.

Click on the bar labeled JSF Validators/Converters to see these components. You can select these just like the standard components. When you drag one to the canvas and drop it on top of a component, the validator or converter will bind to that component. (To test this, select the Length Validator and drop it on top of the `userName` text field component. You'll see a length validator `lengthValidator1` defined for the text field's `validator` attribute in the Properties window.)

Note that the components, validators, and converters all have icons next to them. Creator uses these icons consistently so you can easily spot what kind of component you're looking at. For example, reselect the JSF Standard Components bar in the palette and then select the Login button component on the design canvas. Now look at the Application Outline view. You'll see that the icon next to the button component in the JSF Standard Components palette matches the Login button in the Application Outline window.

Application Outline

Figure 2–6 is the Application Outline window for project **Login1**. (Its default placement is in the lower-left portion of the display.) The Application Outline window is handy because it shows both visual and nonvisual components for the page that's currently displayed in the design canvas. You can select other pages (here we have **LoginGood.jsp** and **LoginBad.jsp**) as well as the preconfigured managed beans, SessionBean1 and ApplicationBean1. These JavaBeans components are handy to hold your project's data that belong in either session or application scope, respectively. (We discuss scope issues for web application

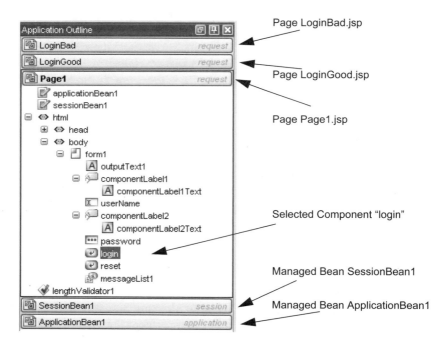

Figure 2–6 **Creator's Application Outline window for project Login1**

objects in "Scope of Web Applications" on page 128.)

Some components are composite components, meaning that they contain nested elements. The Application Outline window will show this structure and allow you to expand and compress the display (using '+' and '-') as needed.

When you placed the length validator component on the userName text field, it appeared here as component lengthValidator1. Delete it by selecting it in the Application Outline view, then right-click and select Delete from the context menu. The validator should disappear from the Application Outline view.

Creator Tip

Once you delete the `lengthValidator1` *component from your project,
Creator will reset the validator attribute for component* `userName` *for you. To
see this, select component* `userName` *in the design canvas. Verify that
attribute* `validator` *is empty in the Properties window.*

Now let's look at the Project Navigator window.

Project Navigator

Figure 2–7 shows the Project Navigator window for project **Login1**. Its default
location is in the lower-right corner. Whereas the Application Outline view displays the components for individual pages and managed beans, the Project
Navigator window displays your entire project. Project **Login1** contains three
JSP pages: **Page1.jsp**, **LoginGood.jsp**, and **LoginBad.jsp**. Double-click on any
one of them to pull it up in the design canvas. When the page opens, Creator
displays a file name tab so you can easily switch among different files in the
design canvas.

When you create your own projects, each page comes with a Java component "page bean." These are Java classes that conform to the JavaBeans structure we mention in Chapter 1 (see "JavaBeans Components" on page 13). To
see the Java files in this project, expand the Java Sources folder (click on the '+'),
then the **login1** folder. When you double-click on any of the Java files, Creator
brings it up in the Java source editor. Without going to the editor, you can also
see the Java classes, fields, constructors, and methods by expanding the '+' next
to each level of the Java file.

The Project Navigator also lists the Resources node, which lives under the
Web Pages node. The Resources node typically holds file `stylesheet.css` and
any image files. The Library References node lists the libraries Creator needs to
deploy your application. These are all of the JSF, Web Services, JDBC Rowset,
and Exception Handler support classes. These class files (compiled Java
classes) are stored in special archive files called JAR (Java Archive) files. You
can see the name of the JAR files by expanding each of the nodes under Library
References.[1] We show you how to add a Library Reference to your project in
Chapter 5 (see "Add a Library Reference to Your Project" on page 133).

By default, the Project Navigator window shows you the Logical View of
your project. Select the project name **Login1**, right-click, and choose Show File-
System View from context menu, shown in Figure 2–8. The FileSystem View

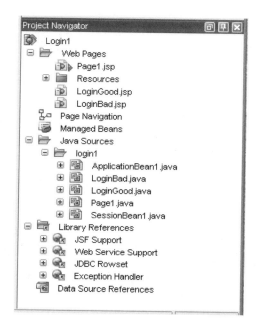

Figure 2–7 **Creator's Project Navigator window for project Login1**

shows all of the files in your project. This is handy for editing a configuration file that doesn't have a "visual editing interface." For example, expand the view until you see file **web.xml**, as shown below. Double-click this file. Creator brings it up in the editor pane. You can close the window again by selecting its File Tab at the top of the editor pane, right-click, and choose Close.

JSP Source Editor

With **Page1.jsp** in the design editor, bring up the JSP for this page by clicking the tab labeled Source at the bottom of the editor pane. Figure 2–9 shows Creator's JSP Source Editor.

---

1. For those of you who are curious about their contents, you can look at these jar files with the Java command-line `jar` command, Winzip or other compatible utility. With Winzip, be sure to specify `*.*` for all file types when opening an archive. The command that produces a file list of a jar archive is `jar tvf *lib.jar.* `The files are found in the directory structure of your project. (Look in `Login1/build/WEB-INF/lib` for the JAR files.)

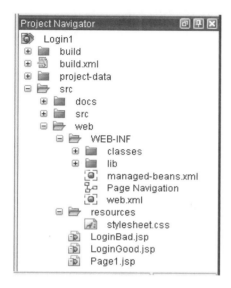

Figure 2–8 **The FileSystem View of the Project Navigator window.**

This is the JSP source that Creator generates for your page. Normally, you will not need to edit this page directly, but studying it is a good way to understand how JSF components work and how you can configure them by managing their properties. You'll see a close correspondence between the JSF tags and the components' properties as shown in the Properties window.

You'll also note the JSF Expression Language (EL) used to refer to methods and properties in the Java page bean. For example, the login button's `action` attribute is set to `#{Page1.login_action}`, which is a method in class **Page1.java**.

Let's look at the Java source for **Page1.java** now. Return to the design canvas for this page (select the tab labeled Design at the bottom of the editor pane). Right-click on the design canvas and select View Page1 Java Class from the menu.

Java Source Editor

You're looking at Creator's Java source editor for Java file **Page1.java**, the page bean for **Page1.jsp**. This Java file is a bean (conforming to a JavaBeans structure). Its properties consist of the components we placed on the page: each component corresponds to a private variable and has a getter and setter. This allows the JSF EL expression to access the properties of the page bean.

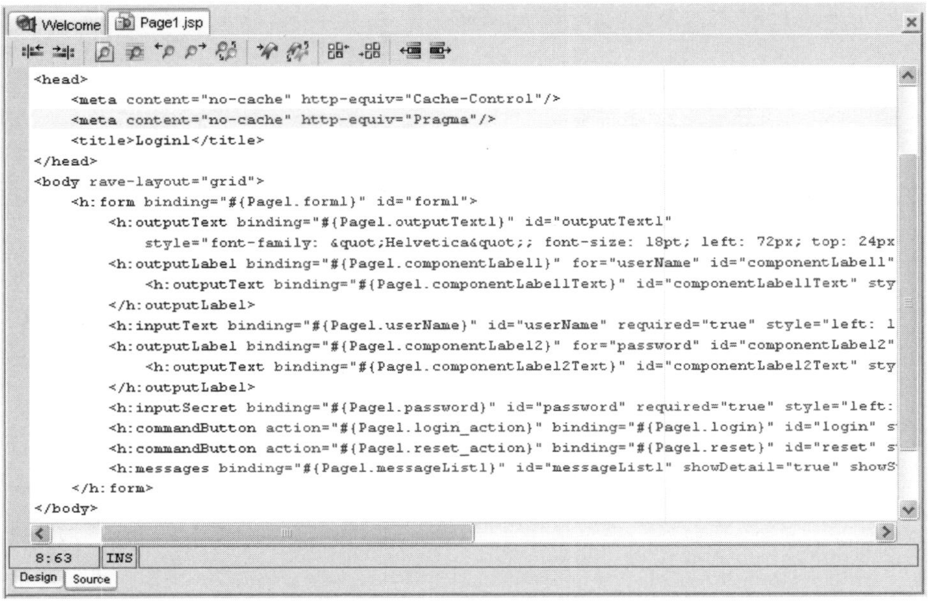

Figure 2–9 **Page1.jsp Source window**

There's a dropdown menu at the top left of the window. You can use this menu to locate a field, method, or constructor in the file. Open the dropdown menu and select method `login_action`. Figure 2–10 shows this view.

There's much to learn about the Java source editor, so we'll just touch on a few tidbits now. First, we enabled line numbers here. To do this for your display, right-click in the margin (on the left-side of the editor window) and select Show Line Numbers. You see that method `login_action()` begins at line 166.

All of Creator's editors are based on NetBeans. The Editor Module is a full-featured source editor and provides code completion (we show an example shortly), a set of abbreviations, and fast import **<Alt-Shift-I>**.

To see the set of abbreviations, select Tools > Options from the menu bar. The Options dialog pops up. Under Options, select Editing > Editor Settings > Java Editor. On the right side of the display, click the small editing box next to Abbreviations. Creator pops up the window shown in Figure 2–11.

The window lists the abbreviations in effect for your Java editor. (You can edit, add, or remove any item.) For example, to add a `for` loop to your Java

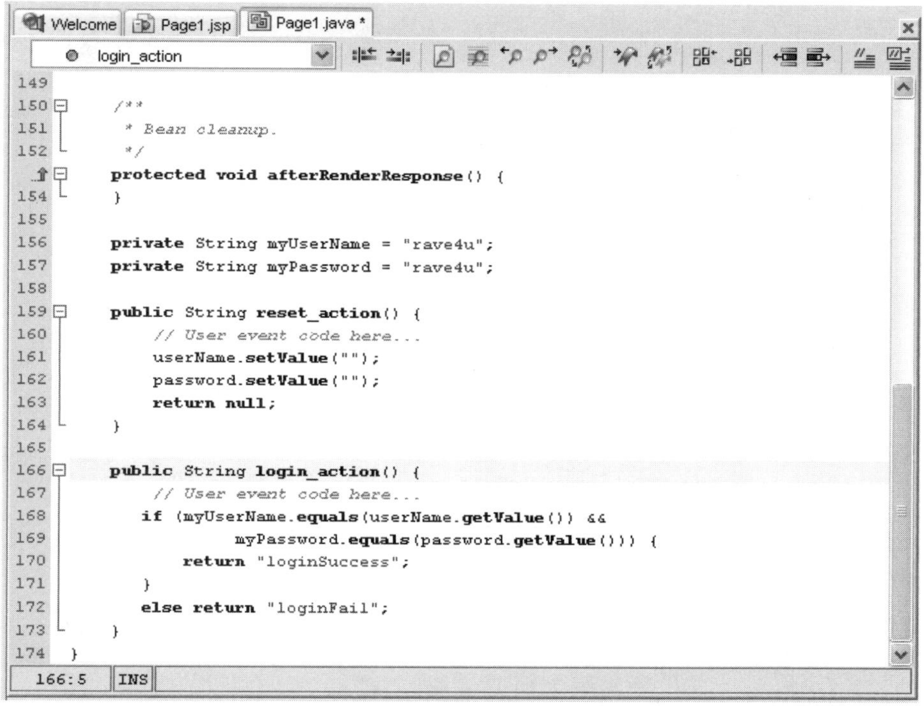

```
Welcome    Page1.jsp    Page1.java *                               X
    login_action                     ▼

149
150   /**
151    * Bean cleanup.
152    */
153   protected void afterRenderResponse() {
154   }
155
156   private String myUserName = "rave4u";
157   private String myPassword = "rave4u";
158
159   public String reset_action() {
160       // User event code here...
161       userName.setValue("");
162       password.setValue("");
163       return null;
164   }
165
166   public String login_action() {
167       // User event code here...
168       if (myUserName.equals(userName.getValue()) &&
169               myPassword.equals(password.getValue())) {
170           return "loginSuccess";
171       }
172       else return "loginFail";
173   }
174 }
    166:5    INS
```

Figure 2–10 **Page1.java Java source editor**

source file, type the sequence **fora** (*for array*) followed by **<Space>**. The editor adds

```
for (int i = 0; i < .length; i++) {
}
```

and places the cursor in front of .length so that you can add an array name. (.length refers to the length of the array object. This code snippet lets you easily loop through the elements of the array.)

The Java source editor also helps you with Java syntax and code completion. All Java keywords are bold, and variables and literal Strings have unique colors (you'll see that in your display; in the text here, it's different shades of gray).

When you add statements to your Java source code, the editor helps you by dynamically marking syntax errors (in red, of course). The editor also pops up

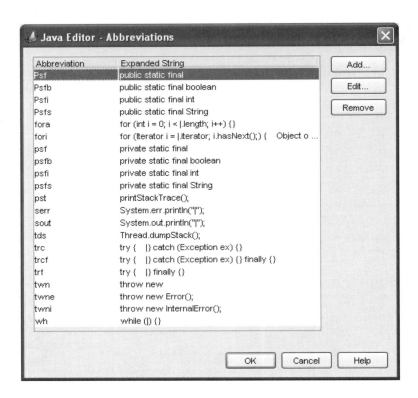

Figure 2–11 Java source editor list of abbreviations

windows to help with code completion or package location for classes you need to reference (press **<Ctrl-Space>** to activate the code completion window). For example, Figure 2–12 shows the code completion mechanism as you start to type a method that begins with "e" for a String object (on line 168).

When you use the down-arrow to select method `equals()`, the help mechanism displays the Javadoc documentation about `equals()` for `java.lang.String`. With method `equals()` highlighted, press **<Enter>**. The code completion does more for you than you really want here. Delete all the characters after "equals" up to the parenthesis in front of "userName." The syntax errors should disappear. (To retrieve Javadoc documentation on any class in your source file, select it and press **<Ctrl-Shift-Space>**.)

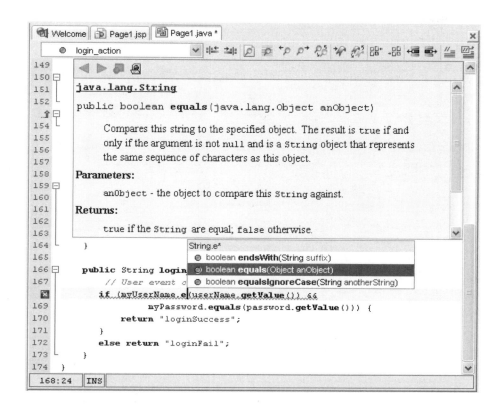

Figure 2–12 Java source editor code completion

Clips Palette

When the Java Source editor is displayed, Creator replaces the component palette with the Clips palette, as shown in Figure 2–13. Here we select the Java Basics Clips. Highlight clip Concatenate Strings. If you hold the cursor over the clip name, Creator displays a snippet window. You can drag and drop the clip directly into your Java source file. We do this when we build our first sample project in the next section.

To view or edit a clip, select it, right-click, and choose Edit. The second window in Figure 2–13 shows the Concatenate Strings clip.

The Clips palette is divided into categories to show sample code for that general topic. For example, if you click Application Data, you'll see a listing of

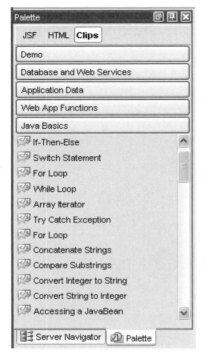
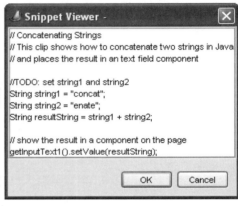

Figure 2–13 Java Basics Clips Palette and Viewer

clips that shows you how to access objects defined in your web application's different scopes.

Page Navigation Editor

Return to the Java Source window and look at method `login_action()`. You'll see that this method returns one of two Strings: either `"loginSuccess"` or `"loginFail"`. These Strings are returned to the action event handler, which then passes them to the navigation handler. The navigation handler manages page flow. Let's look at the Page Navigation editor now.

1. From the top of the Java source window, select the tab labeled **Page1.jsp**. This returns you to the design canvas for this page.
2. Now right-click in the design canvas and select Page Navigation from the context menu. Creator brings up the Page Navigation editor for project **Login1**, as shown in Figure 2–14.

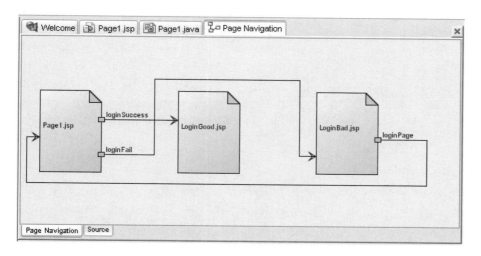

Figure 2–14 **Page navigation editor for project Login1**

We mentioned earlier that there were three pages in this project. The Page Navigation editor displays these pages and indicates page flow logic with labeled arrows. The two labels originating from page **Page1.jsp** correspond to the return Strings we just looked at in the action method `login_action()`.

You learn how to specify Navigation in Chapter 4 (see "Page Navigation" on page 96). The Page Navigation editor is also a handy way to bring up any of the project's pages: just double-click inside the page. As you bring up each page, a corresponding file tab appears at the top of the editor pane. And once you've visited the Page Navigation editor, Creator displays a file tab called **Page Navigation** so you can easily return.

Before we explore our project any further, let's deploy and run the application. From the menu bar, select Build > Run Project. (Or, click the green chevron on the toolbar icon, which also builds and runs your project.)

Build Output Window

Figure 2–15 shows the build output window just as the application is finishing deployment. Creator uses the Ant build tool to control project builds. This Ant build process requires compiling Java source files and assembling the resources used by the project into an archive file called a WAR (Web Archive) file. Ant reads its instructions from a Creator-generated XML configuration file, called **build.xml**, in the project's directory structure.

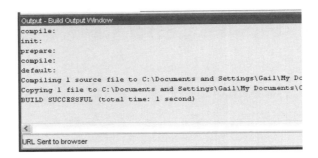

Figure 2–15 **Build Output window for project Login1**

If problems occur during the build process, Creator displays messages in the Build Output window. A compilation error with the Java source is the type of error that causes the build to fail. When the build succeeds (the window will show `BUILD SUCCESSFUL`, as you see above), Creator tells the application server to deploy the application. If the application server is not running, Creator starts it for you. If errors occur in this step, messages come from the application server. Finally, it's possible for the deployment to be successful but for an exception to be shown in the browser's web page. A likely source of this type of error is a problem with JSF tags on the JSP page or a resource that is not available for the runtime class loader.

When the build/deployment process is complete, Creator brings up your browser with the correct URL. (The status window displays "Starting browser for `http://localhost:18080/login1`.") So, to run project **Login1** with the Sun J2EE 1.4 Application Server, Creator uses this web address.

```
http://localhost:18080/login1/
```

You use `localhost` if you're running the application server on your own machine; otherwise, use the Internet address or host name where the server is running. The port number `18080` is unique to Sun's J2EE application server. Another server will use a different port number here.

The Context Root is **/login1** for this application. The application server builds a directory structure for all its deployed applications, and the context root is the "base address" for all the resources that your application uses.

Figure 2–16 shows the **Login1** project deployed and running in a browser. Type in some values for Username and Password. If you leave the Username field empty, you'll get a validation error. The correct Username and Password is "rave4u" for both fields.

Figure 2–16 **Login page web application**

If you type in the correct values and click the Login button, the program displays page **LoginGood.jsp**. Incorrect values display **LoginBad.jsp**. You'll build project **Login1** from scratch in Chapter 4 ("Dynamic Navigation" on page 111).

It's time now to explore the Server Navigator window, located in the upper-left portion of your Creator display. Click the tab labeled Server Navigator.

Server Navigator

Figure 2–17 shows the Server Navigator window after you've deployed project **Login1**. Four categories of servers are listed here: Data Sources, Web Services, Deployment Server, and Database Server.

The Data Sources node is a JDBC database connection. The default database server is PointBase, but you can configure a different one. Creator comes configured with several sample databases, which are visible if you expand the Data Sources node.

Creator Tip

PointBase must be running. You can start it on Windows by clicking the Start button and selecting All Programs > Sun Microsystems > J2EE 1.4 SDK > Start PointBase. You will need to restart Creator.

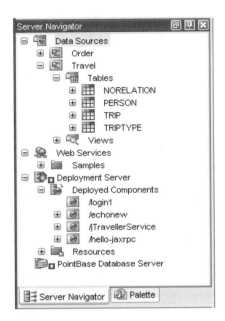

Figure 2–17 **Server Navigator window**

Now expand the Travel > Tables node to see the database tables as shown (there are four). As you select different tables, Creator displays their properties in the Properties window.

You can expand each table further and see the database table field names. If you double-click on the table name, Creator displays the data in the editor pane, as shown in Figure 2–18. You can close the table view by selecting the tab labeled Table View, right-click, and select Close from the context menu. We discuss creating web applications that access databases in Chapter 7 (see "Accessing Databases" on page 204).

The second server type is Web Services, which provides access to remote APIs from Creator applications. This requires the cooperation of several Java technologies, which we discussed in Chapter 1. When you install Creator, it includes a web services API to access Google. In Chapter 6 we show you how to create an application that uses the Google web service API.

The third server type is the Deployment Server, which is the application server. Sun's J2EE 1.4 application server is Creator's default deployment server, which manages the deployment of web applications that you create. To start or stop the server, select the Deployment Server node, right-click, and select Start/ Stop Server. Creator pops up a window that allows you to initiate one of these actions, or you can simply close the window.

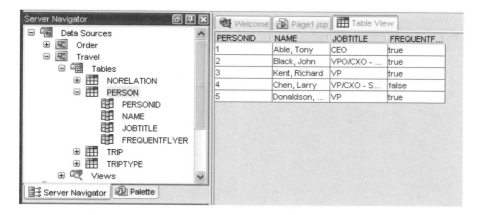

Figure 2–18 Selecting View Data under the Data Sources node

If you expand the Deployment Server node, you'll see the Deployed Components node. Under this node are the deployed applications. The **/login1** application is listed (since you deployed it). You can undeploy an application by right-clicking its node and selecting Undeploy.

The J2EE application server also has administration access through your browser at

```
http://localhost:14848/asadmin/
```

You can get there directly from Creator by selecting the Deployment Server node, right-clicking, and selecting Show Admin Console. (The application server must be running for access to the administration port.) Use user name `admin` and password `adminadmin`.

Debugger Window

Creator has a debugger that lets you trace the call stack, track local variables, and set watches. You can see this window by selecting View > Debugger Window from the toolbar. To run your application in "debug mode," click on Debug > Debug Project from the menu bar. The application server has to stop and restart if it's not already in debug mode. In Chapter 9 we walk you through the debugger options, setting breakpoints, stepping through code, and other debugging activities.

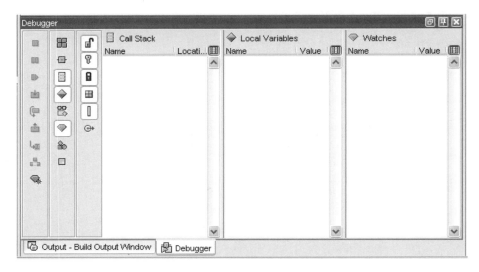

Figure 2–19 **Creator debugger window**

Creator Help System

The Creator Help System is probably the most useful window for readers new to Creator. This help system includes a search capability, contents, and an index. You access the help system by selecting Help > Help Contents in the menu bar. In Figure 2–20 we clicked the Index tab and selected entry "binding data to list components." The relevant information appears in the adjacent window.

2.3   Sample Application

Now that you're comfortable with Creator, let's create a simple web application. Even though this application is simplistic, it hints at some of the power in Creator. Figure 2–22 on page 46 provides a preview of this web application.

Create a Project

Close project **Login1** if it's open.

1. From the Welcome window, select button Create New Project.
2. Specify **Echo** for the Name, then click OK.

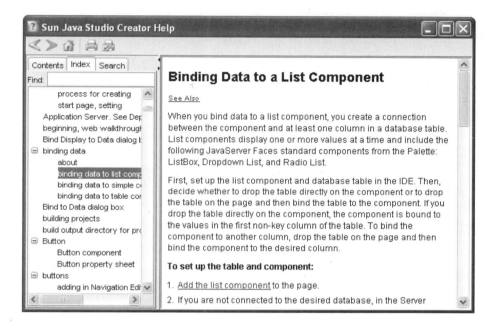

Figure 2–20 **Creator Help window**

Specify Title

Creator initializes a project for you and brings up the design canvas editor. Now you'll be able to add components and modify properties.

1. If the Properties window is not enabled for the page, select the page by clicking anywhere inside the design canvas.
2. In the Properties window under General, change the `Title` attribute to **Echo**. Finish with **<Enter>**.

Add Components

You'll add three components to the page: a component label, a text field, and an output text component. When you created project **Echo** and Creator brought up the design canvas, this made the JSF Standard Components palette visible.

1. From the JSF Standard Components palette, select Component Label and drag it over to the design canvas. Drop it onto the canvas, near the top on the left side. Don't resize it.

Creator Tip

If you resize the component, Creator generates static length and width attributes for your component. If you leave it unsized, the rendering mechanism will dynamically size the component to accommodate the text it needs to display.

2. Component label is a composite component; it contains an embedded (nested) output text component. The output text component displays the label. From the Application Outline view, select the component label's nested output text component, named `componentLabel1Text`.

Creator Tip

Creator provides an enhanced selection mechanism for composite components (such as component label). In the design canvas, select the component label and look in the Properties window to see which component is selected. Now click the component again and you'll see a different component's properties. For component label, you switch back and forth between the top-level, label component and the embedded output text component by clicking the component in the design canvas.

3. Now go to the Properties window and select the `value` attribute. Type the label **Type in some text**. Finish with **<Enter>**. The text you type will appear in the component.
4. From the JSF Standard Components palette, select component Text Field and place it on the design canvas underneath the component label you just added.
5. Make sure that it's selected, and in the Properties window, change its `value` attribute to **Echo Text**. Finish with **<Enter>**.
6. Still in the Properties window for the text field, change its `title` attribute to **The text you enter here will be echoed below**. Finish with **<Enter>**. You've just created a tooltip for this component.
7. Now select component label `componentLabel1` (the top-level component) from the Application Outline view.
8. In the Properties window, select the small editing square opposite the `for` attribute. Creator pops up a dialog for you to choose a component id. Select component `textField1` and click OK. This associates the label component with the text field component. You'll see (when you run the web application) that this affects GUI operations such as cursor movement and selection behavior. For example, selecting the label also selects the text field.
9. From the JSF Standard Components palette, select an Output Text component and place it under the text field. (Again, don't resize it.)

You've finished adding the components. Now you will use property binding to bind the text field component `value` property to the output text component `value` property. Here's how.

1. Select the output text component (`outputText1`), right-click, and choose Property Bindings from the context menu. Creator brings up the Property Bindings dialog. (See Figure 2–21.)
2. Under Select bindable property, choose **value Object**.
3. Under Select binding target, expand Page1 > html > body > form1 by clicking the '+' at each level.
4. Select component **textField1** (the text field component you added). Expand the component by clicking '+' on `textField1` and select **value String**. (The properties are listed in alphabetical order, so `value` is near the end.)
5. Click the Apply button. (If you don't click the Apply button, Creator doesn't set the property binding.) Under Current binding for **value** property, you should see the following JSF EL expression

```
#{Page1.textField1.value}
```

6. Click Close to finish.

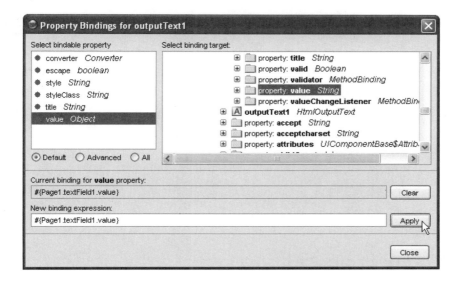

Figure 2–21 **Property Bindings dialog**

So, what did all this accomplish? You've just configured *property binding* on the output text component (id outputText1). This means that JSF gets the value attribute (the text that is displayed on the page) for outputText1 *from* the text field's value (component textField1). This, in turn, means that whatever you type for input will be echoed in the output text's display.

Deploy and Run

You've finished creating the application. Now it's time to build, deploy, and run it. From the menu bar, select Build > Run Project. Creator builds the application, deploys it, and brings up a browser with the **Echo** web application running.

Figure 2–22 shows what the browser window displays after you type **Hello, World Wide Web** inside the text field followed by **<Enter>**.

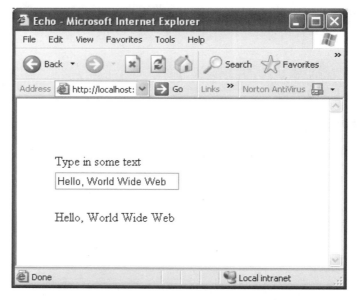

Figure 2–22 **Web application Echo running in a browser**

Modify Project Echo

As promised, let's access the Clips palette and add some Java code to our project. First, we'll add an output text component.

1. Make sure the Creator design canvas is visible.

2. From the JSF Standard Components palette, select Output Text component and place it underneath component `outputText1`. This adds component `outputText2` to your page. (You should see `outputText2` when you look at the Application Outline view of the project.)
3. Make sure component `outputText2` is selected. Note that the word *Text* appears in the component on the design canvas, but the `value` attribute in the Properties window is blank. The word *Text* will not appear on the deployed web page.

Now you will bring up the Java source editor to manipulate the Java page bean for this page.

1. Place the cursor anywhere in the design grid, right-click, and select View Page1 Java Class. This brings up the Java Source editor with file **Page1.java**.
2. Open the dropdown menu at the top of the editor pane and select the constructor, `Page1()`. Creator will place the cursor at the beginning of this method and highlight the line in yellow. (Note that some Creator-managed code is hidden—"folded"—to help keep your editor window uncluttered.)
3. Move the cursor to the end of the following line.

```
// Additional user provided initialization code
```

4. Click the mouse and start a new line by pressing **<Enter>**. Since you're in the Java Source editor, the Clips palette is visible to the left of the editor pane.
5. Select Java Basics > Concatenate Strings. Drag this clip to your Java source and drop it directly underneath the above comment line (where you just added a new line).

Creator adds the following code to your Java source file.

```
// Concatenating Strings
// This clip shows how to concatenate two strings in Java
// and places the result in a text field component

//TODO: set string1 and string2
String string1 = "concat";
String string2 = "enate";
String resultString = string1 + string2;

// show the result in a component on the page
getInputText1().setValue(resultString);
```

Note that the last line is underlined (in red), since it produces a syntax error. Before we fix the error, let's align the newly added code.

1. Select the code you just added by swiping all the lines with the mouse. The selected lines turn gray.
2. At the top of the editor pane, hold the cursor over the icons until you find the icon with the tooltip "Shift Line Right (Ctrl + T)."
3. Click the Shift Right icon until the selected code block is aligned with the line above it.

Let's fix the flagged error now. We need to use method `getOutputText2()` instead of method `getInputText1()`.

1. Change the underlined line above to the following.

```
getOutputText2().setValue(resultString);
```

(Remove `InputText1()` and start typing the replacement text. Then press **<Ctrl-Space>** and see the code completion box, as shown in Figure 2–23. Here we are given two choices. Use the down-arrow key to select method `getOutputText2()` and press **<Enter>**.)

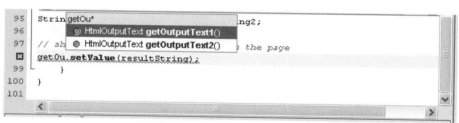

Figure 2–23 **Code completion helping out**

2. Redeploy and run web application **Echo**. You'll see that the String "concatenate" displays in the output text component on the page. We placed this code in Page1's *constructor*. This is where you provide initialization code that is executed before the page is displayed.

This completes our tour of Creator. The next chapter provides a detailed description of the JSF standard components, validators, and converters.

2.4   Key Point Summary

- Creator has multiple windows to give you different views of the project that you're working on. The windows can be sized, docked and undocked, or hidden.
- From the main menu, select View and the desired window name to enable viewing.
- Use the Welcome Window to select a Project to open, or to create a new project.
- The design canvas allows you to manipulate components on a page and control their size and placement.
- Use the components palette to place a component on the design canvas.
- Use the converters/validators palette to select data converters and input validators for your project.
- The Properties window allows you to inspect and edit a component's properties. Each element type displays a different list of properties.
- A component's `value` attribute usually contains text that is displayed (such as labels on buttons or input and output fields). The `title` attribute gives you a tooltip for the component and the `style` attribute lets you change the font characteristics.
- You can apply Property Binding and "connect" the value of one component to another.
- The Application Outline window shows all of the elements on a page, including nonvisual components.
- The Project Navigator displays an entire project, including Java source files. Choose between the Logical view and the FileSystem view by right-clicking the project name.
- The JSP Source editor displays a page's source. Most of the page includes JSF tags for components and their properties. As you make changes in the design canvas, Creator keeps the JSP source (as well as the Java source) synchronized with your changes.
- The Java Source editor displays the Java source for each "page bean," the JavaBeans component that manipulates each page's elements. You typically place event handler code or custom initialization code in the Java page bean.
- The Java Source editor includes a code completion mechanism that provides pop-up windows with possible method names (use **<Ctrl-Space>** to invoke) and Javadoc documentation for classes and objects in your program (use **<Ctrl-Shift-Space>** to invoke). It also includes a dynamic syntax analyzer to warn you about compilation errors before you compile.
- The Clips palette provides sample Java code to accomplish common programming tasks. The Clips are organized into categories based on function.

- The Page Navigation editor lets you specify page flow. It builds a navigation configuration file, **navigation.xml**.
- When you build your project, the Build Output window provides diagnostic feedback and completion status.
- The Server Navigator window displays the Data Sources, Web Services, Deployment Server, and Database Server nodes.
- You can start and stop the application server and undeploy running web applications from the Deployment Server node.
- You can view Table data by expanding the Data Sources node and selecting individual tables. Creator displays the data in the editor pane when you right-click the table name and select View Data.
- The Debugger Window displays several views that are helpful when you are debugging your project. You can monitor the call stack, local variables, and watches, for example.
- The Creator Help system provides a table of contents, an index, and a search mechanism to help you use Creator.

JSF Standard Components

Topics in This Chapter

- JSF Component Attributes and Configuration
- Data-Aware Components
- Component Nesting
- Action and Navigation Components
- JSF Standard Converters and Validators
- Components for Error Messages
- Validation, Conversion, and the JSF Life Cycle

Chapter 3

S un Java Studio Creator's design palette presents a wide variety of JSF standard components to choose from. These components include input and output text fields, checkboxes, listboxes, hyperlinks, images, database tables, and so on—in short, anything you need to design a web page. You can select a component, drag it to the design canvas, and drop it at the location of your choice. In addition, you can choose validator components to verify user input and converter components for data conversions. Creator maintains a design canvas with your web page layout and generates Java code for you, along with JSP and XML statements to help configure and deploy your application.

In this chapter we present a catalog of the JSF standard components, validators, and converters. We also provide references to examples in this book where they are used. The examples will help you understand how to use the JSF components in your Creator projects.

3.1 JSF Overview

The JSF API provides a rich set of UI components that let you handle events, validate and convert user input, define page navigation, and support internationalization. JSF also has custom tag libraries that connect components to server side objects. Let's start with the architecture of JSF to give you the "big picture" of what's going on.

JSF Architecture

Figure 3–1 shows the architecture used with JSF.

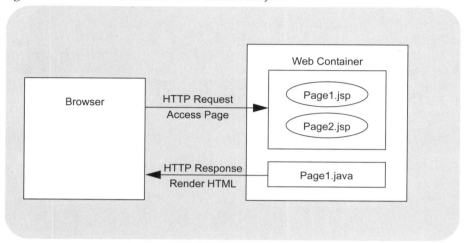

Figure 3–1 **JSF architecture**

Your browser interacts with the web container through one or more JSP pages (**Page1.jsp** and **Page2.jsp**). These are JSP pages containing JSF tags. The supporting page bean (**Page1.java**) manages the objects referenced by the JSP pages. Note that the JSP pages handle HTTP requests when a page is accessed, whereas the Java files render HTML for the HTTP response.

The JSP Page

Suppose a web page has an output text component (outputText1) that displays "In what year were you born?", a button to click (button1), and an input text field (textField1) for the year (restricted to the range 1900 to 1999). When these components are moved from the palette to the design canvas, Creator generates the JSF tags in the JSP file. Each JSF component also becomes a property in the generated Java page bean. To understand how this all works, let's start with how the output text component is defined in **Page1.jsp**.

```
<h:outputText id="outputText1"
    binding="#{Page1.outputText1}"
    style="font-size: 18pt; left: 96px; top: 96px;
        position: absolute"
    value="In what year were you born?"/>
```

The JSP file is expressed in XML. Creator generates this file for you and keeps it synchronized with your page design. As you modify your components with the Properties window, Creator updates the JSP code as well as the Java code as necessary. Creator generates the required JSF tags for your components in the JSP page. You can always access the JSP page by selecting the tab labeled Source below the editor pane design canvas.

In this example, the output text component displays "In what year were you born" on the page. Its `id` attribute (unique page identification) is `outputText1` and its `binding` attribute (the corresponding property in the Page1 page bean) is also `outputText1`. The `style` attribute specifies its location on the page with the left and top settings in pixels. This attribute also makes the text appear in 18-point font size.

JSF Expression Language (EL)

JSF uses a specialized syntax to access JavaBeans components with its tags. For example, the notation

```
#{Page1.outputText1}
```

references the `outputText1` property in JavaBeans component Page1. In the JSP file (**Page1.jsp**), the generated component tags reference properties in the supporting page bean, as follows.

```
binding="#{Page1.outputText1}"
```

Now let's see how the button component is referenced in **Page1.jsp**.

```
<h:commandButton id="button1"
    binding="#{Page1.button1}"
    action="#{Page1.button1_action}"
    style="left: 72px; top: 168px; position: absolute"
    title="Click for your age" value="Submit"/>
```

Elements `binding` and `action` are JSF tag library attributes whose values are set with JSF EL. Element `binding` is the button component's page bean reference, and `action` references a special action event method `button1_action()`, also in Page1. Here, method `button1_action()` is called when the users clicks the button controlled by JSF component `button1`.

Converters and Validators

What about the input text field component? Recall that this component must read a year (in the range 1900 to 1999) from the user. Here's how the input text field component is configured in **Page1.jsp**.

```
<h:inputText id="textField1"
    binding="#{Page1.textField1}"
    converter="#{Page1.integerConverter1}"
    style="left: 192px; top: 168px; position: absolute"
    validator="#{Page1.longRangeValidator1.validate}"/>
```

Text field components display and accept text, but `textField1` must work with integer numbers in this example. Consequently, a JSF conversion component (`integerConverter1`) is necessary to convert String input to integer values. Input is restricted to a specific range of numbers (1900 to 1999), so we'll need a JSF validator (`longRangeValidator1`) for the input, too.

```
converter="#{Page1.integerConverter1}"
validator="#{Page1.longRangeValidator1.validate}"
```

In both cases, JSF EL references the components that perform the conversion and validation.

Event Handling

JSF uses a well-known delegation event model to handle events generated by user actions (clicking a button, changing a selection in a dropdown list, pressing **<Enter>** after editing a text field, for example). It's helpful to have an understanding of the pieces that work together to make responding to events a well-behaved system.

The Event Source is a component that is capable of generating an event. Different components generate different event types. Button components and link action components generate action events. Dropdown list components generate value change events.

Event Objects are generated by components (the Event Source). An Event Object is basically a message that is passed from the Event Source to an Event Listener. The Event Object contains information about the Event.

Event Listeners are specialized objects created by JSF that know what to do when an event is generated. Different types of listeners can respond to different types of events. For example, ActionEventListeners respond to action events and ValueChangeListeners respond to value change events.

Using the "Publish-Subscribe" design pattern, Event Listener Registration keeps track of which objects "care about" an event occurring. Objects that "care" are those that register themselves through the Event Listener Registration. After registering with the Event Source, Event Listeners are notified when an action occurs. Notification means their special event method is called with the event object as a parameter. Fortunately, Creator generates all the method stubs, event listeners, and event registration for you. Here is an example of a value change method that JSF calls when a value change event is generated from a dropdown list component.

```
public void dropdown1_processValueChange(
      javax.faces.event.ValueChangeEvent vce) {
  // User event code here. . .
}
```

Web application developers provide the specialized event-processing code (whatever actions your web application must perform in responding to the value change event).

Action events are common with most applications and Creator generates the action event handlers for you. Action events can be used to write processing code in response to a button click. In addition, action events return String values to a navigation handler, which allow you to move to a different web page. Here is the stub Creator generates when you request event processing for a button.

```
public String button1_action() {
  // User event code here...
  return null;
}
```

Note that action events implement navigation by returning String values. A null string means you stay on the same page. A different String ("Button-Click", for example) instructs the navigation handler to go to a new page.

Java Page Bean

Now let's show you the Java page bean file, **Page1.java**. Creator generates Java code in the Java page bean for the components you select from the design palette. Each component becomes a property of the supporting page bean, and the component instance is bound to that property.

Here's the **Page1.java** file for our simple web application with two text fields and a button. Again, Creator generates this file for you.

```
public class Page1 extends AbstractPageBean {
   private HtmlOutputText outputText1 = new HtmlOutputText();
   private HtmlCommandButton button1 = new HtmlCommandButton();
   private HtmlInputText textField1 = new HtmlInputText();

   private IntegerConverter integerConverter1 =
       new IntegerConverter();
   private LongRangeValidator longRangeValidator1 =
       new LongRangeValidator();

   // getters and setters for components here...

   public Page1() {// page constructor
     // Creator-managed initialization code
   }

   public String button1_action() {// event handler
     // User event code here...
     return null;
   }
}
```

Note that Page1 extends AbstractPageBean. The private fields define the JSF components and the getter and setter methods make them accessible as properties. Here are the getters and setters for the output text component.

```
public HtmlOutputText getOutputText1() {
    return outputText1;
}
public void setOutputText1(HtmlOutputText hot) {
    this.outputText1 = hot;
}
```

In our example the `Page1()` constructor sets the minimum and maximum ranges for the JSF validator component (`longRangeValidator1`). When you set these values for the validator by using Creator's Properties window, Creator generates the statements in the constructor to configure the validator for you.

```
public Page1() {
  // Creator-managed initialization code
    try {
       longRangeValidator1.setMinimum(1900);
       longRangeValidator1.setMaximum(1999);
    }

    catch (Exception e) {
       log("Page1 Initialization Failure", e);
       throw new FacesException(e);
    }
  // User provided initialization code
}
```

3.2 Components

Creator allows you to select components from the JSF standard components palette for your application. These components are implemented with a JSP custom tag library for rendering components in HTML (part of JSF). Therefore, all of the JSF standard components are rendered as HTML tags.

When you select a component and drag it to the design canvas, Creator generates code in the page's JSP source as well as support code in the associated Java page bean. Furthermore, Creator displays each component in the Application Outline view, including any support components that may not be visible. Once you place a component on the design canvas, you can modify its attributes and behavior through the Properties window, through the JSP code, or through modifications to the Java page bean. In general, it's preferable to edit attributes of a component with Creator's Properties window. However, writing code to control navigation or including Java statements to handle action and value change events must be done in the Java page bean file.

Common Attributes

This chapter presents a catalog of the JSF standard components so that you can easily look up their behavior and use them in your application. Many components share common attributes and code generation features, however. Let's start with the definitions of these attributes so that you can see how they're used by the JSF components.

value

The `value` attribute stores a component's main characteristics. Its meaning depends on the component. For example, `value` stores the text of a button label, the display text of an output text component, or the input for a text field. The `value` attribute can also store the text for a secret field and hidden field components. For a hyperlink component, `value` stores a target URL name. For an image component, `value` holds the name of an image file.

The `value` attribute is a Java `Object` type. Creator allows you to bind a component's `value` attribute to a JavaBeans property, a data source, or even a localized message in a properties file.

title

The `title` attribute is a text string for a JSF component's tooltip.

style

The `style` attribute holds CSS Style Sheet strings for attributes such as font family, font size, and position parameters. These determine the type of font used, its point size, and placement on the design canvas.

id

The `id` attribute is a page-unique string that identifies a component on the web page. Creator generates the component's `id` for you, but you can use the Properties window to change it. We recommend renaming the default `id` when you have more than one component on the same page that requires action methods (buttons, for example). Providing meaningful names for the `id` attribute makes Creator generate associated action methods with meaningful names. This makes your Java code easier to read.

action

The `action` attribute is important for button and link action components. This attribute references a method in the page bean that returns a String for JSF's navigation handler. The application writer may provide application-specific statements in the action method, process information to determine page flow, or both. Chapter 4 discusses page navigation in detail.

binding

Creator generates the `binding` attribute for all components you place on the page. The `binding` attribute binds the component instance to a property in the page bean. For example, if you add a button component to a web application's initial page (**Page1.jsp**), the default `binding` attribute for the button component is

```
binding="#{Page1.button1}"
```

This JSF EL expression references the `button1` property of managed bean Page1 and binds the component instance to the bean property. Now you can write code in the **Page1.java** page bean to access the button component and dynamically control its properties.

Input Components

Components that collect input (text field, secret field, multiline text area, drop-down list, multiselect list, for example) share common attributes to control and validate input. Let's look at some of these attributes now.

validator

The `validator` attribute references a method that performs validation on its value. JSF provides three standard validators: a length validator for strings, a long range validator for integral types, and a double range validator for floating types. You can also write your own custom validation method. See "Add a Validation Method" on page 294 (Chapter 8).

converter

The `converter` attribute references a converter component that builds the correct type of object. Once the conversion has taken place, you can retrieve the object by casting it to the desired type.

maxlength

The `maxlength` attribute limits input to a specified number of characters. (This is *not* the same as length validation.) Setting attribute `maxlength` causes a component to stop accepting input after the user has typed in the maximum characters allowed. No error messages are produced.

required

Boolean `required` attribute specifies whether or not input is necessary for the component. If the user leaves an input component's field empty and `required` is set, an error message is produced during the validation phase.

valueChangeListener

A value change event occurs when an input component's selection changes or its text changes. If you want to perform processing based on input change, select the component in the design canvas, right-click, and select Edit Event Handler > processValueChange from the context menu. Creator generates a processValueChange() event method for you in the Java page bean. You can add your own processing code to this method if needed.

onchange

To set the onchange attribute, select a component in the design canvas, right-click, and choose Auto-submit on change. This sets the onchange attribute to the JavaScript element this.form.submit(). When the selection or input value of a component changes, the page request is submitted, allowing immediate processing (instead of waiting for a button click or a link action).

Table Components

The data table component and grid panel component build table elements. Here are the attributes that control their appearance.

bgcolor

The bgcolor attribute sets the component's background color.

border

The border attribute specifies the line width of a table or a grid's border.

cellspacing

The cellspacing attribute specifies the amount of space around the cells.

cellpadding

The cellpadding attribute specifies the amount of padding inside the cells.

columns

The columns attribute specifies the number of columns in a table or grid.

Data-Aware Components

Creator offers a selection of data-aware components that you can bind to a database table selected through the Server Navigator window. The data table component is particularly suited for displaying data, but you can also choose from among the dropdown list, checkbox list, listbox, multi select listbox, multi select menu, or radio button list components.

Creator automatically supplies a converter for non-String data fields when you bind to a database table. However, if there are any unexpected conversion errors, you will only see error messages if you have placed a message list component on the page.

Creator Tip

We recommend placing a message list or inline message component on the page when you're using the data-aware components, especially during development.

3.3 Component Catalog

The following catalog of JSF components describes each component and gives you common usage scenarios. To show you how a component can be useful in a Creator project, we also point you to relevant examples in other chapters of this book. The components are listed alphabetically for easy lookup.

Button

The button component is an example of a "command component." Buttons perform an action when they are activated (clicked). This can happen during server-side processing (a method that processes an action event) or with a navigational action that determines page flow. The button component is one of the most-often-used components in web design. By default, it is rendered as an HTML `<input type=button>` tag.

Buttons can be used for "simple" or dynamic navigation between web pages. With simple navigation, a button's `action` method returns a String that matches a case label in the navigation rules generated for the application. We show you how to create this type of navigation in "Add Page Navigation" on page 102. Dynamic navigation is useful when you need to figure out the next page based on some sort of processing. In this case, the `action` method returns a String based on the processing. See "Enable Page Navigation" on page 117 for an example of dynamic navigation.

In Creator, you connect the click of a button (an action event) to a method for processing the event by double-clicking the button component in the Creator design canvas. This brings up the matching `button_action()` method (where button is the component's id attribute) in the Java page bean so that you can add your processing code.

The button's value attribute is its label. You can bind this value to a database table if you want to update the label dynamically. You can also change the appearance of a button by setting the button's image attribute to an image file-name.

Book Examples

- "Add Button Components" on page 101 (Chapter 4). Uses a button to initiate navigation.
- "Place Button and Output Text Components" on page 158 (Chapter 5). Uses a button to initiate a page request.
- "Add a Button Component" on page 169 (Chapter 6). Uses a button to invoke an action event method.
- "Add Button and Image File" on page 193 (Chapter 6). Uses an image with a button component.
- "Add a Button and an Output Text Component" on page 293 (Chapter 8). Configures a button for internationalization.

Checkbox

The checkbox component provides a boolean on/off setting. Checkboxes are particularly useful in conjunction with component labels. By associating a component label with a checkbox (using the component label's for attribute), you enable a user to check or uncheck the checkbox in two ways, either by selecting the label or by clicking directly on the checkbox component.

All JSF standard components have value attributes that return Object types, so a Java cast is necessary to treat a checkbox value as a boolean. To see how this works, let's look at the following code fragment. Here, we verify whether a checkbox component called checkbox1 is "checked" or not. The checkbox component's getValue() method returns an Object type, so you need to cast it to a Boolean type to call its booleanValue() method. This enables you to use the checkbox expression inside an if statement.

```
if (((Boolean)checkbox1.getValue()).booleanValue())
    feedback.setValue("Email confirmation will be sent to " +
        email.getValue().toString());
else
    feedback.setValue("No confirmation will be sent.");
```

Here, we use a feedback output text component to display an email confirmation message if checkbox1 is checked. If not, a different message appears.

Example

Figure 3–2 shows part of a page with a checkbox component and its associated label. Selecting the label is the same as checking/unchecking the checkbox component. To obtain this behavior, set the component label's `for` attribute in the Properties window to the `id` attribute of the checkbox.

☑ Check here for email confirmation

Figure 3–2 **Using checkbox with a component label**

Checkbox List

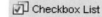

The checkbox list component groups a set of checkboxes. You can specify their items through the Properties window or dynamically fill them from a database or JavaBeans component. When you use a checkbox list, the user may select any number of the checkbox options (including none unless the `required` attribute is checked). A checkbox list component is appropriate when you want to give the user a list of choices with the phrasing "please check all that apply."[1] The selection items may be hardcoded with the Properties window or generated dynamically at run time. Creator automatically supplies a converter for non-String data fields when you fill the list from a database source. This component also accepts data binding. The `value` attribute of the checkbox list returns an array of `Objects` consisting of the checked selections.

Adding a checkbox list component to your web page creates three elements: the checkbox list component, an embedded selection list, and a "default items" list used for initializing the selection choices. To specify the choices, select `checkboxList1DefaultItems` from the Application Outline view. In the Properties window, click the editing box opposite attribute `items`. Creator pops-up a dialog so that you can add, edit, or remove items. (This is the same dialog that you use to specify items for the Listbox component. See Figure 3–9 on page 78.)

Example

Figure 3–3 shows a checkbox list component on a web page. A user can select as many of the choices as he or she wants (including none or all of them).

---

1. If you'd like to limit the choice to only one from a list, use the radio button list component (see "Radio Button List" on page 85).

Figure 3–3 **Using checkbox list**

Here is the Java code to display the choices selected from the checkbox list (whose `id` attribute is `checkboxList1`) in an output text component. Note that we assign the selected values to String array `sides`. Casting is necessary since the `getSelectedValues()` method returns an `Object` array. We use a `for` loop to concatenate the selected values with vertical-bar delimiters. This code is placed in the button event handler method.

```
public String button1_action() {
  // User event code here...
  String choices = null;
  String[] sides =
          (String[])checkboxList1.getSelectedValues();
  for (int i = 0; i < sides.length; i++) {
    choices = choices + " ||" + sides[i] + "|| ";
  }
  outputText2.setValue(choices);
  return null;
}
```

Component Label

A component label associates with another component (using its `for` attribute) to provide label information and additional selection behavior. For example, if you associate a component label with a text field, you can select the text field by clicking *either* the label *or* the text field.

Component label is a composite component. This means it has a nested output text component to hold the label's text. You typically set the text with Creator's Properties window. You can also specify data binding with a data source, property binding with a JavaBeans property, or text from a resource bundle. A component label's outer component contains the attributes that control the label's behavior and rendering.

Book Examples

- "Create the Form's Input Components" on page 113 (Chapter 4). Uses component labels associated with text fields.
- "Add Components for Input" on page 289 (Chapter 8). Nests component labels in a grid panel. Sets the text for its label from a localized **.properties** file.

Data Table

The data table component is complex. First of all, it's a composite component with nested columns, which in turn contain nested display components (such as output text components, buttons, or text fields). The data table component is typically filled dynamically with data from a data source or from JavaBeans properties. When you fill a data table component with data from a data source, Creator lets you control the result, including the columns to display, the number of headers and footers, and the component you want to display the text. You can also apply data converters to any field in a data table component.

When you drop a data source on top of a data table component in the design canvas, Creator automatically binds the table with the data and generates the number of columns from the database. Creator also generates headers from the field names and uses the database table's metadata to apply the necessary converters.

Figure 3–4 shows Creator's design canvas with a data table component bound to the TRACKS table from our Music Database in Chapter 7. This table has three columns (with headings from the database metadata). Creator shows the column's data type as "123" for numeric data and "abc" for String data. If the data are not text, Creator applies a converter for you as well.[2] In this table, an embedded output text component is used for the display.

Creator Tip

Creator provides an enhanced selection mechanism for composite components (such as the data table). In the design canvas, select the data table component and look in the Properties window to see which component is selected. Now click the component again and you'll see a different component's properties. For the data table, you traverse the components' nesting levels by successive clicking over the component.

---

2. For example, if a primary key field is integer data, Creator applies an Integer converter to the component. Creator performs this action for all the data-aware components.

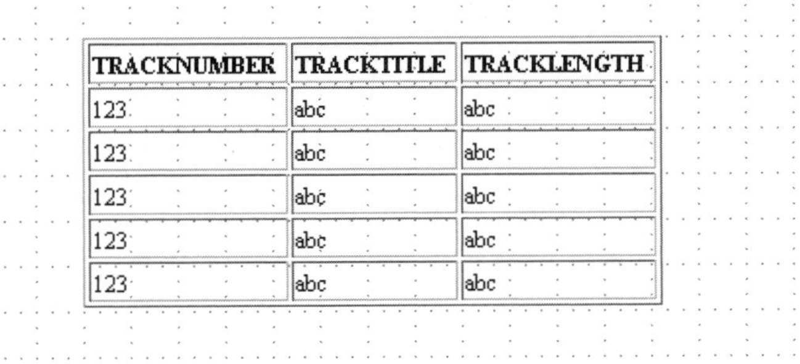

Figure 3–4 **Binding component data table with an external database table**

Creator automatically sizes the columns and dynamically generates the correct number of rows. When you bind a data table component to a database table, Creator generates a default query for you. You can modify this query by selecting the associated rowset from the nonvisual display. We show you how to work with database queries in Chapter 7 (see "Modify the SQL Query" on page 220.)

Figure 3–5 shows Creator's dialog for manipulating a data table format. Here, the dialog shows the columns from the TRACKS database table. You can choose which columns to display, the header and footer text, and the underlying component that holds the data. To bring up this dialog, select the data table component in the Application Outline view, right-click, and choose Table Layout.

Figure 3–6 on page 70 shows Creator's dialog for specifying page controls for database queries that produce many rows. Click the Paging tab in the Table Layout dialog. Now check Enable paging and then specify Page size. If you'd like page navigation buttons, check the box Display page navigation buttons. Next to each button, specify the button's label. At the bottom of the dialog, select where you want Creator to place the page control buttons using the dropdown list. After making your selections, click Apply, then OK.

Book Examples

- "Add a Data Table" on page 217 (Chapter 7). Builds a master-detail relationship using data binding with a data table component.
- "Add a Second Data Table" on page 228 (Chapter 7). Shows how to build an SQL Inner Join query by using multiple database tables and the JSF data table component.

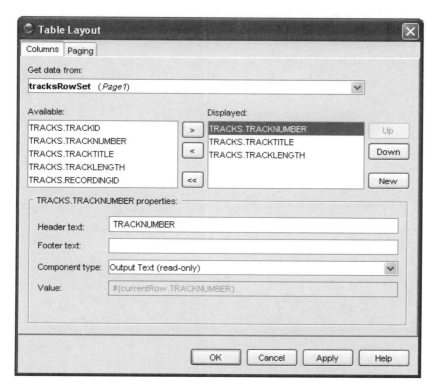

Figure 3–5 Table Layout dialog: specifying columns

Dropdown List

Dropdown List

The dropdown list component is an extremely versatile JSF component, rendered as an HTML `<select>` element (a dropdown list). A dropdown list allows a user to select one item from a set of items. The selection items can be hardcoded with the Properties window or generated dynamically at run time. Creator automatically supplies a converter for non-String data fields when you fill the list from a database source. This component also accepts data binding. The `value` attribute of the `selectOneMenu` JSF tag maps to the property that holds the value of the currently selected item.

When a dropdown list component is used with data table binding, you typically bind the data table's primary key field with the dropdown component's `value` field. You select an appropriate field from the data table for the dropdown component's display field. Thus, the display field may contain a person's

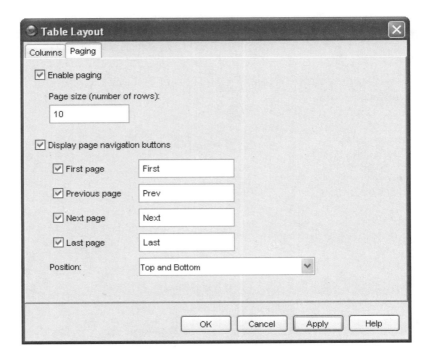

Figure 3–6 **Table Layout dialog: specifying paging**

name, whereas the dropdown component's `getValue()` method will return the primary key. This is useful for setting SQL query parameters from a listbox component's selection value. (See "Add Query Criteria" on page 221.)

The dropdown component contains an embedded `selectItems` tag that represents the items in the list (this is a nonvisual component appearing in the Application Outline view). The nonvisual component named `dropdown1-DefaultItems` supplies text for the selections. To make this happen, select the `dropdown1DefaultItems` element in the Application Outline view and click the `items` attribute in the Properties window. A dialog pops up that lets you type in text for each selection (see Figure 3–9 on page 78).

When the user makes a new selection from a dropdown component, the system generates a value change event. Creator allows you to toggle the `Auto-submit on change` attribute for this event. When it's on, the system invokes the `this.form.submit()` JavaScript function. This function updates the page and resubmits it when a user changes the dropdown list selection.

Finally, the `processValueChange()` event handler is where you add your statements when a value change event is detected. If you right-click the dropdown component and select Edit Event Handler > processValueChange, Creator creates the stub for the event handler method in the Java page bean.

Book Examples

- "Add a Dropdown List" on page 108 (Chapter 4). Uses a dropdown list with navigation.
- "Add a Dropdown List Component" on page 213 (Chapter 7). Fills the selection list from a database data source.
- "Add a Dropdown List Component" on page 276 (Chapter 8). Uses a dropdown list to specify locale.

Formatted Output   📋 Formatted Output

The formatted output component helps web developers display concatenated messages by using a specialized message format pattern. The MessageFormat class (in package java.text) produces language-independent messages. (You can read more about the MessageFormat class in the Java J2SE documentation at http://java.sun.com/j2se.) This type of formatted output can be very useful when you are constructing messages for localized or internationalized web applications. The MessageFormat class is set up to use either the default locale or a locale passed as an argument to its constructor.

The value attribute of a formatted output component specifies the MessageFormat pattern, which is typically a keyed string in a resource bundle. You provide param tags to specify the substitution parameters for the message.

Suppose, for example, your web application uses a counter to display the number of users currently logged on. You'd like to display one of the following messages on your page.

```
There are no other users logged on.
There is one other user logged on.
There are 12 other users logged on.
```

As you can see, the words in these messages must be different when the number of users change. (And this is just for English—the text in the resource bundles for other languages have their own patterns!)

Let's look at how you might do this with the MessageFormat pattern. The following statement lives in the **.properties** file referenced in the <f:loadBundle> tag for this project.

```
userCount = There {0,choice,0#are no other users|
    1#is one other user|1< are {0} other users} logged on
```

Here, userCount is the message *key* and everything else is the MessageFormat pattern. The number of users is represented as a parameter (0). Note that three alternatives are specified for the number of users logged on: zero (0), one (1), and many (1<). The expression {0} resolves to the current number of users.

JSF Tags

Here are the JSF tags for the formatted output component and an embedded parameter tag that fetches a number from text field component numberText. We show the text field component's tags as well.

```
<h:outputFormat binding="#{Page1.formattedOutput1}"
    id="formattedOutput1"
    style="position: absolute; left: 168px; top: 360px"
    value="#{messages.userCount}">

  <f:param value="#{Page1.numberText.value}"/>
</h:outputFormat>

<h:inputText binding="#{Page1.numberText}"
  converter="#{Page1.integerConverter1}" id="numberText"
  style="position: absolute; left: 168px; top: 312px"
  value="0"/>
```

Book Examples

- "Modify JSF Components for Localized Text" on page 269 (Chapter 8). This example doesn't use a formatted output component, but it shows you how to specify and reference localized text with a **.properties** file.

Grid Panel   *Grid Panel*

A grid panel is a general-purpose container that controls the layout of groups of other components. After placing a grid panel in the design canvas and specifying the number of columns (the default is 1), you can drop other components onto it. Creator fills the panel with your components in a grid (rows and columns) layout. This means the components are placed in the order that you drop them on the grid panel and according to the number of columns you specify.

The grid panel component has several attributes that allow you to control a grid's appearance. These attributes include bgcolor for background color, columns for the number of columns, cellspacing for cell width spacing, and border for the width of the grid's border lines.

Creator Tip

When you create a page with nested components (such as the page in Figure 3–7 on page 74), the Application Outline view is easier to use than the design canvas for placing components on top of the desired target. This is because rendering in the design view often obscures the specific target component that you're trying to drop onto.

Book Examples

- "Add a Grid Panel Component" on page 100 (Chapter 4). Uses a grid panel to hold button components.
- "Adding Components to the Page" on page 288 (Chapter 8). Uses a grid panel to format six components in a 3 by 2 grid.

Group Panel

📇 Group Panel

A group panel is another general-purpose container that controls the layout of groups of other components. Whereas the grid panel places components in a grid configuration (you specify the number of columns), the group panel uses a flow layout. Depending on the width of the panel, group panels arrange components one after the other in a flow. When there's not enough room in the first row, Creator continues with placement in a second row. As with the grid panel, placement is determined by the order in which you drop the components on the panel.

Group panels are handy for grouping nested components. It's possible, for example, to place a group panel inside cells of a grid panel. This technique lets you create interesting web pages by placing groups of components in each cell of a grid panel. From the grid panel's perspective, these nested components are treated as a single cell.

Examples

Figure 3–7 shows nested components in a web page that uses an outer grid panel, three columns of nested group panels, and individual components in each group. The first column is a nested grid panel that controls the spacing of the component labels. In the second column, we adjust the width of another nested group panel so that each text field ends up on its own line. The third column contains another group panel with a single message list component.

Figure 3–8 on page 75 shows the Application Outline view for this arrangement. The outer grid panel (gridPanel1) contains three nested group panels, groupPanel1, groupPanel2, and groupPanel3. Inside groupPanel1, a nested grid panel (gridPanel2) contains three component labels. The groupPanel2

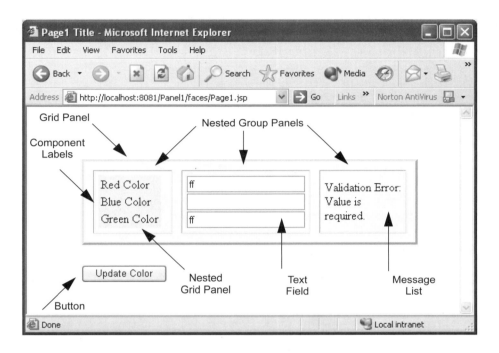

Figure 3–7 **Component nesting with grid panel and group panel**

component has three text fields and the `groupPanel3` component has a message list.

Hidden Field

The hidden field component allows web developers to include a hidden variable in a web page. The hidden field component is generated as an HTML `<input type=hidden>` element. This means hidden fields are not displayed in the browser. Hidden fields that you drop onto the design canvas in Creator show up in the nonvisual tray below the editor pane. Hidden fields can also pass to the server special form-processing information that the user cannot see or change. Note that hidden fields are "hidden" in the sense that they are not rendered by the browser. Anyone can still examine an HTML document's source to locate a "hidden" field, however. Hidden fields, like secret fields, are extended from the same component classes as text field and therefore have the same configurable attributes.

Figure 3–8 **Application Outline with component nesting**

Hyperlink

Hyperlink components link to other pages or a location on a page without generating an action event. A hyperlink component is useful when a page's URL information is data driven and no processing is necessary. In general, the hyperlink component takes an embedded output text component to display textual information to the user.

The hyperlink is rendered as an HTML `<a>` element and its text is underlined in a web page.

Book Examples

• "Add a Hyperlink Component" on page 171 (Chapter 6). Uses a hyperlink component to provide a link to URLs returned from a Google web services search.

Image

Image components display graphics from a file or a URL. Their value is the file or URL containing the image. The image component is rendered as an HTML `<img>` element.

When you select an Image component from the design palette, Creator pops up a Set URL Value dialog. To set the filename, make sure the File tab is selected and browse to the desired file. Select OK. Creator displays the image you select on the design canvas and copies the file to the project under the **Resources** node (you can view this in the Project Navigator window). Alternatively, you can specify a URL and either link to it or maintain a copy in your project's **Resources** folder. If you need to reference an image in Creator, use **images/***image_filename* where *image_filename* is the image file. Be sure to include the **.gif** or **.jpg** extension (these are the two types of image files that browsers can typically display). Once the image component is on the design canvas, you can reposition it.

If you'd like an image to initiate an action, use a button and set its `image` attribute to the filename. (You won't be using an image component for this.)

Book Examples

- "Add the Google Logo" on page 167 (Chapter 6). Puts an image on the page.
- "Add Button and Image File" on page 193 (Chapter 6). Uses an image with a button component.

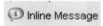 ## *Inline Message*

The inline message component displays messages generated by other components. Typically, these messages are data conversion errors or validation errors. When these types of errors occur, the validator or converter sends a message to the JSF context on behalf of the component. Inline message components can retrieve and display these messages. You attach an inline message component to a source component by using the inline message component's `for` attribute. (For situations in which you'd like to use a single component to retrieve messages originating from more than one component, use the Message List component instead. See "Message List" on page 79.) You can also use the inline message `style` attribute to format the appearance of your error messages.

Book Examples

- "Use Validators and Converters" on page 154 (Chapter 5). Uses an inline message component to report data conversion errors for a text field component.

- "Add an Inline Message Component" on page 183 (Chapter 6). Uses an inline message component to report validation errors for a text field component.
- "Add Components for Input" on page 289 (Chapter 8). Uses an inline message component to report validation errors from a custom validator method.

Link Action

The link action component can initiate an action, just like a button component. Its `action` attribute corresponds to an action method that returns a String. The return String can be used for page navigation, and the method can be used for general processing. The link action component is a composite component consisting of a top-level link action part and an embedded text component. The link action part controls the `action` attribute (like the button component), whereas the embedded output text component holds the textual label of the hyperlink. The link action component is rendered as an HTML `<a href>` element and its appearance is a hyperlink (underlined text). When you are working with the link action component in the design canvas, an easy way to select it is through the Application Outline view.

To add event handling code associated with clicking the link action component, select the link action component in the design canvas (the main, top-level node), right-click, and select Edit Event Handler > action. This brings up the `linkAction1_action()` method (where `linkAction1` is the component's id attribute). This is where you add your processing code to the Java page bean file.

Book Examples

- "Add Components to Page LoginBad" on page 121 (Chapter 4). Uses a link action component with navigation.
- "Modify JSF Components for Localized Text" on page 269 (Chapter 8). Configures a link action component for localization.

Listbox

The listbox component allows users to select one item from a set of items. The selections are displayed in a box (so that they're all visible at once). If the list is too long to display, a vertical scrollbar provides access to the hidden selections. A listbox is similar to a dropdown list.

The selection items can be hardcoded with the Properties window or generated dynamically at run time. The listbox component also accepts data binding. The `value` attribute of the `selectOneListbox` JSF tag maps to the property that holds the value of the currently selected item.

When a listbox component is used with data table binding, you typically bind the data table's primary key field with the listbox component's value field. Creator automatically supplies a converter for non-String data fields when you fill the list from a database source.

You select an appropriate field from the data table for the listbox component's display field. Thus, the display field may contain a person's name, whereas the listbox component's `getValue()` method will return the primary key. This is useful for setting SQL query parameters from a listbox component's selection value. (See "Add Query Criteria" on page 221.)

The listbox component contains an embedded `selectItems` tag that represents the items in the list (this is a nonvisual component appearing in the Application Outline view). To supply text for the selections, use the nonvisual component named `listbox1DefaultItems`. Select the component in the Application Outline view and click the `items` attribute in the Properties window. A dialog pops up that lets you type in text for each selection (see Figure 3–9).

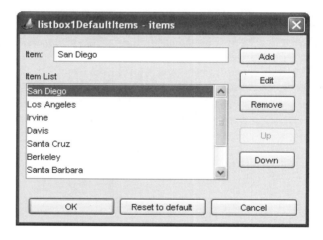

Figure 3–9 **Supply text for selection items for a Listbox component**

When the user makes a new selection, the system generates a value change event. Creator allows you to toggle the listbox `Auto-submit on change` attribute. When it's selected, the system invokes the JavaScript function `this.form.submit()`, which updates the page and resubmits it when the user changes the listbox selection.

To add the `processValueChange()` event handler method to the Java page bean file, right-click the listbox component and select Edit Event Handler > processValueChange. Creator generates the `processValueChange()` event handler method for you. You can then add event processing code to this method.

Book Examples

- "Add a Listbox Component" on page 214 (Chapter 7). Fills the selection list from a database data source. Uses listbox for a master-detail database read.
- "Create the Form's Components" on page 251 (Chapter 7). Fills the selection list from a database data source.

Message List

Although similar to the inline message component, a message list component displays JSF messages originating from *more* than a single component. If a message list component's for attribute is undefined, all messages from the page are displayed. Conversely, when a message list component's for attribute identifies a component id, only that single component's messages are displayed. You can use the message list style attribute to format the appearance of your error messages. (See also "Inline Message" on page 76.)

Creator Tip

A message list is a good component to routinely place on your page. JSF writes FacesException messages to the JSF context. These will only be displayed if a message list or inline message component is on the page. (For example, a conversion error may cause unexpected behavior. If a message list is on the page, you'll see the conversion error.)

Book Examples

- "Add a Message List Component" on page 116 (Chapter 4). Uses a message list component for all the page's components.

Multi Line Text Area

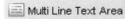

The multi line text area component gathers textual information for multiple lines. This component is similar to a text field, but you build it with rows and columns (see Figure 3–10). Its standard look displays several lines, and a vertical scrollbar appears if the number of lines exceeds the number of rows. The getValue() method retrieves the text and setValue() sets it. With a multi line text component, you can specify its size, provide text for a tooltip, and use data or property binding.

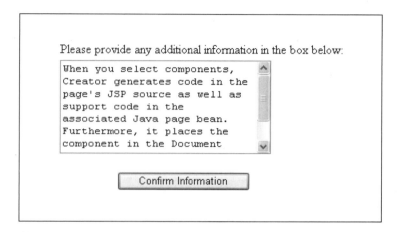

Figure 3–10 **Multi line text area component on a web page**

Multiline text areas are common with web applications that solicit free-form text. This includes such things as composing letters, listing comments, sending email, posting to guest books, filing bug reports, or reviewing user products.

Like the listbox, multiline text areas work with value change events and the `processValueChange()` event handler. To access this method, right-click the multi line text area component and select Edit Event Handler > processValueChange. Creator generates the event handler method in the Java page bean for you. This is where you add your event processing code.

Multi Select Listbox

The multi select listbox component is similar to a listbox except that you can select more than one item at the same time. The selections are displayed in a box (so that they're all visible at once). If the list is too long to display all the items, a vertical scrollbar provides access to the hidden selections.

The selection items can be hardcoded through the Properties window or generated dynamically at run time. Creator automatically supplies a converter for non-String data fields when you fill the list from a database source. Multi select listbox components also accept data binding. The `value` attribute of the `selectManyListbox` JSF tag maps to the property that holds the currently selected items.

A multi select listbox component contains an embedded `selectItems` tag that represents the items in the list (this is a nonvisual component appearing in the Application Outline view). To supply text for the selections, use the nonvisual component named `multiSelectListbox1DefaultItems`. Select the component in the Application Outline view and click the `items` attribute in the

Properties window. A dialog pops up that lets you type in text for each selection (see Figure 3–9 on page 78).

When the user makes a new selection from a multi select listbox component, the system generates a value change event. Creator allows you to toggle the `Auto-submit on change` attribute for this event. When it's on, the system invokes the `this.form.submit()` JavaScript function. This function updates the page and resubmits it when a user changes the list selection.

Finally, the `processValueChange()` event handler is where you add your processing statements when a value change event is detected. If you right-click the multi select listbox component and select Edit Event Handler > processValueChange, Creator creates the stub for the event handler method in the Java page bean.

Example

Figure 3–11 shows a page with a multi select listbox component and several items selected at once. Press **<Ctrl-Click>** to select nonadjacent items.

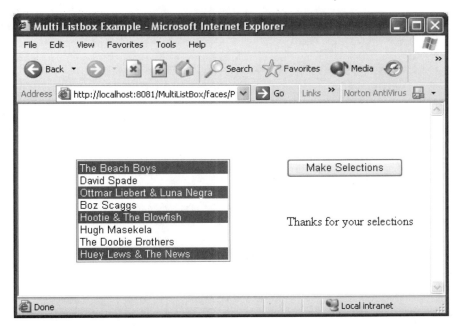

Figure 3–11 **Multi select listbox allows multiple and nonadjacent selections**

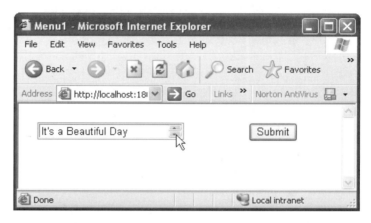

Multi Select Menu

The multi select menu component is similar to a dropdown list except that you can select more than one item at the same time. The selections are displayed in a single line component and the user controls the selections with up and down arrows (see Figure 3–12).

Figure 3–12 **Multi select menu allows multiple and non-adjacent selections**

The selection items can be hardcoded through the Properties window or dynamically generated at run time. Creator automatically supplies a converter for non-String data fields when you fill the list from a database source. Multi select menu components also accept data binding. The `value` attribute of the `selectManyMenu` JSF tag maps to the property that holds the currently selected items.

A multi-select menu component contains an embedded `selectItems` tag that represents the items in the list (this is a nonvisual component appearing in the Application Outline view). To supply text for the selections, use the non-visual component named `multiSelectMenu1DefaultItems`. Select the component in the Application Outline view and click the `items` attribute in the Properties window. A dialog pops-up that lets you type text for each selection (see Figure 3–9 on page 78).

When the user makes a new selection from a multi select menu component, the system generates a value change event. Creator allows you to toggle the `Auto-submit on change` attribute for this event. When it's on, the system invokes the `this.form.submit()` JavaScript function. This function updates the pages and resubmits it when a user changes the list selection.

Finally, the `processValueChange()` event handler is where you add your processing statements when a value change event is detected. If you right-click

the multi-select menu component and select Edit Event Handler > processValueChange, Creator creates the stub for the event handler method in the Java
page bean.

Example

When you apply data binding to a data-aware component, you can specify the
field from the database RowSet component that is displayed and the field that
is returned with a `getValue()` call. Figure 3–13 shows the Fill List from Database dialog. Here, the user chooses RECORDINGARTISTID for the Value field
and RECORDINGARTISTNAME for the Display field.

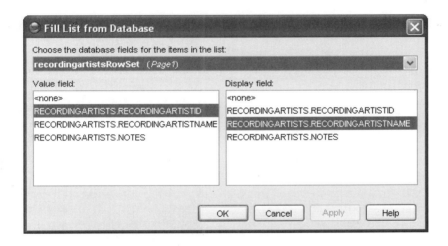

Figure 3–13 **Fill List from Database dialog applied to multi-select menu component**

Output Text

Of all the JSF components, the output text component is probably used the
most often in web pages. It's useful for putting up titles on a page or displaying
any kind of textual information. Output text components display String data,
but you can bind them to other types. With data converters and formatters,
output text components can display almost any type of data. They may be
embedded in data table components, link action or hyperlink components, and
component labels.

The `value` attribute of an output text component stores the text that is displayed. From a user's point of view, output text components are read-only. The
`setValue()` method sets its text and `getValue()` reads it. You can resize out-

put text components on the design page, but Creator expands them if you leave them unsized.

An embedded output text component is the default for a data table component. You can also bind an output text component to a JavaBeans property.

Output text components are rendered as plain text, which may include HTML formatting tags. Thus, you can build entire HTML pages by concatenating a string of HTML tags with text and assigning it to the component's `value` attribute. To enable correct rendering of HTML tags, make sure you set the `escape` attribute to `false` in the Properties window.

Book Examples

- "Place Button and Output Text Components" on page 158 (Chapter 5). Binds an output component to a JavaBeans property and applies a number converter.
- "Add Output Text Components" on page 171 (Chapter 6). Uses an output text component to store HTML text.
- "Build HTML Output" on page 188 (Chapter 6). Uses an output text component with HTML formatting.

Page Fragment Box

The Page Fragment Box component generates a JSP directive that includes a JSP file fragment in your page. This features allows you to build web pages that have consistent form. When you select this component, Creator pops up a dialog so that you can select a page fragment that already exists or you can create one. Figure 3–14 shows the Select Page Fragment dialog.

Figure 3–14 **Select Page Fragment dialog**

Once you create a page fragment box, you can add visual elements to it, such as output text components or image components. A typical use is a page fragment that consists of a banner with a company's logo (an image component), for example. As you create pages in your web application, drag a page fragment box component to the page, position it, and specify the page fragment name.

Creator Tip

When adding components to a page fragment, make sure that the components' id names don't conflict with any of the components' id names on the including page.

Radio Button List

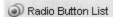
Radio Button List

The radio button list component enables you to group radio buttons on a page. With a radio button list, the user can make only one selection from a group of choices; changing the choice deselects the previous choice. This means only one button within the group is "on" at a time.[3] The selection items can be hardcoded with the Properties window or dynamically generated at run time. Creator automatically supplies a converter for non-String data fields when you fill the list from a database source. This component also accepts data binding. The `value` attribute of the radio button list returns the selected item.

Adding a radio button list component to your web page creates three elements: the radio button list component, an embedded selection list, and a "default items" list used for initializing the selection choices. To specify the choices, select `radioButtonList1DefaultItems` from the Application Outline view. In the Properties window, click the editing box opposite attribute `items`. Creator pops up a dialog so that you can add, edit, or remove items. (This is the same dialog box used to specify items for the Listbox component. See Figure 3–9 on page 78.)

Example

Figure 3–15 shows the design canvas of an application that obtains breakfast selections from the user. The application uses radio button list components for the beverage and entree choices, respectively. A checkbox list handles the optional side dishes (from which the user may select more than one item). With radio buttons, the user is limited to a single choice from the beverage and entree selections.

Figure 3–16 shows this application running in a browser. Note that the two radio button list components have a single item selected, whereas the checkbox list allows multiple selections.

---

3. If you need multiple-item selections, use the checkbox list component (see "Checkbox List" on page 65.)

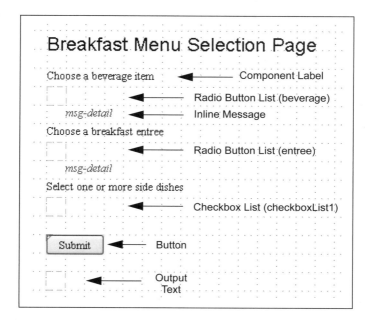

Figure 3–15 **Using radio button list components on the design canvas**

Here is the code in the button's event handler that displays the user's selections in the output text component. The code that accesses the radio button list components is bold.

```
public String button1_action() {
   // User event code here...
   String choices = null;
   choices = "You chose . . . " + beverage.getValue()
       + " and " + entree.getValue()
       + " and your side dishes are:";

   String[] sides =
       (String[])checkboxList1.getSelectedValues();
   for (int i = 0; i < sides.length; i++) {
      choices = choices + " ||" + sides[i] + "|| ";
   }

   outputText2.setValue(choices);
   return null;
}
```

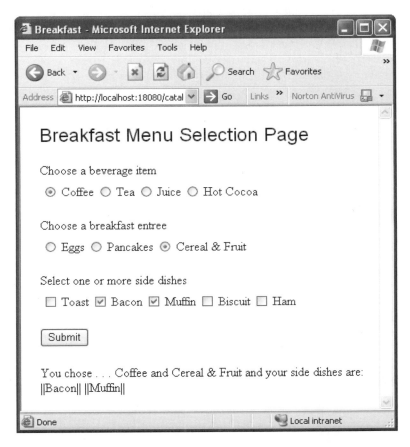

Figure 3–16 **Using radio button list components in an application**

Secret Field

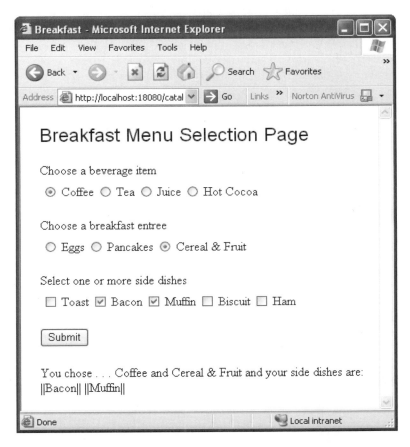

The secret field component allows users to input a single line of text. Echoed text is replaced by a single character, such as a black dot or an asterisk. When a secret field is rendered, its previous value is always cleared. Secret field components are useful for handling sensitive data input, like passwords and PIN numbers.

In all other respects, a secret field component behaves just like a text field. The input string is stored in the component's `value` attribute. Whenever you change the text, a value change event is generated. The secret field's `getValue()` method reads the text and `setValue()` sets it.

You can also attach validators to secret field components. Length validators, required validators, and range validators (to convert input text strings to numerical values) can be used to check input text. Note that value change events occur only if no validation errors are detected. When data conversion and formatting is needed, you can attach data converters to secret field components.

When a secret field component generates a value change event, the JSF implementation invokes the value change event handler for that component. The secret field component is rendered as an HTML `<input type=password>` element.

With secret fields, a component label typically appears with the label text on a page. It's a good idea to use an inline message component with secret fields to report validation or conversion errors. To create a tooltip, set the secret field's `title` attribute.

Book Examples

- "Create the Form's Input Components" on page 113 (Chapter 4). Uses a secret field to gather input for a password field.
- "Bind Input Components" on page 140 (Chapter 5). Shows property binding with the secret field component.
- "Modify JSF Components for Localized Text" on page 269 (Chapter 8). Shows how to localize an application that contains a secret field.

Text Field

The text field component enables users to input a single line of text. The input string is stored in the component's `value` attribute, and a value change event is generated when you change the text. The component's `getValue()` method reads the text and `setValue()` sets it. With text fields, you can attach a length validator, a required validator, or range validators (to convert text strings to numerical values). Value change events occur only if no validation errors are detected.

You can also attach a data converter to a text field. To do this, select the convertor you want from the Properties window under Data. When you apply a data converter, the type of the `value` attribute changes from the default String to the converted type.

A text field component can be embedded in a data table component. You can bind text field components to data, either by themselves or by embedding them in data table components. You can also bind a text field to a property in a Java-Beans component (see Chapter 5, "Property Binding with Components" on page 132). Figure 3–17 shows Creator's Property Bindings dialog box for binding a text field component to a JavaBeans property. Here, we bind text field `blueInput` with the `blueColor` property in the JavaBeans component Color-Bean.

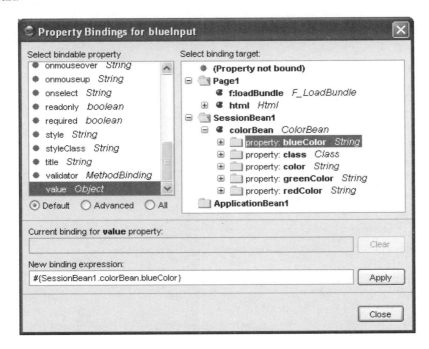

Figure 3–17 **Property Bindings dialog with text field component**

When the text field component generates a value change event, the JSF implementation invokes the value change event handler for that component. The text field component is rendered as an HTML `<input type=text>` element.

With text fields, a component label typically appears with the label text on a page. Inline message components are handy for reporting validation or conversion errors with text fields. To create a tooltip, set the text field's `title` attribute.

Example Page

Figure 3–18 shows Creator's design canvas for a page with text fields, component labels, and inline message components. Each text field has an associated component label, allowing users to select either the label or the text field component (this makes the text field active). Inline message components appear next to the text fields requiring input. This makes it easy for the user to see errors made during input.

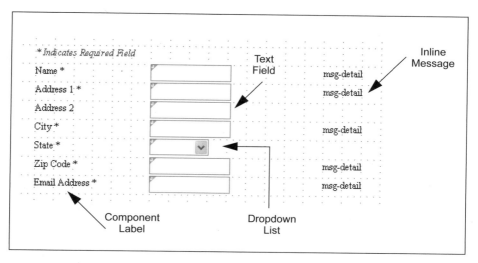

Figure 3–18 **Using text field components with other components**

Note that in this example, a dropdown list handles State input codes. Presumably, each text field has a tooltip to help users input data correctly. The zip code text field component should only accept zip codes with a 5-character maximum length. Set the `maxlength` attribute of the text field component to limit input to 5 characters.

Book Examples

- "Bind Input Components" on page 140 (Chapter 5). Shows binding properties with a text field.
- "Create the Form's Input Components" on page 153 (Chapter 5). Shows text fields with converters and validators.
- "Add a Text Field Component" on page 168 (Chapter 6). Shows validators.
- "Create the Form's Input Components" on page 242 (Chapter 7). Uses text fields to gather input for database row insert operations.
- "Add Components for Input" on page 289 (Chapter 8). Uses text fields with a custom validator method.

3.4   JSF Validators

JSF provides a set of standard objects that validate user input gathered through JSF components. The JSF architecture builds validation into the page request life cycle process, making validation an easy task for the developer to specify.

Validation Model

In Creator, you attach a validator object to a JSF component by selecting a validator from the design palette and dropping it onto the component in the design canvas. Validators also have properties that you can manipulate.

The JSF life cycle (see Figure 6–5 on page 185) includes a Process Validation phase. For components that have registered validators, JSF will validate the component's data. When validation errors occur, the affected component is marked "invalid" and an error message is sent to the JSF context.

Validation errors affect the life cycle process. Validation errors cause the page to proceed directly to the Render Response phase, skipping the Update Model Values phase and Invoke Application phase. This means events such as button clicks are not processed. When a page has multiple components with registered validators, all input is validated. This is helpful to the user since feedback (error messages) for the entire page can be displayed.

Table 3.1 lists the choices you have for validators in JSF. There are three standard validators: a Double Range Validator for floating types, a Length Validator for strings, and a Long Range Validator for integral values. You can also write your own custom validation method. Note that each standard validator has attributes that let you specify minimum and maximum values. The Length validator works with String data, and the Double Range and Long Range validators are typically used with converters to convert a component's data to the correct type.

Table 3.1 also points you to examples in the book that show you how to use the validators. This includes an example of a custom Validate Method called `validateHexString()` that checks for a 2-digit hexadecimal string.

3.5   JSF Data Converters

JSF strives to maintain a separation of presentation data (the data that users read and possibly modify) from internal data or model data. To accomplish this, you should use JavaBeans components, JDBC rowsets, and other application-specific structures as much as possible in your models. JSF also makes sure that any data conversions between the two views are consistent and well-defined.

Conversion Model

A JSF component that is type `UIOutput` or is subclassed from `UIOutput` can take a data converter to convert its data to a specific type. Typically (but not always), the component may be bound to a JavaBeans property of that type. For example, in project **Payment1** (see "LoanBean Component" on page 144),

Table 3.1 Validation choices

Name	*Description*	*Example*
Double Range Validator	Specify minimum and maximum values.	"Use Validators and Converters" on page 154 (Chapter 5). Uses a Double Range Validator with a text field to check the range of a double.
Length Validator	Specify minimum and maximum values. Does not detect empty input fields (you use required attribute of component).	"Add a Validator" on page 181 (Chapter 6). Uses a Length Validator with a text field.
Long Range Validator	Specify minimum and maximum values.	"Place Interest Rate and Term Components" on page 156 (Chapter 5). Uses a Long Range Validator with a text field to check the range of an Integer value.
Custom Validate Method	`validate-HexString()` method checks for a 2-digit hex string	"Add a Validation Method" on page 294 (Chapter 8). Shows how to implement your own validation method.

we bind a text field component (`loanAmount`) to the `amount` property of Loan-Bean. Property `amount` is a Double, so we apply a Double converter to the text field component.

Like the validation process, JSF sets aside specific times to perform conversions. Conversion errors may occur after the Process Validation phase or the Update Model phase. When errors occur, the affected component is marked "invalid" and conversion errors are sent to the JSF context. JSF proceeds to the Render Response phase in this case.

Creator will apply converters automatically to data-aware components when the source data type is not a String.

Table 3.2 lists the JSF standard converters available on Creator's palette. Most of the JSF converters are straightforward and provide a conversion that's obvious from their name. Note that all converters use wrapper classes (subclassed from `Object`) instead of the primitive types. This allows the `value` attribute (type `Object`) to accept all of these types. Two converters require a bit more explanation, however: the Date Time Converter and the Number Converter, so let's do that now.

Date Time Converter

The Date Time Converter converts a component's data to a `java.util.Date`. When you apply a Date Time Converter to a text field, the textual input is con-

Table 3.2 JSF converters

Name	*Description/Example*
Boolean Converter	Convert String data to Boolean.
Byte Converter	Convert String data to Byte.
Character Converter	Convert String data to Character.
Date Time Converter	(See below.)
Double Converter	"Use Validators and Converters" on page 154 (Chapter 5). Shows a double converter with an interest rate value and a loan amount value.
Float Converter	Convert String data to Float.
Integer Converter	"Place Interest Rate and Term Components" on page 156 (Chapter 5). Shows an integer converter with a loan term value.
Long Converter	Convert String data to Long.
Number Converter	"Place Button and Output Text Components" on page 158 (Chapter 5). Shows a number converter with a currency value.
Short Converter	Convert String data to Short.

verted. The field on the page is updated with a standard format during the Render Response phase. You can always configure a Date Time Converter's format if you need to. If you don't specify a locale, the Date Time Converter uses the default locale (see "A Word About Locales" on page 265).

The Date Time Converter uses the format rules and patterns of the `Date-Format` class. See the tutorial at `http://java.sun.com/docs/books/tutorial/i18n/format/dateFormat.html` for more information on formatting; see also the Javadoc for the DateFormat class at `http://java.sun.com/j2se/1.4.2/docs/api/java/text/DateFormat.html`.

The Date Time Converter uses a default pattern if you don't configure it differently. The data are assumed to be a date (as opposed to time) using the pattern MMM d, yyyy. Although full names for the month are accepted, the Date Time Converter shortens it to three letters and rejects numerical values. On input, you must supply a comma.

Of course, your choices for other formats are flexible. Figure 3–19 shows the Date Time Converter with the `dateStyle` attribute set to `default` for a text field component and to `medium`, `long`, and `full`. The second column shows formatting with two different *patterns* (appearing above the output text components). Each component has its own registered Date Time Converter to manipulate the converter's attributes separately. All the output components are bound to a single text field.

Figure 3–19 **Using the Date Time Converter**

Number Converter

A Number Converter enables you to manipulate numerical data in all sorts of interesting ways. Since numbers as well as date information are sensitive to language and locale, a Number Converter can use locale.

The Number Converter uses a pattern with separate attributes for manipulating a format (such as currency symbol, integer digits, fraction digits, and locale). To learn how a Number Converter can convert a double to a dollar value (including a dollar sign with a comma to separate thousands and hundreds and two digits to the right of the decimal point), see "Place Button and Output Text Components" on page 158.

3.6 Key Point Summary

- Creator's design palette contains JSF standard components, validators, and converters.
- JSF components are rendered in HTML.
- The JSF components share many attributes in common, such as `value`, `title`, `style`, `id`, and `binding`.
- JSF components that have a `UIOutput` type (output text components) or subclassed from `UIOutput` (such as text fields) can accept converters to convert text information.
- Input components share common attributes, such as `validator`, `maxlength`, `required`, `valueChangeListener`, and `onchange`.
- A value change event occurs when an input component's selection changes or its text changes.
- Creator generates a `processValueChange()` method for you when you write event processing code for a value change event.
- The `onchange` attribute allows you to specify a JavaScript element that is invoked with a value change event.
- Table components (data table and grid panel) have attributes to control appearance, such as `bgcolor`, `border`, `cellspacing`, `cellpadding`, and `columns`.
- JSF provides component binding with data sources, JavaBeans properties, and other JSF components. With component binding, converters, and validators, you can build web applications without writing any event processing code.
- A data table component is data aware and offers sophisticated layout choices. By specifying headers, footers, and embedded component types for its columns, the page designer can build a custom page for displaying data.
- You can enable paging controls with data table components. This is useful for database queries that produce more than a single page of data.
- JSF has data converters that encourage the separation of model and presentation data. The standard converters seamlessly convert presentation data to and from model data.
- The JSF validators validate user input before events are processed. Validation and conversion errors short-circuit the normal life cycle request mechanism and re-render the page with error messages.
- Use an inline message or message list component to display validation or conversion errors on a web page.
- You can write your own custom validation method and hook it into the JSF validation cycle.

PAGE NAVIGATION

Topics in This Chapter

- JSF Navigation Model
- Page Navigation Editor
- Navigation Rules
- Command Components and Navigation
- Action Event Handlers
- Noncommand Components
- Simple Navigation
- Dynamic Navigation

Chapter 4

M
ost web applications consist of multiple pages. A significant design task in building web applications is deciding page flow: that is, how you get from one page to another. Many commercial web sites consist of a "main" (or home) web page with links to other pages. These are frequently static links that simply bring up the requested page without any processing or decision making. Other web sites require more flexibility in their page navigation. Even if the next page is known, the web application may perform bookkeeping tasks or other processing before launching the next page. Finally, clicking a button may involve dynamic processing whose outcome determines the next page. For example, a login sequence results in either a successful login (and you go to the Welcome page) or a failed login (where you are rebuffed or are invited to try again).

Fortunately, Creator excels at page navigation. It uses the JavaServer Faces navigation model in concert with an easy-to-use Page Navigation editor that lets you draw page flow action arrows to define navigation rules. Creator generates the underlying configuration files for you. You retain the needed flexibility through coding the action methods that return outcome Strings to the navigation handler. Let's see how this works.

4.1 Navigation Model

JSF navigation is a rule-based system. Each application contains a navigation configuration file, **navigation.xml**, that has rules for choosing the next page to display after a user clicks a button or a link action component. Like the other configuration files, **navigation.xml** consists of XML elements. Here is a sample rule for changing pages from Page1 to MusicBrowser.

```
<navigation-rule>
      <from-view-id>/Page1.jsp</from-view-id>
      <navigation-case>
        <from-outcome>musicBrowse</from-outcome>
        <to-view-id>/MusicBrowser.jsp</to-view-id>
      </navigation-case>
</navigation-rule>
```

Element `from-view-id` identifies the origination page and `to-view-id` identifies the target page. Element `from-outcome` specifies the String value that is returned from an action method associated with a command component. Clicking that component generates the String which is passed to the navigation handler. With these rules, the navigational handler can then identify the target page.

In Creator, you specify the navigation rules by connecting your web pages with labeled page flow arrows in the Page Navigation editor. For each rule you construct, Creator generates an origin page, a destination page, and the outcome label that identifies it. Creator assumes that your origin page contains either a link action component or a button component that generates an action event when the user clicks it. The action event implements the navigation. That is, it returns the String that matches the label associated with that navigation rule.

Figure 4–1 is a UML activity diagram summarizing the steps in the navigation system.

Creator implements dynamic navigation. Often you need to process information before you can determine which page to invoke (for example, a login scenario can succeed or fail). To do this, the component's action property specifies an action *method*. The action method returns a navigation label that depends on the results of its processing.

By the way, the navigation model understands a default rule. If the action method returns null (its default in the initial definition Creator generates for you), the navigation model renders the same page. You'll see this behavior if you add a button to your page but do not define an action method. Or, if you don't change the default return value of null. When you click the button, it

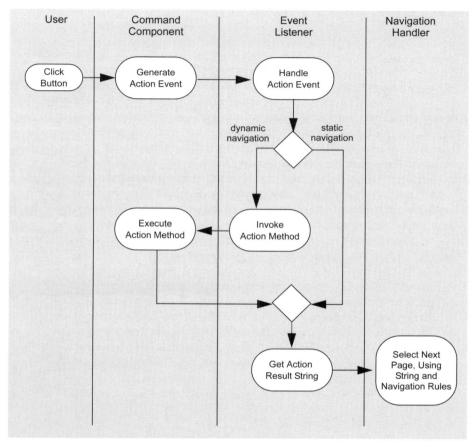

Figure 4–1 JSF Navigation Model: Page Navigation UML activity diagram

appears as if nothing happens. However, JSF invokes the page request life cycle process and the current page is redisplayed.

4.2 Simple Navigation

The first example we work through illustrates simple navigation. That is, each button component (or you could just as easily use a link action component) takes the user to one page. No processing is involved after the user clicks the button. The action event handler invokes an action method on behalf of the button; that method always returns the same String.

Create a New Project

- In the Welcome Page, click Create New Project. Specify the project name as **Navigate1**. The selected project type is J2EE Web Application. Click OK.

Specify Title

After creating the project, Creator comes up in the design view of the editor pane. You can now set the title.

1. Click anywhere in the design canvas.
2. Select attribute `Title` in the Properties window and type the text **Navigate 1**. Finish by pressing **<Enter>**. (Alternatively, if you click in the small square opposite the property name, a pop-up dialog lets you edit the title. Click OK to complete editing.)

Add an Output Text Component

You now use an output text component to place a heading title on the page.

1. From the JSF Standard Components palette, select Output Text. Drag it over to the design canvas and place it near the top of the page. Don't resize it.
2. Make sure that it's selected and type in **Welcome to the Music Store**, ending with **<Enter>**. This changes the `value` attribute. The component should now display these words.
3. In the Properties window under Appearance, edit the `style` attribute. Add the following.

```
; font-family: Helvetica; font-size: 18pt
```

Press **<Enter>**. The output text should now appear with its new style characteristics. (Again, it's probably easier to click the small square opposite the property name. A pop-up dialog lets you edit the `style` attribute. Click OK to complete editing.)

Add a Grid Panel Component

A grid panel component is a container that holds nested components, organized as a grid. You'll use it to hold two button components in a single row. (Adding a grid panel component for this project is optional.)

1. Select Grid Panel from the JSF Standard Components palette and drag it to the design canvas. Place it underneath the output text component. Creator builds a grid panel component with `id` attribute `gridPanel1`.

2. Make sure the grid panel is selected. In the Properties window under General, specify **lightyellow** for attribute `bgcolor`.
3. Still in the Properties window, change `cellpadding` to 3, `cellspacing` to 3, `border` to 3, and `columns` to 2.

Creator Tip

Grid panel is a container component that uses a grid layout. It places the components in the container in the order that you drop them on the panel. A grid panel dynamically creates rows to hold the components according to how many columns you've specified. (If you don't specify the number of columns, it defaults to 1.) After you add the button components, you'll see them nested beneath the grid panel node in the Application Outline view.

Add Button Components

You now add two button components to the grid panel.

1. From the JSF Standard Components palette, select Button and drag the component to the design canvas. Drop it directly on top of the grid panel you added previously. Change its `id` attribute to **browseMusic** and its `value` attribute to **Browse Music Titles**. Note that the grid panel automatically resizes itself as you add components to it.

Creator Tip

Changing the `id` *attribute is important here because you want more meaningful names than those generated by Creator. When you have multiple components that generate action events, it is much easier to work with meaningful method and property names in the Java page bean.*

2. Select a second Button and drop it onto the grid panel. Creator will place the second button to the right of the first.
3. Change the button's `id` attribute to **loginButton** and its `value` attribute to **Members Login.**

Besides buttons, you can also use link action components. These components have action methods and can be used with the JSF navigation model, too.

Creator Tip

You cannot, however, use the hyperlink component with the navigation model. The hyperlink component does not generate an action event, which is required in order to return a String label to the navigation handler. Use the hyperlink to hold a literal URL address, or hold a link that is data driven. For an example of using the hyperlink component, see the Google Web Services example ("Add a Hyperlink Component" on page 171).

Deploy and Test Run

Your web application is only partially done, but this is a good point at which to deploy and run it. Note that the page is redisplayed when you click the buttons; that's because there are no navigation rules yet. Figure 4–2 shows what the initial page looks like.

Figure 4–2 **Simple navigation web application**

Add Page Navigation

Creator makes it particularly easy to add page navigation to your web application. In this section, we show you how to do this with the Page Navigation editor. Let's enhance your application to have a total of three web pages. The first page, **Page1**, contains all of the components you just added, which include two buttons that take the user to separate pages in the application. Here are the steps to create the new pages and add page flow definitions with Creator's Page Navigation editor.

1. From the design canvas view, place the mouse in the canvas (anywhere in the background), right-click, and select Page Navigation. This brings up the Page Navigation editor. You see the initial web page, **Page1.jsp**, in the Page Navigation editor pane.
2. Place the mouse anywhere in the editor pane (in the background area) and right-click. From the context menu select New Page. Provide the name **MusicBrowser** instead of the default (Page2). This creates a new page called **MusicBrowser.jsp**.
3. Repeat this process to create another page called **LoginStart**.

The Page Navigation editor now displays the three pages of your application in the editor pane: **Page1.jsp**, **MusicBrowser.jsp**, and **LoginStart.jsp**. (You can see the pages in the Project Navigator window as well, under the Web Pages node.)

There is also a tab at the top of the editor pane labeled **Page Navigation**. This refers to the XML-based configuration file (**navigation.xml**) that contains your application's navigation rules. As you define page flow cases, Creator generates the navigation rules for you.

New Rules!

In this next step, you'll connect the pages and provide navigation case labels that the navigation handler uses to control page flow.

1. Click the mouse inside page **Page1.jsp**. The page changes color, enlarges, and displays its buttons.
2. Position the mouse inside page **Page1.jsp**, click, and drag the arrow to page **MusicBrowser.jsp**. When you unclick, you'll see an arrow with a label. Change the label from case1 to **musicBrowse** (finish by pressing <Enter>).
3. For the second case, start once again inside **Page1.jsp**, click, and drag the arrow to page **LoginStart.jsp**. This time change the label name to **userLogin**.

Figure 4–3 shows the Page Navigation editor pane with the web pages and navigation labels you just created. Note that the page flow arrows originate from **Page1.jsp** and point to the target pages.

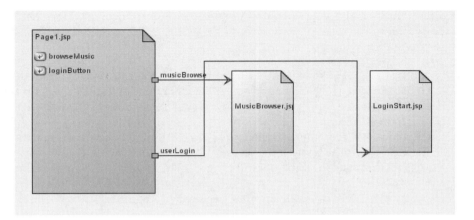

Figure 4–3 **Navigating from page Page1.jsp**

Creator Tip

As you create your navigation rules, Creator displays the attribute values in the Properties window for that rule (see Figure 4–4). You can always use the Properties window to change a selected page flow arrow or rename a label.

Figure 4–4 **Properties window for a navigation rule**

To view the navigation configuration file that Creator generates, select the Source tab at the bottom of the Page Navigation editor pane. Here is the file for this application.

```
<faces-config>
  <navigation-rule>
    <from-view-id>/Page1.jsp</from-view-id>
    <navigation-case>
      <from-outcome>musicBrowse</from-outcome>
      <to-view-id>/MusicBrowser.jsp</to-view-id>
    </navigation-case>

    <navigation-case>
      <from-outcome>userLogin</from-outcome>
      <to-view-id>/LoginStart.jsp</to-view-id>
    </navigation-case>
  </navigation-rule>
</faces-config>
```

This XML code defines one navigation rule with two separate navigation cases. Creator can collapse both cases into a single rule since they share the same origination page (**Page1.jsp**, the value of attribute `from-view-id`). The `from-outcome` attribute corresponds to the labels you supplied to the Page Navigation editor. These are the labels that you'll return from the buttons' action methods.

Add Event Handler Code

Now let's add event handler code for the two buttons on page **Page1.jsp**. Select the tab labeled **Page1.jsp** at the top of the Page Navigation editor pane. Alternatively, double-click inside the **Page1.jsp** page in the Page Navigation editor pane. You are now working in the design canvas for **Page1.jsp**.

1. From the design view, select the Browse Music Titles button, right-click, and choose Edit Event Handler > action. This takes you to the Java page bean, **Page1.java**. Creator generates the event handler method for you and places the cursor inside the method.
2. Change the null return value to **"musicBrowse"** (make sure you include the quotation marks).
3. Repeat the same steps for the second button, using String **"userLogin"**, as follows. Return to the design canvas, select button Members Login, and right-click. Select Edit Event Handler > action. Creator brings up **Page1.java** in the Java source editor. Change the null return value to **"userLogin"**.

The action methods for both buttons follow. Note that the return values (in bold) match the case labels you used in the Page Navigation editor.

```
public java.lang.String browseMusic_action() {
  // User event code here...
  return "musicBrowse";
}

public java.lang.String loginButton_action() {
  // User event code here...
  return "userLogin";
}
```

Action methods have a consistent format: they are always public methods that return a String and take no parameters. A null return value is ignored by the navigation handler (and therefore redisplays the same page).

When you define action method components, Creator generates the necessary JSP source for the button components. Here are the tags. Note that the `action` property references the event method in the page's Java page bean.

```
<h:commandButton action="#{Page1.browseMusic_action}"
  binding="#{Page1.browseMusic}" id="browseMusic"
  value="Browse Music Titles"/>

<h:commandButton action="#{Page1.loginButton_action}"
  binding="#{Page1.loginButton}" id="loginButton"
  value="Members Login"/>
```

Add Output Text Components

Before testing the application, you'll now add output text components to both target pages (**MusicBrowser.jsp** and **LoginStart.jsp**). You can access the design canvas of each page by double-clicking the page in the Page Navigation editor, by selecting the page name in the tab at the top of the editor pane (if it has been opened previously), or by double-clicking the page name in the Project Navigator window.

1. For each page, select it and bring up its design canvas editor.
2. From the JSF Standard Components palette, select Output Text component and drag it to the design canvas.
3. Modify its `value` attribute so that it displays a title that indicates which page you navigated to.
4. Optionally, modify the style attributes to manipulate the text font.

Deploy and Run

Go ahead and deploy the application. When you click a button, the system displays the appropriate page. You can use the browser's back arrow to return to the main page. If you'd prefer to have a button or link action component to navigate back, you can easily add these components to each of the target pages. Of course, you'll need to define the additional navigational rules in the Page Navigation editor. Figure 4–2 on page 102 shows the initial page in this web application.

Creator Tip

When you navigate to one of the target pages, the page loads slowly the first time. This is because the application server must generate Java source from the JSP, compile, and execute the code. It will be faster after the first time because the code has already been generated and compiled.

4.3   Noncommand Components

The JSF navigation model is set up to work with command components (those components that generate action events). Action event handlers return a String that the navigation handler uses to determine which page to launch next.

However, you can use other components to initiate navigation, although it's not quite as seamless. Basically, you need to provide a String directly to the navigation handler that matches the navigation rules you defined. Let's modify the **Navigate1** project to use a dropdown list component instead of buttons to hold the navigation choices.

Copy the Project

To avoid starting from scratch, copy the **Navigate1** project to a new project called **Navigate2**. This step is optional. If you don't want to copy the project, simply skip this section and continue making modifications to the **Navigate1** project.

1. Bring up project **Navigate1** in Creator, if it's not already opened.
2. Click anywhere inside the design canvas.
3. From the File menu, select Save Project As and provide the new name **Navigate2**. You'll make changes to the **Navigate2** project.
4. Click anywhere in the design canvas of the **Navigate2** project. In the Properties window, change the page's `Title` attribute to **Navigate 2**.

Delete the Buttons

1. From the design canvas of the first page **Page1.jsp**, select and delete the two button components. (Make sure you select the buttons and not the grid panel. Use the Application Outline view to select and delete them if you want.)
2. Right-click in the background of the design canvas and select View Page1 Java Class to bring up the Java page bean.
3. In the Java source, remove the action methods associated with the button components you just deleted. These are `browseMusic_action()` and `loginButton_action()`.

Add a Dropdown List

1. Return to the design canvas by selecting the tab labeled **Page1.jsp** at the top of the editor pane. From the JSF Standard Components, select Dropdown List and drop it on top of the grid panel component. (If you elected not to use the grid panel component, just drop Dropdown List onto the page.)
2. In the Application Outline view, select the `dropdown1DefaultItems` element (at the very bottom of the view).
3. In its Properties window, click the small editing square opposite attribute `items`. An editing dialog box appears. Replace the default items with the *three* choices: type in **Home** and click Add. Then change the input field to **Browse Music Titles** and click Add again. Finally, add the third choice, **Members Login**, followed by Add. Now select each of the default strings and click Remove. When you're done, click OK.
4. In the design canvas, select the dropdown list component. Right-click and check `Auto-submit on change` (it's currently *unchecked*). This tells JSF to initiate the page request cycle when the user changes the dropdown list component's selection.

Value Change Event vs. Action Event

Before we go any further, an explanation is warranted for adding three navigation choices to the dropdown menu component. Why is this necessary? Remember, the event type is called value *change*. If we present the user with a dropdown menu item that contains navigation choices and one of the choices is preselected, this preselection prohibits the user from selecting it with an accompanying value *change* event. Simply, there is no change in value since it is already selected. Therefore, we create an initial (preselected) choice, **Home**, representing the current page.

When users return to this page by clicking the browser Back button, **Home** is no longer preselected. Now selecting **Home** *does* cause a value change event and the string "Home" is passed to the navigation handler. Since **Home** doesn't match any of the navigation rules, no page change occurs.

A page designer has another choice. You can always place a button next to the dropdown menu. After the user makes a selection (whether it be a value change or not), he or she clicks the button and the button's action event handler can return the dropdown menu selection's String value.

Creator Tip

When you key off a value change event, the event handler will only be called if the selection component has actually changed. The event handler will not be called when you select the displayed choice.

Match the Navigation Labels

In the previous example, you used navigation labels that are not the same as the text you're using for the dropdown list component. The dropdown list component's `getValue()` method returns the text you just put into the `dropdown1DefaultItems` element. Therefore, you'll need to modify the navigation labels so they match the text you used in the dropdown list.

1. Bring up the Page Navigation editor: right-click in the design canvas and select Page Navigation from the context menu.
2. Select the page flow arrow that points to the **MusicBrowser.jsp** page. In the Properties window, change the `Outcome` attribute to **Browse Music Titles**.
3. Now select the second page flow arrow and change its `Outcome` attribute to **Members Login**. The labels are case sensitive. It's all right to have embedded spaces in the Strings.
4. Click the Source tab at the bottom of the editor pane. You'll see that Creator updated the navigation configuration file, as follows.

```
<navigation-rule>
  <from-view-id>/Page1.jsp</from-view-id>
    <navigation-case>
      <from-outcome>Browse Music Titles</from-outcome>
      <to-view-id>/MusicBrowser.jsp</to-view-id>
    </navigation-case>

    <navigation-case>
      <from-outcome>Members Login</from-outcome>
      <to-view-id>/LoginStart.jsp</to-view-id>
    </navigation-case>
</navigation-rule>
```

Add Event Handler Code

When the user changes the selection in a dropdown list component, a value change event is generated. A value change event is not hooked into the navigation system the way that an action event is. But in the event handler, we can grab the new value and pass it directly to the navigation handler. You'll be adding code to do this.

Creator Tip

The code you are about to add will cause the Java source editor to complain because it doesn't have all of the necessary import statements. After you add the code, we'll show you a shortcut for adding the imports.

1. Return to the design canvas for **Page1.jsp**.
2. Select the dropdown list. Right-click and select Edit Event Handler > processValueChange. Creator brings up the Java page bean and puts the cursor in the newly generated event handling method for the dropdown list component, dropdown1_processValueChange().
3. Add the code from the book's download examples (copy and paste file **FieldGuide/Examples/Navigation/snippets/Navigate2_valueChange.txt**). This code "gets at" the context and application objects associated with this web application to access the navigation handler. The last statement sends the navigation String (the value in the dropdown list component) to the navigation handler. The added code is bold.

```
public void dropdown1_valueChangeListener(
javax.faces.event.ValueChangeEvent vce) {
    // User event code here...
    FacesContext context = FacesContext.getCurrentInstance();

    Application application = context.getApplication();
    NavigationHandler navigator =
          application.getNavigationHandler();
    navigator.handleNavigation(context,null,
          (String)dropdown1.getValue());
}
```

Your code will be underlined in red because the Java file is lacking import statements. Here's how to add the needed import statements.

1. First, click anywhere inside the word FacesContext and type **<Alt-Shift-I>**. Creator pops up the Import Class dialog and displays package name javax.faces.context. Choose radio button Import Package and Click OK.

2. Repeat this by clicking inside the word `Application` in your code. Again, press **<Alt-Shift-I>**. Choose radio button Import Package and click OK. Figure 4–5 shows the Import Class dialog box at this point.

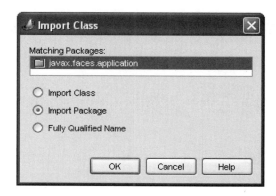

Figure 4–5 **Import Class dialog**

When you're finished specifying the code imports, Creator adds the following packages to your file.

```
import javax.faces.application.*;
import javax.faces.context.*;
```

This procedure will eliminate the red underlines in your code and any "unresolved symbol" errors in the event handler code.

Deploy and Run

Deploy and run the application. Figure 4–6 shows the dropdown list component with the page navigation choices. You can see that command components (button and link action) are easier to use for navigation, but with a bit of extra coding you can make other components work too.

4.4 Dynamic Navigation

You've seen an example of simple navigation, in which each component's action event returns a label that corresponds to a navigation rule. Now you're going to work through an example that shows dynamic navigation. Here, an

Figure 4–6 **Using a dropdown list component for navigation**

action method can return a different label depending on some processing it performs. You'll see that dynamic navigation is also straightforward with Creator.

This example sets up a login sequence whereby the user is required to give a username and password to gain access to the next page. We've simplified the processing criteria to concentrate on the navigation issues, but in the next chapter we expand this example for an improved architectural configuration (using JavaBeans component architecture).

Create a New Project

Creator Tip

In this section, you will use the same name (Login1) as the project we showed you in Chapter 2 ("Creator Basics"). However, this time you'll build the project from scratch. If project Login1 is already included in your default Creator Projects directory, you may want to delete it or move it before continuing.

- In the Welcome Page, select button Create New Project. Specify project name as **Login1**. The selected project type is J2EE Web Application. Click OK.

Specify Title

After creating the project, Creator comes up in the design view of the editor pane. You can now set the title.

1. Click in the middle of the design canvas.
2. Select `Title` in the Properties window and type in the text **Login 1**. Finish by pressing **<Enter>**.

Add an Output Text Component

You'll use an output text component to place a heading title on the page.

1. From the JSF Standard Components palette, select Output Text. Drag it over to the design canvas and place it near the top of the page.
2. Make sure that it's selected. Start typing **Members Login** and press **<Enter>**. The `value` attribute in the Properties window will show these words and the output text component will display them.
3. In the Properties window under Appearance, edit the `style` attribute. Click the small square opposite the `style` attribute. A pop-up dialog allows you to edit the attribute. After the current settings, add the following.

```
; font-family: Helvetica; font-size: 18pt
```

Click OK. The output text should now appear with its new style characteristics.

Create the Form's Input Components

The application uses the next set of components to gather input for the member's username and password. For the username, you'll add a component label to display a label and a text field to gather the data. Figure 4–7 shows the design canvas with all the components added to the page.

1. From the JSF Standard Components palette, select Component Label and add it to the design canvas. This is a composite component with a nested output text to display the label's text.

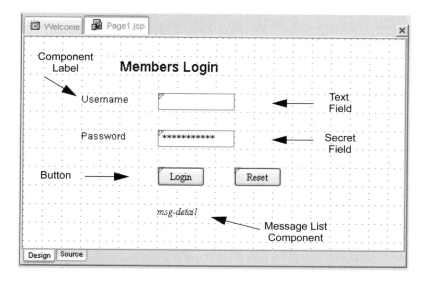

Figure 4–7 Design canvas showing components for project Login1

2. In the Application Outline view, select the embedded output text component (`componentLabel1Text`) and change its `value` attribute to **Username**.
   Under `style`, add

```
font-family: Helvetica
```

3. From the JSF Standard Components palette, select Text Field and add it to
   the design canvas. Change its `id` attribute to **userName**. Position it next to
   the label component you just added.
4. In the text field's Properties window under Data, check the `required`
   attribute. This prevents an empty input field. Now when you process the
   input in the event handler, you don't have to worry about checking for null
   values.
5. Still in the Properties window, change its `title` attribute to **Please type in
   your username**. The `title` attribute supplies text to the component's tooltip
   mechanism.
6. In the Application Outline view, select component `componentLabel1` (the
   top-level component of the component label element you added).
7. In the Properties window, click the editing box next to the `for` attribute and
   from the list of components, select `userName` (the text field component).
   Click OK. This step binds the label component to the text field component,

affecting GUI operations such as mouse selection. For example, clicking the mouse over the label's text puts the cursor in the associated text field's input box.

For the password field, you'll need a secret field component in addition to a label component to display the label. The secret field component performs several functions that make it particularly suitable for gathering sensitive data. First, it replaces the text that you enter with a constant character (the default is a black dot or an asterisk). Second, when the page is refreshed or you return to the page, the field is cleared. Thus, if you leave your workstation and someone else uses your computer, the new user can't "borrow" your password entry by simply selecting the browser's back button until the login page is reached.

Place the password components directly underneath the username components added above. You will follow the same procedure.

1. From the JSF Standard Components palette, select Component Label and add it to the design canvas.
2. In the Application Outline view, select the embedded output text component (`componentLabel2Text`) and change its `value` attribute to **Password**. Under `style`, add

```
font-family: Helvetica
```

3. Add a Secret Field component and change its `id` attribute to **password**. Position it next to the label component you just added.[1]
4. Still in the Properties window, change its `title` attribute to **Please type in your password** for the tooltip.
5. In the Application Outline view, select component `componentLabel2` (the top-level component of the component label element you added).
6. In the Properties window, click the editing box next to the `for` attribute and from the list of components, select `password` (the secret field component) to associate the label with the password secret field. Click OK.

To check the placement of the components on the page, right-click in the design canvas and choose Preview in Browser. Creator renders the JSF components in a page in your browser.

---

1. Unlike the username field, *don't* check the `required` attribute for password. Since the component clears its field every page request, requiring input interferes with the reset button that you will add in the next section.

Add Button Components

This application uses two button components: one to submit the form data to be processed for logging in. The second button clears the two input fields so that the user can start over. After adding the components, you'll add page navigation rules and code for the button event handlers.

1. From the JSF Standard Components palette, select the Button component and drag it to the design canvas. Position it under the two text field components. Change its component name (`id` attribute) to **login**.
2. Make sure it's selected and bring up its Properties window. Under Data, change its `value` attribute to **Login** and press **<Enter>**. The button's label should now change.
3. Repeat these steps and add a second button to the design canvas. Change its `id` attribute to **reset**.
4. Make sure it's selected and bring up its Properties window. Under Data, change its `value` attribute to **Reset** and press **<Enter>**. The button's label should now reflect this label name.

Add a Message List Component

Since the `required` attribute is checked for component `userName`, you need to tell the user that input is required if they leave the field empty. Creator has two components that help you do this. The inline message component is bound to a single component and listens for and displays messages generated by that component. If you choose this component, use one for each component that has user input validation. Because you place each inline message component near its associated input field, users know right away where the problems are.

The second choice is the message list component. In this case, a single component will display the error messages generated from all the page's components. The message list component is appropriate for this example because we have only one component that requires input.

1. Select the Message List component from the JSF Standard Components palette and drag it onto the design canvas. Position it under the two buttons you just added.
2. In its Properties window under Appearance, select the `style` attribute and add the following.

```
; font-style: italic
```

3. In the Properties window under General, make sure attribute `showSummary` is checked. (Attributes `showDetail` and `showSummary` display the same message text here.)

Deploy and Test Run

Although you haven't yet added any functionality to the button components, it's a good idea to deploy and run the application now. Go ahead and click the green chevron in the toolbar. When the login page comes up, type in user-names and passwords. Of course, clicking the buttons won't do anything, but you should see an error message if you leave an input field empty. Figure 4–8 shows the initial page of the **Login1** web application. The user is holding the cursor over the secret field to display the tooltip.

Figure 4–8 Login page web application

Enable Page Navigation

This application has a total of three web pages. The first page, **Page1**, contains all of the components you have just added, including a Login button that will take the user to either a **LoginGood** page (if the login process succeeds) or **Log-inBad** page (if the login process fails). The easiest way to build this is to go to the Page Navigation editor, create the two new pages, and connect them with labeled navigation arrows. When you've done all this, you can then add the code in the button event handlers to return the correct String values for the navigation rules.

1. From the design canvas view, place the mouse in the canvas (anywhere in the background), right-click and select Page Navigation. The Page Navigation editor comes up. You see the initial web page, **Page1.jsp**, in the Page Navigation editor pane.
2. Place the mouse anywhere in the editor pane (in the background area) and right-click. From the context menu select New Page. Provide the name **LoginGood** instead of the default. This creates a new page, **LoginGood.jsp**.
3. Repeat this process, creating another page. Call it **LoginBad**. In the Project Navigator window, you see your application's three web pages: **Page1.jsp**, **LoginGood.jsp**, and **LoginBad.jsp**.

In the next three steps, you'll connect the pages and provide navigation case labels that you can use in your event handling code to control the page flow. This step is exactly the same as in the previous example.

1. Place the mouse inside page **Page1.jsp**, click and drag the arrow to page **LoginGood.jsp**. When you unclick, you'll see an arrow with a label. Change the label from case1 to **loginSuccess**.
2. Once again, select **Page1.jsp** and drag the arrow to page **LoginBad.jsp**. This time change the label name to **loginFail**.
3. Finally, you'll add a third rule. Create an arrow from **LoginBad.jsp** back to the initial page, **Page1.jsp**. Change its label to **loginPage**.

Figure 4–9 shows the Page Navigation editor pane with the web pages and navigation labels you just created.

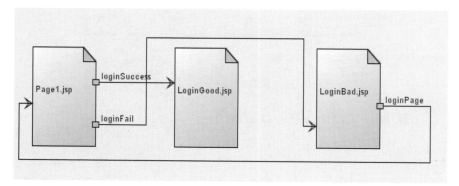

Figure 4–9 **Page Navigation editor pane with three navigation rules**

Behind the scenes Creator is generating code for its Navigation Rules in file **navigation.xml**. To see what it generates, select the Source tab at the bottom of the Page Navigation editor pane. Here is the file.

```
<faces-config>
  <navigation-rule>
    <from-view-id>/Page1.jsp</from-view-id>
      <navigation-case>
        <from-outcome>loginSuccess</from-outcome>
        <to-view-id>/LoginGood.jsp</to-view-id>
      </navigation-case>

      <navigation-case>
        <from-outcome>loginFail</from-outcome>
        <to-view-id>/LoginBad.jsp</to-view-id>
      </navigation-case>
  </navigation-rule>

  <navigation-rule>
    <from-view-id>/LoginBad.jsp</from-view-id>
      <navigation-case>
        <from-outcome>loginPage</from-outcome>
        <to-view-id>/Page1.jsp</to-view-id>
      </navigation-case>
  </navigation-rule>
</faces-config>
```

This XML file has two rules originating from **Page1.jsp** and one rule from page **LoginBad.jsp**. The `from-outcome` attribute corresponds to the labels you supplied to the Page Navigation editor. You'll use these labels when you write the event handling code in the Java page bean.

Add Event Handler Code

You added two button components to the **Page1.jsp** page. Now let's add event handler code to both of them.

1. Select the tab labeled **Page1.jsp** at the top of the Page Navigation editor pane. Alternatively, double-click inside the **Page1.jsp** page in the Page Navigation editor pane. You are now in the design canvas for **Page1.jsp**. The button components should be visible.
2. From the design view, double-click the Reset button. This takes you to the Java page bean, **Page1.java**. Creator generates the event handler method for you and places the cursor inside the method. The following code clears the

input components. Add it to the Reset button event handler, reset_action(). (The added code is bold.)

```
public java.lang.String reset_action() {
    // User event code here...
    userName.setValue("");
    password.setValue("");
    return null;
}
```

3. Return to the design view by selecting the **Page1.jsp** tab at the top of the editor pane. Double-click the Login button component. Creator now generates the event handler for the Login button. This takes you to the Java page bean, **Page1.java**.

4. Add the following code to the Login button event handler, login_action(). Copy and paste from file **FieldGuide/Examples/Navigation/snippets/ Login1_loginAction.txt**. The added code is bold. (Be sure to delete the return null statement.)

```
public java.lang.String login_action() {
    // User event code here...
    if (myUserName.equals(userName.getValue()) &&
      myPassword.equals(password.getValue())) {
        return "loginSuccess";
    }
    else return "loginFail";
}
```

(Ignore the errors flagged in red for now.) The "loginSuccess" and "login-Fail" String values correspond to the page's navigation rules for going to page **LoginGood.jsp** and **LoginBad.jsp**, respectively. This is called "dynamic" navigation because the event handler dynamically figures out the outcome according to the result of the if statement.

5. Add the following two lines of code (place them above method login_action()). These statements define values for private variables myUserName and myPassword. These are the "correct" values the user must supply for a successful login. Choose whatever values you'd like for testing the application (and they don't have to be the same). Here's the code. (After you add this code, the errors flagged in red will disappear.)

```
private String myUserName = "rave4u";
private String myPassword = "rave4u";
```

Add Components to Page LoginBad

When the login process fails because the values typed into the input fields do not match the Strings stored in the Java page bean, the system loads page **LoginBad.jsp**. Here you display a failure message to the user and include a link action component to return to the login page, **Page1.jsp**.

1. In the Project Navigator window under Web Pages, double-click the web page **LoginBad.jsp**. You're now working in the design canvas for this page.
2. From the JSF Standard Components palette, select component Output Text and drag it onto the design canvas. Position it at the top.
3. Make sure the component is selected and type **Invalid username or password. To try again, click**. Finish by pressing **<Enter>**. This changes the `value` attribute.
4. Now select the Link Action component from the components palette and drag it onto the design canvas. Position it directly under the output text component.
5. Note that just like component label, the link action component results in a composite component, as shown in the Application Outline view. The link action component contains a nested output text component.
6. In the Application Outline view, select the nested output text component `linkAction1Text`, and change its `value` attribute to **HERE**.
7. Now select the link action component in the Application Outline view and change its `id` attribute in the Property view to **loginpage**. The component's name should reflect this change in the Application Outline view.

Add Event Handler Code

1. Return to the Application Outline view and select the link action component, `loginpage`. Right-click and from the context menu select Edit Event Handler > action.
2. This brings up the Java page bean for this page, **LoginBad.java**, and places the cursor at the generated event handler method.
3. Add the following navigation case label to the event handler. (Replace the word `null` with the text in bold. Be sure to include the quotation marks.)

```
public java.lang.String loginpage_action() {
   // User event code here...
   return "loginPage";
}
```

Recall that in the Page Navigation editor, you assigned this label to the navigation case going from page **LoginBad.jsp** to the initial page, **Page1.jsp**.

Add a Component to Page LoginGood

Before deploying and testing the web application, you need to add a component to the successful login page, **LoginGood.jsp**.

1. From the Project Navigator window under Web Pages, double-click **Login-Good.jsp**.

   You should now be working in the design canvas view of the **Login-Good.jsp** page.

2. From the JSF Standard Components palette, select component Output Text and drag it onto the design canvas. Position it at the top.
3. Make sure the component is selected and type in **Welcome to our Members-Only Page**. Finish by pressing **<Enter>**.
4. In the Property window under Appearance, modify the `style` attribute to include the following font values after the other style characteristics.

```
; font-family: Helvetica; font-size: 18pt
```

Deploy and Run

Deploy and run the application by clicking the green chevron on the toolbar. Go ahead and type in test usernames and passwords. Check both the failure and success cases, as well as leaving one or more of the input fields blank. Also, note that when you return to the login page, the password input field (the secret field component) is cleared. Figure 4–8 on page 117 shows the login page.

Design Tip

The `login_action()` *event handler performs a simple String comparison between the input field values and the private variables in the Java page bean. We elected to show you this code because it is simple and we really wanted to emphasize page navigation. However, it is better to remove the computation for determining the "success" of a login from the action method and encapsulate it in a JavaBeans component. The changes are small, but the architectural advantages are striking. In the next chapter, we show you how to encapsulate this computation.*

4.5 Key Point Summary

- JSF navigation is a rule-based system. When you create page flow links, Creator generates the rules for you and stores them in the XML configuration file, **navigation.xml**.
- Creator supports both simple and dynamic navigation.
- In simple navigation, the command component's action event handler returns a String that matches a navigation case label.
- In dynamic navigation, the command component's action event handler performs some processing that affects the String value that it returns.
- The action event listener passes the String associated with clicking a button or link action component to the navigation handler.
- You can use other components with navigation, but you have to manually code their event handlers to pass an appropriate String to the navigation handler.
- Dynamic navigation provides more flexibility than simple navigation. With dynamic navigation you can add processing in the event handler (to determine the next page or just to perform some housekeeping updates).
- With Creator's Page Navigation editor, you can create new web pages and connect the pages in your application with page flow case labels. Creator generates the navigation rules that the navigation handler uses to manage your application's page flow.

JAVABEANS
COMPONENTS

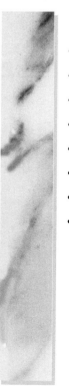

Topics in This Chapter

- JavaBeans Properties
- Managed Beans in Creator
- Object Scope
- Property Binding
- Creation of Java Classes and Packages
- Using JAR Files
- Examples of Using Converters and Validators
- Separation of Business Logic and Presentation Code

Chapter 5

J SF's architecture includes the concept of *managed beans*. A managed bean is a JavaBeans component whose life cycle and scope is controlled by JSF. By carefully defining its public methods, you can make your managed bean and all of its properties available to the pages of a web application.

Creator projects support JavaBeans components. In our first example (LoginBean), you'll make the JavaBeans component a *property* of a managed bean. You'll also add its JAR file to your project as a library reference. In the second example (LoanBean), the JavaBeans component itself will be a managed bean and you'll add the source directly to your project with the Project Navigator. Either way, once you make your JavaBeans component available to Creator, you can bind JSF components directly to your JavaBeans component's properties.

This chapter shows you how to build Creator projects with JavaBeans components. In addition, you can find examples in other chapters (see "Localizing an Application" on page 263 and "Creating Custom Validation" on page 279). The first step is to learn what a JavaBeans component is.

5.1 What Is a Bean?

A JavaBeans component (bean) is a Java class with certain structure requirements. When a Java class conforms to this structure, other programs (like Creator) can access the bean and inspect it intelligently. Furthermore, programs can inspect instances (objects) of the bean.

Because they follow certain design conventions, beans can be reused as components in various applications. The JSF architecture is set up to allow the JSF components to access JavaBeans components.

Properties

One the most important characteristic of a bean is its ability to define and manipulate *properties*. A JavaBeans property is a value of a certain type. With a bean, you provide public methods to access a bean's properties. A property is frequently implemented by an instance variable, but not always. Sometimes properties are derived from the values of other instance variables in the Java class (especially with read-only properties). Properties can also be tied to events and have listeners that detect a change to a property's value.

Properties usually contain a single value. These are called *simple properties*. They can also be represented by an array of values. These are called *indexed properties*.

Setters and Getters

The public setters and getters define a bean's properties. A setter provides write access to a property and a getter provides read access. The names of these access methods are set by convention and determine the name of the property.

A getter is a public method that returns a reference to an object of the property's type (or if the type is a built-in type, it returns a value). It combines the word "get" with the property name, capitalizing its first letter. For example, if a JavaBeans component implements a property called customer (a String), its getter is

```
public String getCustomer() {
   return customer;
}
```

Similarly, a setter is a public method that takes an object of the property's type and returns void. Using the same convention, setters combine the word "set" with a property name whose initial letter is capitalized. A setter for the above customer property is

```
public void setCustomer(String c) {
   customer = c;
}
```

A boolean property's getter may have one of two forms. Suppose a Java-Beans component has a property called `onMailingList` (a boolean). Its getter can be implemented as

```
public boolean isOnMailingList() { ... }
```

or the traditional

```
public boolean getOnMailingList() { . . . }
```

Note that what determines a bean's properties is the accessor methods you provide. When you create a JavaBeans component through Creator's IDE, Creator enforces these conventions.

Default Constructor

There is one important rule to remember with JavaBeans components. A bean *must* define a public default constructor, that is, a constructor with no arguments.[1] Typically, JavaBeans components are instantiated by a mechanism that precludes passing arguments to the constructor. The constructor's job is to provide any necessary initialization steps for the bean, including default values for the bean's properties.

Binding

When you write a JavaBeans component that conforms to these design conventions, you can use them with Creator and bind JSF components to JavaBeans properties. This provides a powerful link between a GUI component and the application's "model," that is, the business data that the application manipulates.

The binding is specified by the JSF EL (Expression Language). Typically, the value property of either a text field component or an output text component is bound to a JavaBeans property. Creator provides a Property Bindings dialog that allows you to select an object's bindable property and a binding target (see Figure 5–4, "Property Bindings dialog" on page 140). After you've applied the binding, Creator generates the necessary code in the page's JSP source. Here is an example of an output text component called `cost` bound to the `payment`

---

1. A public class with *no constructor* is also considered to have a public default constructor.

property of LoanBean, which we show you later in this chapter. The binding
with the LoanBean component is in bold.

```
<h:outputText binding="#{Page1.cost}"
   converter="#{Page1.numberConverter1}" id="cost"
   style="position: absolute; left: 264px; top: 264px"
   value="#{LoanBean.payment}"/>
```

This binding means that the output text's `value` is updated with the Loan-
Bean's `payment` property during the page's request cycle. The binding generates code to invoke the `payment`'s getter method of the LoanBean,
`getPayment()`. In this example, the LoanBean object is a managed bean and
has session scope. We explain later how this all works in more detail. But first,
we discuss object scope in web applications.

Scope of Web Applications

When a web application runs on the server, it consists of various programming
objects whose life cycles depend on their *scope*. For example, a page generally
lives in request scope and exists during the life cycle of a single request. Certain
data, however, are available throughout the entire session. When a user puts
items in a shopping cart, for example, the cart and all of its contents are generally in session scope. Each user running the application has his or her own session objects.

Sometimes data need to be shared among all users of a web application. For
example, suppose a counter keeps track of how many users have accessed a
web application. Such a counter needs to be accessible throughout all sessions
and therefore must have application scope. Since it's important to understand
object scope in your Creator projects, we define the different kinds for you.

Session scope means the object is available for one user across multiple pages
in a single session. Each user of the web application is given his or her own
instance of any object with session scope.

Application scope means the object is available for all sessions within an
application. A component with application scope usually contains application-
wide data or processing, since all sessions share the same object.

Request scope means the object is available for only the page that references it.
If another page needs an object of the same type, the system instantiates a
unique object for that page (in the new request scope). An object with request
scope is *not* shared with other pages in the same session.

An object with scope *none* is instantiated each time it is referenced. This
means that the object is not saved in any scope. You would use scope none
when an object is closely tied to and dependent on another object. For example,
an AddressBean with scope none is instantiated when a CustomerBean references it.

If one object references a second one, the allowable scope of the second object depends on the scope of the first object. Table 5.1 lists the allowable bindings in a JSF application.

Table 5.1 Well-behaved bindings between objects

Object1's Scope	*May Refer to Object2 in This Scope*
none	none
application	none, application
session	none, application, session
request	none, application, session, request

In general, (except for scope none) an object with a longer-living scope should not refer to an object with a shorter life span. For example, an object with session scope should not reference an object with request scope. On the other hand, an object of request scope may refer to an object stored in session scope because session scope has a longer life span. Objects with scope none may only reference other objects of the same scope (none).

Why is all this important? First of all, you need to understand scoping rules to create your JavaBeans components properly in a Creator project. Then you must understand scoping rules to correctly instantiate and access your Java-Beans components in the correctly scoped managed bean. Later in this chapter, we show you how to do this with the LoginBean in session scope (see "Modify Event Handler" on page 141).

Predefined Creator Java Components

If you open any Creator project (or create a new one) from Creator's Project Navigator window, you'll see at least three Java source files (expand the Java Sources node, then the "package name" folder): **ApplicationBean1.java**, **Page1.java**, and **SessionBean1.java**. These are all JavaBeans components installed as *managed beans* with application scope, request scope, and session scope, respectively.

Page1.java is the page bean for the first page of your application (unless you rename it). Each page has its own page bean. The page bean is a JavaBeans component containing properties for all the components you add to your page. Creator generates the Java source for this file, and you can add code to it (such as event handler methods or user-defined initialization statements). Page1, therefore, is a JSF managed bean with request scope.

SessionBean1.java defines a Java class that is an almost-empty shell by default. This is where you place objects with session scope. Here is its source.[2]

```
package project_name;
import com.sun.jsfcl.app.*;

public class SessionBean1 extends AbstractSessionBean {
    . . . Creator-managed Component Definition . . .

  public SessionBean1() {
        . . . Creator-managed Component Initialization . . .
        // Additional user provided initialization code
  }

  public ApplicationBean1 getApplicationBean1() {
    return (ApplicationBean1)getBean("ApplicationBean1");
  }
}
```

Inside SessionBean1, you call operator new to create your JavaBeans component and store its reference in a private class variable. You also need to provide getter and setter methods to make the component accessible to your project as a property (we show you how to do all this in our first example). When SessionBean1 is instantiated, all of its added components are instantiated, too. Since SessionBean1 has session scope, all of its instance variables will have session scope as well.

ApplicationBean1.java has the same structure. You use ApplicationBean1 as a holder for objects with application scope. Here is its source.

```
package project_name;
import com.sun.jsfcl.app.*;

public class ApplicationBean1 extends
                        AbstractApplicationBean {

    . . . Creator-managed Component Definition . . .

    public ApplicationBean1() {
        . . . Creator-managed Component Initialization . . .
        // Additional user provided initialization code
    }
}
```

---

2. Creator hides (or "folds") some of the Creator-managed code by default to keep your editor pane uncluttered. To see this code, click the '+' in the editor pane's margin.

There's a lot more to tell you about using JavaBeans components in Creator projects, so let's get started.

5.2 LoginBean Component

In our first example using managed beans with Creator, you'll start with the web application you built in the previous chapter (project **Login1**). You will add a reusable component called LoginBean. LoginBean is a bean with the structure described in the previous section. LoginBean's purpose is twofold: it holds user login information and it processes a login request. By encapsulating both the login data and the processing procedure, the client (which is the JSF web application you are building) is shielded from the implementation details. Furthermore, by making LoginBean a JavaBeans component with session scope, you can access it from any JSP page you define in your project.

LoginBean Outside View

Let's begin by examining the LoginBean from its outside view, that is, the view from your application. Then we'll look at its source and show you how to install it in your project.

A bean that represents a user logging in should store the user's name and password. Therefore, the LoginBean will have two properties, one for `username` (a String) and another for `password` (also a String). To access these properties from JSF tags, use a JSF EL expression, as follows.

```
#{SessionBean1.loginBean.username}
```

Note that `username` is a property of `loginBean`, which in turn is a property of SessionBean1 (the default managed bean with session scope). Likewise, the expression

```
#{SessionBean1.loginBean.password}
```

references `loginBean`'s `password` property in SessionBean1. In Java code, these map to the property's accessor methods: `getUsername()`, `setUsername()`, `getPassword()`, and `setPassword()`.

Once a user of your web application types a username and password and these values are stored in the LoginBean, the bean can tell you if that user's login information is valid. The LoginBean has a boolean property for that, called `loginGood`. Since this is a read-only property, you'll need to provide getter `isLoginGood()`.

Note that a client does not need to know how LoginBean determines whether a login is valid, making it easier for bean providers to change how this is done. For example, our initial implementation of LoginBean compares the web application user's login data with constants stored in the Java source. Another implementation could access a database and look up the user's name and password. To the client, however, the calling method is unchanged. You still invoke method isLoginGood().

Advantages of JavaBeans Components

In the previous chapter, we said that using a JavaBeans component offers striking advantages over placing code in a Java page bean. We were referring to the ability to change a JavaBeans component's implementation without affecting its clients, as well as the ability to encapsulate business logic and data. For example, in project **Login1** you placed the code for a valid login sequence inside the action event handler of the Java page bean, **Page1.jsp**. In general, it's not a good idea to put business logic in the Java page bean. Instead, you should encapsulate all business logic inside business components implemented as beans. This approach separates the presentation code (GUI components and event handlers in the Java page bean) from the model code (business logic).

Reusability is another big advantage of JavaBeans components that implement business logic. Because you don't put any GUI-specific code (such as output formatting, for example) in LoginBean, there's no reason why another web application cannot easily use it.

Property Binding with Components

When objects are implemented as JavaBeans components, it's easy to use binding with the JSF components you define on your page. This means you don't need to write explicit Java code to set the LoginBean properties to the values using the component's getValue() method. By binding the component's value property to a property in LoginBean, you're essentially performing the Java code implicitly. Suppose, for example, the following code appears in an event handler that reads a text field component called username.

```
loginBean.setUsername(userName.getValue());
```

Or, in the beforeRenderResponse() method, you might use the following code to display the value that's stored in the LoginBean instance.

```
userName.setValue(loginBean.getUsername());
```

With object binding, however, all of this is accomplished behind the scenes (we show you how to specify binding shortly). Creator generates the JSF tags for you. For example, to bind the text field component userName to the user-name property of LoginBean, Creator generates the following JSF tag (the relevant attribute is bold).

```
<h:inputText binding="#{Page1.userName}" id="userName"
   required="true"
   style="position: absolute; left: 240px; top: 96px"
   value="#{SessionBean1.loginBean.username}"/>
```

Binding this JSF component to LoginBean means that JSF displays the text that's in the username property of LoginBean in the JSF's component's input field. And conversely, JSF puts the text that's in the value property of the text field component in the username property of LoginBean.

Let's use LoginBean to upgrade the **Login1** project from the previous chapter. Here's a step-by-step approach.

Copy the Project

To avoid starting from scratch, copy the **Login1** project to a new project called **Login2**. This step is optional. If you don't want to copy the project, simply skip this section and continue making modifications to the **Login1** project.

1. Bring up Creator and open the project you created in the previous chapter, **Login1**. Creator displays the design view for **Page1.jsp**.
2. Click anywhere inside the design grid.
3. From the File menu, select Save Project as . . . and provide the new name **Login2**. You'll make changes to the **Login2** project.

Specify Title

In the design view of the editor pane, change the title.

1. Click in the middle of the design canvas.
2. Select Title in the Properties window and type the new title **Login 2**. Finish by pressing **<Enter>**.

Add a Library Reference to Your Project

LoginBean is a reusable JavaBeans component that you will configure with *session scope*. Session scope means that the component is available for one user across multiple pages. Each user of the web application is given his or her own instance of the LoginBean object.

Both the class file (the compiled Java code) and the source file are in a component JAR file in your Creator book's example files. Let's add the JAR file to your project now.

1. Open up the Project Navigator window. This window displays all the resources, pages, Java sources, and references used by your project.
2. Expand the Library References node (if it's not already expanded). Creator lists several different libraries used by your project. You're going to add the **asg.jar** file as a new library reference.
3. Right-click the Library References node and select Create New Library Reference. Creator pops up the Create New Library Reference dialog. (See Figure 5–1.)

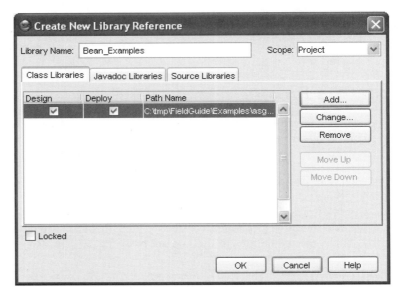

Figure 5–1 **Create New Library Reference dialog**

4. For Library Name, specify **Bean_Examples**. Scope should be set to Project.
5. Select tab Class Libraries and click Add. The Open dialog is displayed.
6. Browse to the location of your Creator book's examples. Under directory **FieldGuide/Examples** select **asg.jar** and click Open. Creator adds the JAR file path to the Path Name field. Click OK.[3]

---

3. Note that Creator uses an *absolute pathname* for the library reference. If you open a project created on another system, make sure the JAR file has the same pathname or recreate the library reference.

Bean_Examples now appears under the Library References node. If you expand it, you'll see the added JAR file, **asg.jar**.

Add a LoginBean Property to SessionBean1

You've added the library reference that contains the LoginBean class file, but now you need to make it accessible within your project. Since LoginBean should have session scope, let's add it to managed bean SessionBean1 as a property. This will enable JSF to automatically instantiate it when it instantiates SessionBean1. It will also make it available to the GUI components as a SessionBean1 property.

1. In the Project Navigator window, expand the Java Sources folder and then the project's default package folder. You'll see the Java page bean source for your project, **Page1.java**.
2. You'll also see "template" beans **ApplicationBean1.java** and **Session-Bean1.java** for beans at application and session scope, respectively.
3. Right-click the file node **SessionBean1.java** and select Add > Property. This pops up the New Property Pattern dialog (see Figure 5–2).

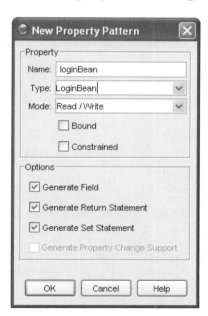

Figure 5–2 **New Property Pattern dialog**

4. Fill in the dialog as follows. Under Name specify **loginBean**, under Type specify **LoginBean**, and under Mode, select **Read/Write**.

Creator Tip

Since Name and Type are case sensitive, make sure you copy the capitalizations exactly.

5. Make sure that options Generate Field, Generate Return Statement, and Generate Set Statement are all checked. Click OK to add property `loginBean` to SessionBean1.
6. Still in the Project Navigator window, double-click the file node **SessionBean1.java**. This brings up the file in the Java source editor. Here are the getter /setter methods Creator generated.

```
/**
  * Getter for property loginBean.
  * @return Value of property loginBean.
  */
public LoginBean getLoginBean() {
   return this.loginBean;
}
/**
  * Setter for property loginBean.
  * @param loginBean New value of property loginBean.
  */
public void setLoginBean(LoginBean loginBean) {
   this.loginBean = loginBean;
}
```

You'll note that the code is marked with syntax errors. This is because type LoginBean is unknown in the current compilation scope. Let's use the fast import shortcut to fix these errors.

1. In the Java source editor for file **SessionBean1.java**, place the cursor over the LoginBean class reference (in any of the lines) and click the mouse.
2. Press the shortcut keys **<Alt-Shift-I>**. Creator's Java source editor displays the Import Class dialog box as shown in Figure 5–3.
3. Make sure that `asg.bean_examples.LoginBean` and radio button Import Class are selected. Click OK.

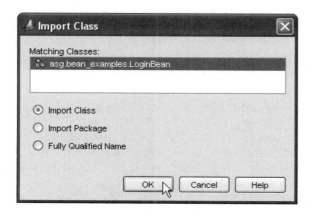

Figure 5–3 **Import Class dialog box**

This adds an import statement for the LoginBean class near the top of source file **SessionBean1.java**, as shown below. The red underlines should disappear.

```
import asg.bean_examples.LoginBean;
. . .
```

Now you'll add Java code that instantiates (with operator new) the Login-Bean object.

1. In the Java source editor (you're still editing file **SessionBean1.java**), add instantiation with operator new for property loginBean inside the SessionBean1() constructor.
2. Place it after the comment, as follows.

```
// Additional user provided initialization code
loginBean = new LoginBean();
```

An Aside About Initialization Code

You must specify the instantiation of properties that you add to any Creator managed bean. It is recommended that you place any initialization code in the constructor instead of modifying the Creator-generated declaration with (for example),

```
// Creator-managed Component Definition
// Not recommended
private LoginBean loginBean = new LoginBean();
```

Placing initialization code in the constructor is preferable because

- you don't have to unfold and modify Creator-generator code;
- if you need to add more initialization steps, your instantiation code will already be in the constructor and you can keep all initialization code together;
- if you have several properties in your bean, the initialization of all the properties is in one place instead of spread out in the component definition section;
- in general it's a poor idea to modify Creator-generated code.

The code that you added to **SessionBean1.java** makes the loginBean object a property of SessionBean1. Thus, to access the username property of login-Bean (for example), use the following JSF EL expression.

```
#{SessionBean1.loginBean.username}
```

This is how you'll bind LoginBean's properties with the GUI components on your web page. Before you specify binding for the components, it's time to look at the source for **LoginBean.java**.

LoginBean.java Code

The source for **LoginBean.java** is included in the **asg.jar** JAR file. Since the JAR file is installed in your project as a library reference, you can easily view the file in Creator's Java source editor.

1. In the Project Navigator window under Library References, expand nodes Bean_Examples > asg.jar > asg > bean_examples.
2. Double-click file **LoginBean.java**. Creator brings it up in the Java source editor as a read-only file for you.

We show **LoginBean.java** in Listing 5.1.

Listing 5.1 LoginBean.java

```java
// LoginBean.java
package asg.bean_examples;

public class LoginBean {
    private String username;
    private String password;

    private String correctName;
    private String correctPassword;

 /** Creates a new instance of LoginBean */
    public LoginBean() {
        username = "xxx";
        password = "xxx";
        correctName = "rave4u";
        correctPassword = "rave4u";
    }

    public boolean isLoginGood() {
        return (username.equals(correctName) &&
            password.equals(correctPassword));
    }

    public void setUsername(String name) {
        username = name;
    }
    public void setPassword(String word) {
        password = word;
    }

    public String getUsername() {
        return username;
    }
    public String getPassword() {
        return password;
    }
}
```

LoginBean has three properties, `username`, `password`, and `loginGood`. It also has two additional fields (`correctName` and `correctPassword`), but these fields are not properties. LoginBean's default constructor sets the four fields with initial values. (Property `loginGood` is read-only and does not correspond to an instance variable.)

Boolean method `isLoginGood()` returns true if the login information in `username` and `password` is valid. Our implementation checks the property values against the internal fields `correctName` and `correctPassword`. Other implementations of valid login information are possible; change the initialization code in the constructor (to access a database, for example).

The remaining methods implement the setters (`setUsername()` and `setPassword()`) and getters (`getUsername()` and `getPassword()`) for the bean's other properties.

Bind Input Components

To implement binding for both the text field and the secret field components, return to the design canvas (select the tab **Page1.jsp**) at the top of the editor pane.

1. From either the design canvas or the Application Outline view, select text field `userName`.
2. Right-click and choose Property Bindings from the menu. Creator displays the Property Bindings dialog as shown in Figure 5–4.

Component `userName` appears in the Property Bindings dialog title.

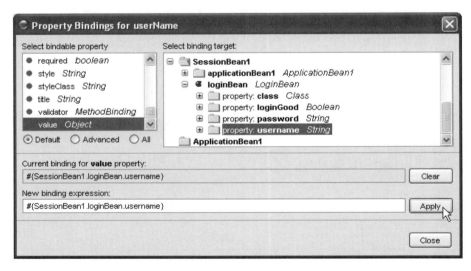

Figure 5–4 **Property Bindings dialog**

3. In the Select bindable property window, choose *value Object*.

4. In the Select binding target window, expand the `SessionBean1` and `login-Bean` nodes.
5. Select the `username` property under `loginBean`. Click Apply. The following expression is displayed under Current binding for *value* property.

```
#{SessionBean1.loginBean.username}
```

6. Click Close.
7. Repeat steps 1 to 6 to bind the component `password` to the `Session-Bean1.loginBean.password` property.

Creator Tip

You can also edit the component's `value` attribute in the Properties window to specify binding using the JSF EL expressions above.

Modify Event Handler

You also need to update the **Page1.java** event handler to invoke the Login-Bean's `isLoginGood()` method. To do that, you have to access the LoginBean component. First bring up **Page1.java** in the Java source editor. Here are the steps.

1. Right-click in the background of the **Page1.jsp** page and select View Page1 Java Class. Or, select **Page1.java** under Java Sources in the Project Navigator and double-click. (Make sure the Project Navigator window is in Logical View if you do this.)
2. Remove the private variables `myUserName` and `myPassword` from the code.

```
private String myUserName = "rave4u";
private String myPassword = "rave4u";
```

3. From the dropdown menu at the top of the editor pane, select method `login_action`. Creator puts the cursor at the start of this event handler. (You'll notice that the editor has underlined some of the code in red since you deleted the private variable declarations. We'll fix that soon.) Move the cursor to the end of the comment line and press **<Enter>** to add a new line.
4. Add the following statement to obtain a reference to the LoginBean object from SessionBean1.

```
LoginBean login = getSessionBean1().getLoginBean();
```

Method `getSessionBean1()` returns a reference to the SessionBean1 object. We access this to get at SessionBean1's `loginBean` property.

5. We've once again introduced syntax errors because of LoginBean. Use the fast import shortcut **<Alt-Shift-I>** to have Creator add the import class statement to your source file.

```
import asg.bean_examples.LoginBean;
```

6. Modify the `if` statement to call LoginBean's getter, `isLoginGood()`.

```
if (login.isLoginGood()) {
. . .
```

At this point, no red underlines should appear in your source code. If you still see them, check the syntax again before moving on. Listing 5.2 shows the complete method.

Listing 5.2 Action event handler `login_action()`

```
public java.lang.String login_action() {
  // User event code here...
  LoginBean login = getSessionBean1().getLoginBean();

  if (login.isLoginGood()) {
    return "loginSuccess";
  }
  else return "loginFail";
}
```

After calling getter `isLoginGood()`, the event handler returns either `"login-Success"` or `"loginFail"`. These are the labels you used when you specified navigation page flow for the project in the previous chapter.

Modify Page LoginGood.jsp

Because the LoginBean has session scope, it's available to other pages in your application. The successful login page, **LoginGood.jsp**, will access LoginBean to personalize the welcome greeting for the user. You can do this simply enough by binding an output text component to the LoginBean's `username` property. Here's how.

1. In the Project Navigator window, select the top node **Login2**, right-click, and select Show Logical View (if it's not currently in Logical View).

2. Double click page **LoginGood.jsp**. This brings up the design canvas for this page.
3. Select the output text component `outputText1`.
4. In the Properties window, click the small editing box opposite the `value` attribute. A dialog pops up. Under Current value setting, change its value to

```
Welcome, #{SessionBean1.loginBean.username}
```

5. Click OK.

Note that you've concatenated a plain string with a property binding expression. You can also concatenate one or more property binding expressions together. The string and binding expression now appear inside the output text component on the design canvas.

6. Click the Source tab at the bottom of the editor pane. Here is the updated JSP tag for the output text component you placed on the **LoginGood.jsp** page. The property binding is in bold.

```
<h:outputText binding="#{LoginGood.outputText1}"
  id="outputText1"
  style="font-family: Helvetica; font-size: 24pt;
  position: absolute; left: 24px; top: 48px"
  value="Welcome, #{SessionBean1.loginBean.username}"/>
```

Deploy and Run

Deploy and run the application by clicking the green chevron on the toolbar. Figure 5–5 shows the login page when the web application first comes up.

Note that the Username text field component displays "xxx." This is because the LoginBean constructor initializes the `username` field with "xxx." When you specify binding, JSF automatically instantiates LoginBean and updates the text field component's `value` field with the initialized value in LoginBean's `user-name` field.

The same initialization occurs with the secret field component and Login-Bean's `password` field. However, because the rendering mechanism of the secret field component clears its `value` property for display, you don't see Log-inBean's default initialization here.

Go ahead and type in various usernames and passwords. Again, check both the failure and success cases, as well as leaving one or more of the input fields blank. Also, note that when you return to the login page, the Password input field (the secret field component) is cleared.

Figure 5–6 shows page **LoginGood.jsp** after a successful login scenario. (Type **rave4u** for both the username and password.) The page displays the

Figure 5–5 Login web application that uses LoginBean

Username, thanks to the binding of the output component with the Login-Bean's `username` property.

5.3 LoanBean Component

In the previous example, you added a library reference to your project and made the JavaBeans component LoginBean a property of the SessionBean1 managed bean. Although we looked at LoginBean's source code, all you really need is the JAR file that contains its class (compiled) file. However, sometimes you'll want to create the JavaBeans component yourself. Instead of adding a pre-compiled class file (or files) in a JAR file, you can also create a managed bean using Creator's interactive dialogs. In this example, you'll create a Loan-Bean component and make it a managed bean (instead of installing it as a property of one of the default managed beans that Creator provides).

The project that you'll build in this section uses a JavaBeans business component called LoanBean. The LoanBean component is interesting because we accomplish the web application's functionality completely through binding properties with converters and validators to manage input and output. Once

Figure 5–6 **A successful login session**

you install LoanBean as a managed bean in the application, there is no code to write! All the hard work is accomplished by the architecture of the JSF components, the functionality of the converters and validators, and the ability to plug in an application-specific bean. Furthermore, the LoanBean code is compact and straightforward. This is a poster-child example for using layered technologies in an IDE environment.

LoanBean Outside View

The LoanBean component computes a monthly payment for a long-term, fixed-rate loan based on a loan amount, annual interest rate, and term (the length of the loan in years). The monthly payment is returned from getter `getPayment()`, making `payment` a property of LoanBean. Although `payment` is a property of LoanBean, it is a *derived* property. This means its value is computed from the values of the bean's other properties. Since `payment` is a derived property, LoanBean does not require a setter method for it.

LoanBean's other three properties are `amount` (the loan amount), `rate` (the annual interest rate), and `years` (the loan's term). Following the conventions of building a conforming JavaBeans component, LoanBean contains setters and getters for each of these three properties.

To build this application, you'll be placing text field components on the design canvas to allow the user to specify amounts for the LoanBean's properties. You'll use converters to convert String input into the necessary data types and validators to control the range of these values. You'll also bind the components' `value` properties to the LoanBean properties.

After supplying input parameters for the loan, the user clicks a Calculate button to see the monthly payment. The application displays the payment information in an output text component that is bound to the LoanBean's `payment` property. With the help of converters and formatters, JSF updates the page automatically. Figure 5–7 shows what this web application looks like.

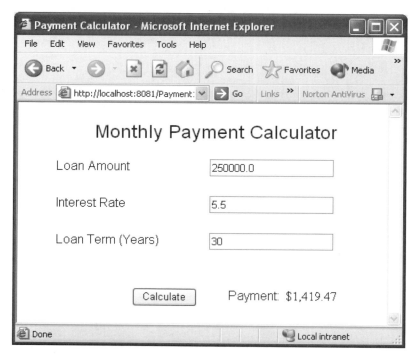

Figure 5–7 **Project Payment1 running in a browser**

Create a New Project

To build this application, you create the project, place a title on the page, and add the LoanBean managed bean to the project. After configuring the Loan-Bean component, you add the other components to gather input and report a monthly payment amount. This involves adding labels, specifying tooltips, applying converters and validators, and specifying binding between the user interface components (the "presentation" components) and the JavaBeans component (the "model"). Let's begin.

- From Creator's Welcome Page, select button Create New Project. Specify project name **Payment1**. The selected project type is J2EE Web Application. Click OK.

Specify Title and Background

After initializing the project, Creator comes up in the design view of the editor pane. You can now set the title.

1. Click anywhere in the middle of the design canvas and select `Title` in the Properties window. Change the title to **Payment Calculator**. Finish by pressing **<Enter>**.
2. Change the page's background color. In the Properties window, select the small editing square next to attribute `Background`. Creator pops up a color selection dialog. Choose the yellow swatch in the top row. This corresponds to RGB value 255, 255, 204 (a variation of yellow).

Add an Output Text Component

You'll need an output text component to put a heading on the page.

1. From the JSF Standard Component palette, select Output Text component and drag it to the top of the page.
2. When you drop it onto the design canvas, it remains selected and you can begin typing its value. This is a Creator shortcut to set a component's value. Type in **Monthly Payment Calculator**. Finish with **<Enter>**. (Don't resize the component; Creator will stretch it to fit the text.)
3. Under Appearances in the Properties window, edit the `style` attribute. Add the following after the `position` settings.

```
;  font-family: Helvetica; font-size: 18pt
```

The output text should now appear with its new style characteristics on the design canvas.

Add LoanBean to Your Project

These steps create the LoanBean Java source file and add it to your project as a managed session bean.

1. Select the Project Navigator window.
2. Expand the Java Sources folder and then the `payment1` folder. You'll see the Java page bean for your project, **Page1.java**, as well as the "template" Java beans **ApplicationBean1.java** and **SessionBean1.java**.
3. Select the Java Sources folder, right-click, and select New > Package from the menu. Creator displays the New Wizard - Package dialog.
4. Specify name **asg** and click Finish. This adds package **asg** under node Java Sources.
5. Now select the **asg** node and add package **bean_examples** (following the same steps you did for package **asg**).
6. Select package **bean_examples**, right-click, and select New > Managed Session Bean from the menu. Creator displays the New Wizard - Managed Session Bean dialog.
7. Specify name **LoanBean** and click Finish. You've just added a stub for class **LoanBean.java**, which Creator brings up for you in the Java source editor.

You now define LoanBean's properties and specify custom code for its constructor and one of its getters.

1. The first property you will add is property `amount`. In the Project Navigator window, expand folder **bean_examples** and select file **LoanBean.java**.
2. Right-click node **LoanBean.java** and select Add > Property. Creator displays the New Property Pattern dialog as shown in Figure 5–8.
3. Fill in the dialog. For Name, specify **amount**, for Type select **Double**[4], and for Mode select **Read/Write**. Verify that the default Options (Generate Field, Generate Return Statement, and Generate Set Statement) are all checked.
4. Click OK. You see that Creator has added the code to **LoanBean.java** for property `amount`.

You will add three more properties to LoanBean. Table 5.2 displays the property name, type, mode (read/write or read-only), and options for each property in **LoanBean.java**. Use the table as a guide to add the three remaining properties using the New Property Pattern dialog. Note that property `payment` is read only.

You must now supply initialization code for the constructor and payment calculation code for method `getPayment()`.

1. The Java source editor should still be active with file **LoanBean.java**.

---

4. Note that you specify type as *Double* (the wrapper class), not *double* (the primitive type).

Figure 5–8 **New Property Pattern dialog**

Table 5.2 Properties for LoanBean component

Name	*Type*	*Mode*	*Options*
amount	Double	Read/Write	Generate Field Generate Return Statement Generate Set Statement
rate	Double	Read/Write	Generate Field Generate Return Statement Generate Set Statement
years	Integer	Read/Write	Generate Field Generate Return Statement Generate Set Statement
payment	Double	Read Only	Generate Field Generate Return Statement

2. Find the folded code box in the constructor labeled Creator-managed Component Initialization. Place the cursor in a new line after the comment

```
// Additional user provided initialization code
```

3. Add the constructor initialization code shown. Copy and paste from your Creator book's file **FieldGuide/Examples/JavaBeans/snippets/Payment1_constructor.txt**. The added code is bold.

```
// Additional user provided initialization code
amount = new Double(100000);
rate = new Double(5.0);
years = new Integer(15);
```

4. Add the getPayment() calculation code. Select getPayment from the drop-down menu in the upper-left corner of the editor pane. Creator puts the cursor at method getPayment().
5. Copy and paste from your Creator book's file **FieldGuide/Examples/JavaBeans/snippets/Payment1_getPayment.txt**. The added code is bold.

```
public Double getPayment() {
   double monthly_interest = rate.doubleValue() / 1200;
   int months = years.intValue() * 12;
   payment = new Double(amount.doubleValue() *
      (monthly_interest/(1-Math.pow(1+monthly_interest,
            -1*months))));
   return payment;
}
```

This completes the source for LoanBean. When you specified LoanBean as a managed session bean, Creator generated the configuration information for you.

Managed Beans Configuration File

Creator provides a **managed-beans.xml** file to store managed bean configuration details. This is where Creator specifies LoanBean's configuration as a managed bean for your project. There's nothing more you need to do, but let's look at the configuration file anyway.

1. In the Project Navigator window, select node Managed Beans.
2. Open the file in Creator's XML editor by double-clicking the node.

Listing 5.3 shows the **managed-beans.xml** file with the configuration information for LoanBean at the end.

Listing 5.3 Configuration file **managed-beans.xml**

```
<faces-config>
    . . .
   <managed-bean>
      <managed-bean-name>Page1</managed-bean-name>
      <managed-bean-class>payment1.Page1
         </managed-bean-class>
      <managed-bean-scope>request</managed-bean-scope>
   </managed-bean>
  <managed-bean>
      <managed-bean-name>asg$bean_examples$LoanBean
         </managed-bean-name>
      <managed-bean-class>asg.bean_examples.LoanBean
         </managed-bean-class>
      <managed-bean-scope>session</managed-bean-scope>
   </managed-bean>
</faces-config>
```

The `<managed-bean-name>` element identifies the LoanBean component within your web application. This is the name you use when you specify binding values for some of the components on your page.

The `<managed-bean-class>` element identifies the Java class file when JSF builds and instantiates the objects in your project. Note that this element includes the package name as well as the Java class name.

Finally, the `<managed-bean-scope>` element specifies the bean's scope. Here, Creator specified session scope since you created LoanBean as a Managed *Session* Bean. Session scope is appropriate here because JSF creates LoanBean only once per session (instead of with each request). (See "Scope of Web Applications" on page 128 for a more detailed discussion of object scope.)

LoanBean.java Code

Listing 5.4 contains the source for **LoanBean.java**. You've already seen the source in the Java source editor, but we show it here for completeness. We omit most of the Creator-generated comments.

Listing 5.4 LoanBean.java

```
package asg.bean_examples;
import com.sun.jsfcl.app.*;
```

Listing 5.4 LoanBean.java *(continued)*

```java
public class LoanBean extends AbstractSessionBean {
    private Double amount;
    private Double rate;
    private Integer years;
    private Double payment;

    public LoanBean() {
        try {
        }
        catch ( Exception e) {
            System.err.println(
                    "LoanBean Initialization Failure" + e);
        }

        // Additional user provided initialization code
        amount = new Double(100000);
        rate = new Double(5.0);
        years = new Integer(15);
    }

    public payment1.ApplicationBean1 getApplicationBean1() {
        return (payment1.ApplicationBean1)
            getBean("ApplicationBean1");
    }

    public Double getAmount() {
        return this.amount;
    }
    public void setAmount(Double amount) {
        this.amount = amount;
    }

    public Double getRate() {
        return this.rate;
    }
    public void setRate(Double rate) {
        this.rate = rate;
    }

    public Integer getYears() {
        return this.years;
    }
    public void setYears(Integer years) {
        this.years = years;
    }
```

Listing 5.4 LoanBean.java *(continued)*

```
public Double getPayment() {
    double monthly_interest = rate.doubleValue() / 1200;
    int months = years.intValue() * 12;
    payment = new Double(amount.doubleValue() *
        (monthly_interest/(1-Math.pow(1+
            monthly_interest,-1*months))));
    return payment;
    }
}
```

Create the Form's Input Components

Our web page requires a set of components to gather input for the parameters of the loan. There are three parameters: the loan amount, the interest rate, and the term. Each parameter has a component label, a text field to gather input, and an inline message component to report validation and conversion errors. Figure 5–9 shows what the design canvas looks like with all of the components added to the page (we've labeled most of them for you).

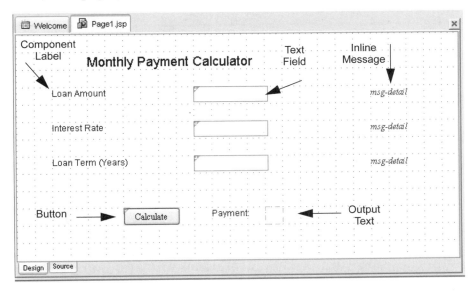

Figure 5–9 **Design canvas showing placement of components for project Payment1**

To create the components for the loan amount parameter:

1. Switch back to the design canvas by selecting the tab labeled **Page1.jsp** at the top of the editor pane.
2. From the JSF Standard Components palette, select Component Label and drag it onto the design canvas. The component label is a composite component with an embedded output text component to hold the label's text.
3. In the Application Outline view (or see the Creator Tip on this page), select the nested output text component, `componentLabel1Text`. In the Properties window, set its `value` attribute to **Loan Amount**.
4. In the Properties window, set its `style` attribute to

```
font-family: Helvetica
```

Creator Tip

Creator provides an enhanced selection mechanism for composite components (such as component label). In the design canvas, select the component label and look in the Properties window to see which component is selected. Now click the component again and you'll see a different component's properties. For component label, you switch back and forth between the top-level, label component and the embedded output text component by clicking the component in the design canvas.

5. From the JSF Standard Components palette, select Text Field and drop it onto the design canvas. Position it to the right of the label component you just added.
6. In the Properties window, change its `id` attribute to **loanAmount**.
7. In the Properties window under Data, make sure the `required` attribute is selected (checked). This ensures that the user supplies input for this field.
8. In the Properties window, set the `title` attribute to **Please supply the loan amount in dollars**. Finish with **<Enter>**. This sets the component's tooltip.
9. In the Application Outline view, select the component label (`componentLabel1`). In the Properties window, click the editing box next to the `for` attribute. Choose component `loanAmount` from the list of components displayed in the pop-up dialog. Click OK.

This associates the label component with the `loanAmount` text field, which affects mouse behavior. Now when the application is running, selecting the label as well as the text field places the cursor in the text field.

Use Validators and Converters

The `loanAmount` text field collects a numerical string that represents the amount of the loan. The string data is used with GUI components for the "presentation" part of the application. Internally, however, you'll store this information as a Double. Therefore, you need to convert the String to a Double and make sure its value is within a reasonable range with validation. To do this, you'll use a JSF `DoubleRangeValidator` for validation and a JSF `DoubleConverter` for conversion. You can add these components to your project from the JSF Validators/Converters palette. Here's how.

1. From the JSF Validators/Converters palette, select Double Converter, drag it to the design canvas, and drop it *on top of* the text field component `loanAmount`. Creator sets the `converter` attribute for `loanAmount` to `doubleConverter1`. Component `doubleConverter1` now appears in the Application Outline view.
2. Repeat this step for the validator. From the JSF Validators/Converts palette, select Double Range Validator, drag it to the design canvas, and drop it on top of the `loanAmount` text field component. Creator sets the `validator` attribute for `loanAmount` to `doubleRangeValidator1` in the Properties window. Component `doubleRangeValidator1` also appears in the Application Outline view.

You've just applied a range validator for the loan amount. Now you specify its range (maximum and minimum).

1. In the Application Outline view, select the validator you just added for the `loanAmount` component, `doubleRangeValidator1`.
2. From the Properties window, set the minimum and maximum values to **1.0** and 1 million (**1000000.0**), respectively (or other values you deem reasonable).

You also need a message component to display error messages during conversion.

1. Return to the JSF Standard Components palette and select Inline Message. Drag it to the design canvas and position it to the right of the text field component `loanAmount`.
2. In the Properties window under General, click the editing box next to the `for` attribute. Choose component `loanAmount` from the list of components displayed in the pop-up dialog. Click OK.

This ties the inline message component to the `loanAmount` text field component. Any error messages generated by the component's validator or converter will be displayed by the message component.

3. Still in the inline message's Properties window, make sure attribute show-
Summary for the message component is checked and add the following to its
style attribute.

```
; font-style: italic
```

Specify Property Binding

Now let's specify binding for the loanAmount text field's value attribute. Make
sure that the loanAmount component is selected.

1. Right-click and select Property Bindings from the menu. A dialog entitled
   Property Bindings for loanAmount pops up. (Figure 5–4 on page 140 shows
   the Property Bindings dialog for the **Login2** project.)
2. In the Select bindable property window, choose *value Object*.
3. In the Select binding target window, choose amount under node **asg/
   bean_examples/LoanBean**.
4. Click Apply. The following binding expression appears in Current binding
   for value property window.

```
#{asg$bean_examples$LoanBean.amount}
```

5. Click Close. This binds the value attribute of the text field component loan-
   Amount to the amount property of the LoanBean.

Place Interest Rate and Term Components

Ok, you've finished placing the components associated with gathering the loan
amount parameter. You'll need to repeat these steps for the interest rate (which
uses a Double converter and a Double range validator) and the loan term
(which uses an Integer converter and Long range validator). Follow the same
steps we showed you for the loan amount input. First grab a component label,
then the text field, converter, and validator, and finally, the inline message component. To make this easier, we've created tables that help you create the components and set their values. You may find it helpful to follow the instructions
and descriptions we gave you for the loan amount parameter.

Table 5.3 lists the components and their properties for the interest rate input.
Be sure to specify binding for interestRate's value attribute with
#{asg$bean_examples$LoanBean.rate}.

Creator Tip

You can use the same Double converter for text field interestRate *that you used with text field* loanAmount. *Instead of dragging a new converter from the JSF Validators/Converters palette, specify* interestRate's *converter in the Properties window. After placing the text field on the design canvas, select the* converter *attribute. From the component selection pop-up, choose* doubleConverter1 *followed by* **<Enter>**.

Table 5.3 Components for interest rate input

Component	Property	Setting
Component Label (componentLabel2)	for	interestRate (set this attribute after you place text field interestRate on canvas)
embedded text field (componentLabel2Text)	value	Interest Rate
	style	font-family: Helvetica
Text Field	id	interestRate
	title	Please specify the interest rate (APR)
	converter	doubleConverter1 (the same converter you used for loanAmount; make sure to press **<Enter>**)
	required	true (checked)
	validator	doubleRangeValidator2 (will be set after you drop the validator onto the component)
	value	#{asg$bean_examples$ LoanBean.rate}
Double Range Validator (doubleRangeValidator2)	minimum	0.001
	maximum	15.5
Inline Message (inlineMessage2)	for	interestRate
	showSummary	true (checked)
	style	font-style: italic

Table 5.4 lists the components and their Properties settings for the loan term parameter. The text field component loanTerm requires an Integer converter

and a Long range validator to control the allowable range. Specify binding
with #{asg$bean_examples$LoanBean.years}.

Table 5.4 Components for loan term input

Component	Property	Setting
Component Label (componentLabel3)	for	loanTerm (set this attribute after you place text field loanTerm on canvas)
embedded text field (componentLabel3Text)	value style	Loan Term (Years) font-family: Helvetica
Text Field	id	loanTerm
	title	Please specify term of loan in years
	converter	integerConverter1 (will be set after you drop the Integer Converter onto the component)
	required	true (checked)
	validator	longRangeValidator1 (will be set after you drop the validator onto the component)
	value	#{asg$bean_examples$ LoanBean.years}
Integer Converter (integerConverter1)		
Long Range Validator (longRangeValidator1)	minimum	1
	maximum	99
Inline Message (inlineMessage3)	for showSummary	loanTerm true (checked)
	style	font-style: italic

Place Button and Output Text Components

On the last line of the web application page, you'll place a button, an output
text component (to hold a label), and a second output text component that
binds to the payment property of the LoanBean. Table 5.5 shows the components you need and their properties that control the payment display. Specify
#{asg$bean_examples$LoanBean.payment} to bind the output text's value
property with the LoanBean's payment property.

Table 5.5 Components for monthly payment output

Component	Property	Setting
Button	id	calculate
	value	Calculate
Output Text (outputText2)	value	Payment
	style	font-family: Helvetica
Output Text	id	cost
	converter	numberConverter1 (this will be set after you drop the Number Converter onto the component)
	value	#{asg$bean_examples$ LoanBean.payment}
Number Converter (numberConverter1)	pattern	$###,###.00

Let's see how the button and output text components work with the Loan-Bean and the Number converter.

The button component does not have an action event handler defined in the Java page bean. The default action submits the page. This begins the life cycle process and updates the fields, including the output text component cost.

Output text component cost is bound to the payment property of the Loan-Bean. Recall that method getPayment() returns a double. When you define a number converter for the output text component, the double generated by the LoanBean component is converted to a String. We want the payment displayed in dollars and cents, however. Fortunately, the number converter has a pattern property that manipulates the double as a comma-separated number with two digits to the right of the decimal point and a dollar sign in front. The pattern that accomplishes this is

```
$###,###.00
```

The number converter has additional properties to help you control the format of the output String, but this pattern fully specifies the format we need.

Deploy and Run

Figure 5–10 shows the Application Outline view of the JSF components, converters, and validators for project **Payment1**. Before deploying, you may find it helpful to compare your Application Outline view with ours in Figure 5–10.

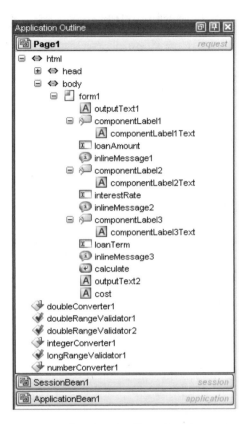

Figure 5–10 **Application Outline view for project Payment1**

Deploy and run the application by clicking the green chevron on the toolbar. Figure 5–11 shows the web application with new values. Note the tooltip display as the user holds the cursor over the interest rate text field component.

The payment amount is computed from the new values. When you change any of the loan parameters and click the Calculate button, a new payment appears. All this takes place because of the bindings between the input text field components and the LoanBean properties (including the LoanBean payment property for output). Of course, the converters and validators play important roles as well.

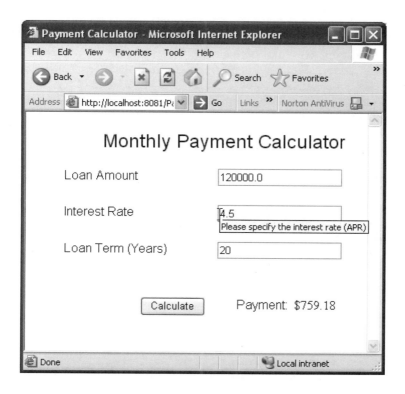

Figure 5–11 **Monthly payment calculator that uses LoanBean**

5.4   Key Point Summary

- You can add a JAR file (a library reference) to your project through the Library References node in the Project Navigator window. JAR files commonly hold libraries of compiled Java classes that address some functionality.
- A JavaBeans component is a Java class that conforms to certain design conventions.
- JavaBeans components implement read-access properties with public getter methods.
- JavaBeans components implement write-access properties with public setter methods.

- A JavaBeans component must have a public default constructor with no arguments.
- A JavaBeans component is a reusable component and helps separate business logic from presentation code.
- A JavaBeans component hides its implementation code by carefully defining its public methods (outside view).
- You can install a JavaBeans component as a property in one of Creator's default managed beans. A JavaBeans component configured as a property of the **Page1.java** page bean has request scope. Configuring it in **SessionBean1.java** gives it session scope and configuring it in **ApplicationBean1.java** gives it application scope.
- You can also install a JavaBeans component in a Creator project as a managed bean and specify its scope explicitly.
- The bean configuration file **managed-beans.xml** contains your JavaBeans component's name, class, and scope. It may also specify other properties of your bean.
- A managed bean with session scope is available across multiple pages for one user.
- A managed bean with request scope is available for only the page that references it.
- To specify a managed bean property within a JSF component tag, use the JSF EL expression

```
#{ManagedBeanName.propertyName}
```

- To specify a JavaBeans component's property that is itself a property of a managed bean, use the JSF EL expression

```
#{ManagedBeanName.javaBeanComponentName.propertyName}
```

- To bind a JSF component's property to a property in a JavaBeans component, select the JSF component, right-click, and select Property Bindings. Creator displays the Property Bindings dialog which lets you specify the JSF component's bindable property and the binding target. The binding target can be a property of another JSF component.

ACCESSING WEB SERVICES

Topics in This Chapter

Chapter 6

W eb services are software APIs that are accessible over a network in a heterogeneous environment. This network accessibility is achieved with a set of XML-based open standards such as the Web Services Description Language (WSDL), the Simple Object Access Protocol (SOAP), and Universal Description, Discovery, and Integration (UDDI). Both web service providers and clients use these standards to define, publish, and access web services.

Creator's default deployment server (J2EE 1.4) provides support for web services. Preinstalled with Creator is the Google Web Service, which appears in the Server Navigator window under node Web Services > Samples > **GoogleSearchService**. The Google Web Service APIs provide a SOAP interface to search Google's index, accessing information and web pages from its cache. With SOAP and WSDL, Google enables clients to access these services in a variety of programming environments (including, of course, Java).

This chapter shows you how to create an application that uses the Google Web Service API. Then, you'll enhance it. After creating a project that uses web services, you'll (hopefully) exclaim, "Is that all?" because the steps are fairly simple. And that's the way technology should be when industry-wide standards are adopted. You'll see that once we drag and drop the web service onto the design canvas in Creator, we spend most of our time showing you elaborate ways to manipulate and display the data that Google returns.

6.1   Google Web Services

We've divided this example into several projects that incrementally build on features of the previous project. With each increment, you'll make a copy of the project so you can go back to a previous project if you want. Alternatively, you can simply create a single project without saving any increments.

Note

You must register with Google before using their web service. You might also want to download the Google Web APIs developer's kit since it has additional documentation. Registration is free and painless. Once you register, Google will email you a key, which is required for access to their service. The Google Web Service URL is at `http://www.google.com/apis/`.

Create a New Project

- From Creator's Welcome Page, select button Create New Project. Specify project name as **Google1**. Click OK.

Let's look at a preview of what you'll be building. Figure 6–1 shows Creator's design canvas with the components you'll add for project **Google1**. The image component holds Google's recognizable logo, a button component initiates the search, and a text field holds the search string. For the results display, output text field `timeCount` displays the search time and results count, the hyperlink component displays the target URL, and the text field called `result` displays the URL's "snippet" description. The Google web services component appears in the nonvisual component tray at the bottom of the editor pane.

Specify Title

After creating the project, Creator comes up in the design view of the editor pane. You can now set the title.

- Select `Title` in the Properties window and type in the text **Google Search 1**. Finish by pressing **<Enter>**. (Alternatively, if you click the small square that appears when you initiate editing, a pop-up dialog appears from which you can edit the title. Click OK to complete editing.)

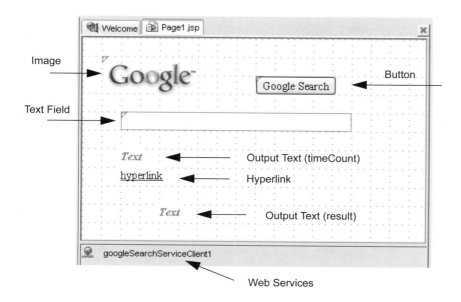

Figure 6–1 Creator's design canvas view showing project Google1's components

Add the Google Logo

It's a nice touch to include the Google logo when building a web application with Google's search service. To do this, let's have Creator load an image component and set its URL to the logo on Google's web site.

1. In the JSF Standard components palette, select component Image and drag it onto the design window in the editor pane. Place the image component in the upper-left corner of the canvas.
2. Creator displays a pop-up window entitled Select File or URL, as shown in Figure 6–2. Choose the tab labeled URL and type the following URL address in the editing box labeled Enter a URL (make sure you use http://).

```
http://www.google.com/logos/Logo_40wht.gif
```

3. Click OK. The editing box disappears, and the Google logo image appears on the design canvas.
4. Alternatively, you may specify a file (instead of a URL) for the image. In the same dialog, select tab File and browse to directory **FieldGuide/Examples/**

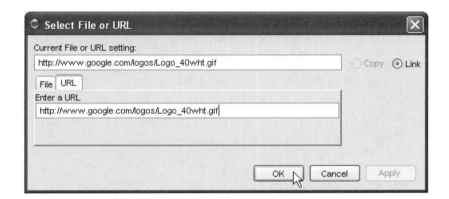

Figure 6–2 **Select File or URL dialog for image component**

WebServices/images in your Creator book download. Select file **Logo_40wht.gif** and click OK. Creator copies the file under the Resources node in the Project Navigator window.

Creator Tip

*When you select the File tab, Creator copies the **.gif** file from its original location to your project's Resources folder. Selecting the URL tab loads the image from Google's web site. You can decide whether to keep a local copy or link to Google's web page. To change the setting, select the Google image on the design canvas. In the Properties window, click the small editing box next to attribute* value. *A dialog pops up that allows you to change the URL/File designation.*

Add a Text Field Component

You'll need a text field component to read the user's search query.

1. In the JSF Standard Components palette, select component Text Field and drag it onto the design window. Place it below the Google logo.
2. Make sure it is selected and stretch it so that it's approximately 10 grid units wide. You'll use this component to obtain the user's search query string.
3. In the Properties window, change its id attribute to **searchString**.
4. To provide a tooltip for this text field, edit its title attribute in the Properties window. Type the text **Type in a search string** followed by **<Enter>**.

Add a Button Component

Button components allow users to initiate some action, like navigating to a different page or submitting data for some sort of processing. In this application, a button component will initiate a search using Google's Web Service API.

1. In the JSF Standard Components palette, select Button and drag it onto the design canvas. Place it to the right of the Google logo.
2. Make sure the button is still selected. Use the Creator shortcut for editing its `value` attribute by simply typing in a new label. When you type **Google Search** followed by **<Enter>**, Creator enables editing for the `value` attribute. Note that Creator resizes the button to accommodate the longer text string, which now appears inside the button on the design canvas.
3. In the Properties window, change the button's `id` attribute to **search**.
4. To provide a tooltip for the button, edit its `title` attribute in the Properties window. Type the text **Search Google for the Search String** followed by **<Enter>**.

Inspect the JSP Source File

When you add components to your web application, Creator generates JSP code in a file by using the JavaServer Faces (JSF) tag libraries. To look at this file, select the tab labeled Source at the bottom of the editor pane. You'll see the following JSF standard components defined in your JSP file (**Page1.jsp**).

```
<h:graphicImage binding="#{Page1.image1}" id="image1"
   style="position: absolute; left: 48px; top: 24px"
   value="images\Logo_40wht.gif"/>

<h:inputText binding="#{Page1.searchString}" id="searchString"
   style="position: absolute; left: 48px; top: 96px;
   width: 240px; height: 22px"
   title="Type in a search string"/>

<h:commandButton binding="#{Page1.search}" id="search"
   style="position: absolute; left: 216px; top: 48px"
   title="Search Google for the Search String"
   value="Google Search"/>
```

Three tags are defined here. The `graphicImage` tag defines an image component, and the `inputText` tag allows users to type in and edit textual information. The `commandButton` tag allows users to initiate an action, typically involving navigation or some kind of request for processing information. Clicking the button generates an event, which in turn invokes the *action method* associated with the component. You haven't yet specified any action associated with this button component, but you will do that shortly.

Let's return now to the design canvas by selecting the tab labeled Design at the bottom of the editor pane.

Add the Google Web Services

1. In the Server Navigator window under Web Services > Samples, click the '+' and select the Google Web Service API, GoogleSearchService.

Creator Tip

The Google Web Service comes preinstalled during Creator's installation process and appears in the Server Navigator window.

2. Drag the GoogleSearchService node and drop it anywhere on the editor pane. Since this is not a visible component, nothing appears in the design canvas. However, you will see **googleSearchServiceClient1** in the nonvisual component tray below the editor pane.
3. Go to the Application Outline view. This window shows all the components (visible and nonvisual) currently in your project. Note that the Google Web Service, **googleSearchServiceClient1**, is listed here.

Add a Web Service to the Server Navigator

The installation process configures the Google web service as well as other web services listed under the Web Services > Samples node in the Server Navigator window. Creator also provides a way to *add* a web service to these selections. Here are the steps to load the Google web service into Creator if it isn't precon-figured. Before you can add a web service, you must provide the location (URL) of its Web Service WSDL. This is the information that describes the particular web service's API.

We're going to step through the process to add the Google Search Service to Creator as an example. Use these steps to add any web service. (Skip this section if the Google web service is already listed in the Server Navigator window.)

1. Go to the Server Navigator.
2. Right-click on Web Services.
3. Select Add Web Service. Creator pops up the Add Web Service dialog.
4. In the URL field at the top, supply Google's WSDL file.

```
http://api.google.com/GoogleSearch.wsdl
```

This is the location of the WSDL (Web Services Description Language) file for the Google Search Service.

5. Click Get Web Service Information. The Google web service API appears in the Web Service Information window.
6. Click Add. The name GoogleSearchService appears under the Web Services node in the Server Navigator window.

Once a web service is listed in the Server Navigator window, you can select it and add it to your Creator project (as you did with the GoogleSearchService).

Add Output Text Components

Next, let's add output text components and a hyperlink to display the search results from Google.

1. From the JSF Standard Components palette, select Output Text. Place it below the text field component, aligning it on the left. Don't stretch it.
2. In the Properties window, change its id attribute to **timeCount**.

   The output text component timeCount will display the amount of time in seconds that the search request took on Google's server, as well as the estimated number of search results found. Although Google's search returns at most 10 results, this number is the estimated total (anywhere from zero to thousands).

3. Repeat step 2 to add a second output text component. Place the second output text component under the first one, indent it slightly, and leave some space above it for a hyperlink (this will be the URL the Google search returns). This second output text component will display the "snippet" returned by the Google search.
4. In the Properties window, change the id attribute to **result**.
5. The snippet that Google returns will contain embedded HTML tags. To display the HTML formatting correctly, *uncheck* the escape attribute in the output text's Properties window.

Add a Hyperlink Component

The hyperlink component allows application writers to set the href attribute in an HTML <a> tag. This in turn allows the user to navigate to an arbitrary URL. The hyperlink's value attribute is the target URL. It uses an embedded output text component to control the text displayed to the user.

Creator Tip

JSF provides two "hyperlink" components: a link action and a hyperlink. The link action component generates an action event that can perform dynamic navigation or some other processing. The hyperlink component does not generate an action event when clicked. Instead, the application simply loads the URL specified in its value attribute.

For this application, the hyperlink component is an easier way to display URL choices for the user. You'll get the URL from the results returned by the Google search method. For now, let's put a hyperlink component in the application.

1. In the JSF Standard Components palette, select Hyperlink and drag it to the design canvas. Position it directly below the first output text component, aligning it on the left. The name will appear as `hyperlink1`.
2. In the Application Outline view, select the `hyperlink1`'s embedded output text component `hyperlink1Text`. Uncheck its `escape` attribute in the Properties window. This allows HTML tags to format the text. Unchecking `escape` results in an `escape="false"` attribute in the corresponding JSP code generation.
3. Look again at the JSP source file (select the Source tab at the bottom of the design canvas). You'll see that the `<h:outputLink/>` tag has an embedded `<h:outputText/>` tag. The `value` attribute of the output text component is the text that's displayed in the hyperlink (by default set to the hyperlink component's name). The `value` attribute of the hyperlink component is the target URL (by default set to `http://www.sun.com/jscreator`).

```
<h:outputLink binding="#{Page1.hyperlink1}" id="hyperlink1"
    style="position: absolute; left: 48px; top: 192px"
    value="http://www.sun.com/jscreator">

  <h:outputText binding="#{Page1.hyperlink1Text}"
    escape="false" id="hyperlink1Text" value="hyperlink1"/>
</h:outputLink>
```

4. Return to the design canvas by selecting the Design tab at the bottom of the editor pane. Right-click inside the design canvas and select View Page1 Java Class from the context menu. Creator now displays the Java page bean source, **Page1.java**.
5. Take a moment to peruse this file. In the Creator-managed code, you'll see private instance variables corresponding to the `binding` attributes of each of the JSF components you created with the GUI editor. (To unfold hidden code, click the '+' near the left margin next to the box labeled Creator-man-

aged Component Definition.) There are also corresponding getter and setter methods. This is the standard way you create properties for JavaBeans component classes. Every component in our application has become a property of the Java page bean.

6. Return to the design canvas by selecting the **Page1.jsp** tab above the editor pane. Go to the Application Outline view. The components `hyperlink1` and `hyperlink1Text` appear in this view along with the previously added components.

Figure 6–3 **Application Outline view of components added to project Google1**

Deploy and Run

Creator Tip

Although you haven't added the calls to the Google Web Service yet, let's build and run the web application anyway. When the application runs, the page is redisplayed when you click the Search Google button (admittedly, not much). However, at this point you know if you've added all of the components to your page correctly.

To run the project, click the green chevron in the toolbar or select Build > Run Project from the main menu. The page should display the Google logo in the upper-left corner, as well as the text field, button, and hyperlink components. Since the hyperlink component has its value set to Sun's Creator web site, clicking it will take you to that site. The output text components are not visible. You can type in a test search string, but clicking the button does not (yet) access the Google web service. It does, however, redisplay the page.

Now it's time to add code to the Java page bean file to do something when you get an action event from clicking the button!

Perform an Action

Our next step is to associate clicking the Search Google button with invoking the appropriate search routine in the Google Web Service API. Recall that components may have event listeners associated with them. When the listened-to event occurs, the system calls the action method associated with that component.

You must tell Creator to listen for an event associated with a specific component. You do this by double-clicking on that component in the design canvas. When you double-click a component, Creator generates an action method stub so that you can provide the correct event processing code. We show you this now.

- In the design canvas, select the button component and double-click. Creator brings up the Java page bean (**Page1.java**) in the editor pane and displays method `search_action()`. (Alternatively, you can right-click with the mouse over the button component and select Edit Event Handler > action from the context menu.) The default implementation of this method is as follows:

```
public String search_action() {
  // User event code here...
  return null;
}
```

When the user clicks the `search` button, the system invokes the `search_action()` method. This is where you want to place the code that invokes Google's search. Before we show you this code, however, let's look at the methods in the Google web service API.

Inspect the Web Service

The Google web service is already included in your application, so let's ask Creator to show you its methods.

- In the Server Navigator window, select and open the folder labeled Web Services > Samples > GoogleSearchService > GoogleSearchPort. Click the '+' to expand the node.

Three methods are available.

```
doGetCachedPage()
doSpellingSuggestion()
doGoogleSearch()
```

You'll be invoking method `doGoogleSearch()` in this application.[1] Now look at the Java page bean, **Page1.java**.

When you added the Google web service to your page, Creator modified the Java page bean file (**Page1.java**) to import the Google web service package, as shown here.

```
import webservice.googlesearchservice.*;
```

This means you'll be able to use the code completion mechanism in the editor to get the package names and methods when you access Google's API.

In the Creator-managed code, you'll see private variable `googleSearchServiceClient1` in the Page1 JavaBean. This is the object that you use to make calls to Google's web service API.

```
private GoogleSearchServiceClient googleSearchServiceClient1 =
        new GoogleSearchServiceClient();
```

Creator Tip

> *At this point, you will undoubtedly find Google's documentation to be helpful. A detailed description of the methods and their parameters can be found on the Google Web Site:* `http://www.google.com/apis/` `reference.html`

Table 6.1 contains a list of the parameters for `googlesearchportDoGoogleSearch()`. The `doGoogleSearch()` method returns a `GoogleSearchResult` object response. Table 6.2 on page 177 contains some of its access methods.

Finally, each response includes an array of `ResultElement` objects. Some of the methods you use to access a `ResultElement` object are listed in Table 6.3 on page 178.

---

1. You access method `doGoogleSearch()` using `googlesearchportDoGoogleSearch()`. See the event handler code in Listing 6.1 on page 178.

Table 6.1 `doGoogleSearch()` **parameters**

Name	Type	Description
key	String	Key provided to you by Google. A key is required for access to the Google service.
q	String	Search query.
start	int	Zero-based index of the first desired result.
maxResults	int	Number of results desired per query. This is at most 10.
filter	boolean	Specifies whether or not you want filtering, which helps eliminate very similar results.
restricts	String	Limits the search to a subset of the Google Web index.
safeSearch	boolean	Enables filtering of adult content.
lr	String	Language Restrict–limits the search to documents with the specified languages.
ie	String	Input Encoding–deprecated.
oe	String	Output Encoding–deprecated.

Add the Java Code to Access the Google Web Service

What should the `search_action()` method do? Here's an overview.

- Invoke the `doSearchGoogle()` method and save the response.
- Display the time it took to complete the search and the estimated number of responses (using output text component `timeCount`).
- For the first result only, display the web site title and create a link to the web site's URL (using components `hyperlink1` and `hyperlink1Text`).
- For the first result only, display the result's "snippet," which is an HTML-formatted string containing the search words in bold (using output text component `result`).

Design Note

Because taking small steps is always better than attempting a giant leap, let's display only the first result on your web page. In a later section, we'll have you display all of the returned results (a maximum of 10).

Table 6.2 `GoogleSearchResult` public methods

Name	*Return Type*	*Description*
`getDirectoryCategories`	`Array`	Array of the Directory Category items corresponding to the ODP[a] directory matches for this search.
`getEndIndex`	`int`	Index (1-based) of the last search result in the `ResultElements` array.
`getEstimatedTotalResultsCount`	`int`	Estimates of the total number of results for the query.
`getResultElements`	`ResultElement[]`	Array containing the results.
`getSearchComments`	`String`	Search comments.
`getSearchQuery`	`String`	Search query you provided.
`getSearchTime`	`double`	Time it took the Google server to compute the results.
`getSearchTips`	`String`	Tips for searching.
`getStartIndex`	`int`	Index (1-based) of the first search result in the `ResultElements` array.
`isDocmentFiltering`	`boolean`	True if document filtering is enabled.
`isEstimateIsExact`	`boolean`	True if the total results estimate is exact.

a. "The **Open Directory Project** is the largest, most comprehensive human-edited directory of the Web. It is constructed and maintained by a vast, global community of volunteer editors." (See About the Open Directory Project, `http://dmoz.org`.)

1. At the top of the editor pane in **Page1.java**, open the dropdown menu and select **search_action**. Creator puts the cursor at the start of this method and marks it in yellow.

Table 6.3 ResultElement public methods

Name	Return Type	Description
getCachedSize	String	Size of the cached document.
getDirectoryCategory	DirectoryCategory	Name of the ODP category in which the result occurs.
getDirectoryTitle	String	Name of the result as it appears in the Open Directory.
getHostName	String	Hostname of the result.
getSnippet	String	Short description of the result page.
getSummary	String	Description of the result as it appears in the Open Directory.
getTitle	String	Page title of the result.
getURL	String	URL of the result page.
isRelatedInformationPresent	boolean	True if there are related documents to this result.

2. Add the following private instance variable after the `Page1()` constructor and in front of the `search_action()` method.

```
private GoogleSearchResult mySearchResult;
```

3. Add the following code to the `search_action()` method. From your Creator book download, copy and paste the file **FieldGuide/Examples/WebServices/snippets/google1_search.txt** into the `search_action()` event handler. The added code is bold.

Listing 6.1 Method `search_action()`

```
public String search_action() {
// User event code here...
   try {
```

Listing 6.1 Method `search_action()` *(continued)*

```
mySearchResult =
googleSearchServiceClient1.googlesearchportDoGoogleSearch(
    "Your Google Key Here",(String)searchString.getValue(),
    0,10,true,"",true,"lang_en","","");
timeCount.setValue("Search Time = " +
    mySearchResult.getSearchTime()
    + " Number of results returned = "
    + mySearchResult.getEstimatedTotalResultsCount());

ResultElement[] myResults =
    mySearchResult.getResultElements();

if (myResults.length > 0) {
    result.setValue(myResults[0].getSnippet());
    hyperlink1.setValue(myResults[0].getURL());
    hyperlink1Text.setValue(myResults[0].getTitle());
}
}

catch (Exception e) {
    log("Remote Connect Failure", e);
    throw new FacesException(e);
}
return null;
}
```

Creator Tip

Make sure you include your Google Web API's License Key as the first argument of the Google search method. Otherwise, your application will throw an exception, as shown.

```
javax.faces.FacesException:
javax.xml.rpc.soap.SOAPFaultException:
Exception from service object:
Invalid authorization key: Your Google Key Here
```

Deploy and Run

It's time to test this initial version of the Google search web application.

- From the menu bar, select Build > Run Project. You can test the Google Search API by typing in various search queries. Click on the URL (displayed as the title) and go to that web page. Figure 6–4 shows a screen shot of the application.

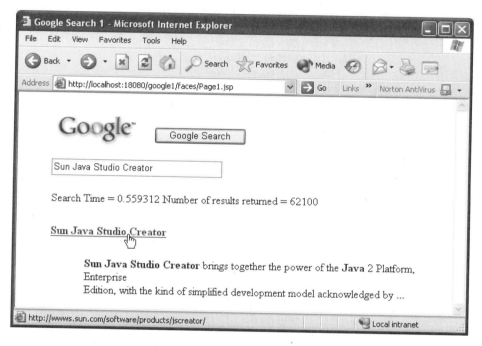

Figure 6–4 **First version of the Google Web Search application**

6.2 Validation

You have created a simple web application that uses a published web service. Now you're going to build on this example and enhance it in the following ways.

- Provide validation for the text field component and require that the user provide something. That is, you want to prevent a zero-length string and require a minimum length for the search string (three characters).

- Make sure all of the output text components values are cleared so that if there is any problem with the Google search (for example, if zero results are returned), the previous results are cleared from the page.
- Place an inline message component on the page to report errors.

Copy a Project

To avoid starting from scratch, copy the **Google1** project to a new project called **Google2**. This step is optional. If you don't want to copy the project, simply skip this section and continue making modifications to the **Google1** project.

1. Bring up project **Google1** in Creator, if it's not already opened.
2. Click anywhere inside the design canvas.
3. From the File menu, select Save Project as . . . and provide the new name **Google2**. You'll make changes to the **Google2** project.
4. Change the title to **Google Search 2**.

Add a Validator

It's always a good idea to validate user input. Among the JSF standard components are a set of validators to help with this task. With text strings, two validators are of interest. First, a length validator can control a String's length. You can specify a maximum and a minimum for the number of characters input. Interestingly enough, if you want to prevent a zero-length string, you cannot use the length validator (and set the minimum to 1). Instead, you must use the component's *required* attribute. The `required` attribute is set in the Properties window for each text field component. If you check it (set it to true) and the component's value is a String, then its length must be greater than zero.

For this example, let's prevent a zero-length string and set a length minimum of three characters and a maximum of 2,048 characters (this is the maximum search query allowed by Google).

Creator Tip

For testing, you'll set the length minimum to 3 and its maximum to 25. Coupled with the required validator, you should get the following behavior. If the user leaves the text field empty, you'll get a message from the required validator saying that a value is required. If you type in a 1- or 2-character text value, you'll get feedback from the length validator saying that it was less than the minimum of 3. Likewise, if you type in more than 25 characters, the length validator will complain that the string was more than the maximum. Note that a zero-length string does not trigger the length validator even if the minimum is set to 1. You must use the required attribute of the component!

Let's add validation to the application now.

1. Make sure Page1 is in the design canvas.
2. Select the text field component, searchString.
3. In the Properties window, click the checkbox for the required attribute. This means the text field component cannot be empty.

Now let's add one of the JSF Validators.

4. From the JSF Validators/Converts palette, select Length Validator, drag it to the design canvas, and drop it on top of the searchString text field component. Creator sets the validator attribute for searchString to lengthValidator1. Component lengthValidator1 appears in the Application Outline view.
5. You've instantiated a length validator for the text field component. Now you have to give it length boundaries: the minimum and maximum allowable. To do this, select lengthValidator1 in the Application Outline view. In its corresponding Properties window, change attribute maximum to 25 and minimum to 3. These values are probably not the limits you'd want to use in your production application, but they're good values for testing. Once you're convinced the length validator is working, set the maximum to 2048, which is the maximum imposed by Google. The advantage of using the validator instead of letting Google complain is that you save a trip to the Google server.
6. Since the validator is a nonvisual component, it does not appear in the design canvas. However, it does appear in the Application Outline view and the searchString component's tags in the source for **Page1.jsp** have been modified as follows.

```
<h:inputText binding="#{Page1.searchString}"
   id="searchString" required="true"
   style="position: absolute; left: 48px; top: 96px;
   width: 240px; height: 22px"
   title="Type in a search string"
   validator="#{Page1.lengthValidator1.validate}"/>
```

Note that the Page1() constructor in the Java page bean has been modified to include the minimum and maximum settings you defined in the Properties window, as follows. (Unfold the Creator-managed Component Initialization block to see the code.)

```
lengthValidator1.setMinimum(3);
lengthValidator1.setMaximum(25);
```

Add an Inline Message Component

The JSF inline message component retrieves messages from the JSF context. As it turns out, the validator sends an error message to the JSF context when it detects nonconforming input. The inline message component just needs to know which component's messages it should retrieve.

1. From the JSF standard components palette, select Inline Message and drag it onto the design canvas. Place it below the output text component called `result`.
2. From the Properties window under General, select the property `for` and select `searchString` from the list of components in the pop-up window. Click OK.
3. Make sure attribute `showSummary` is checked (`showSummary` and `showDetail` display the same message for this validation).
4. Still in the Properties window under Appearances, select attribute `style`. Click the small editing box; an editing pane appears. After the position attributes, add the following font characteristics (this makes the error message appear in italic).

```
; font-style: italic
```

5. Click OK.

Now any messages having to do with component `searchString` will be displayed by the `inlineMessage1` component.

Life Cycle Issues

It's time to delve into the deep, dark crevices of JSF. This section is somewhat advanced, but it's useful nonetheless to help you tweak your applications. If you'd prefer to skip this part and go ahead to the next section, you can do that without jeopardizing your Google application.

Let's explore some of the nuances of the JSF life cycle process. The best way to do this is to "see" the life cycle effects on a running web application.

Run the **Google2** application now. Note that when you supply valid input, the application accesses the Google web service and displays the first result. Subsequently, if you supply invalid input (a search query less than three characters or no input at all) the validation step fails and the inline message component displays the appropriate error message. However, the result from the previous search is still displayed, making for a confusing page at best.

A more pleasing page would make the validation errors appear directly below the text field component, overlapping the output text components. To accomplish this, you must clear the `value` attribute in the output text components from the previous search request. This results in a cleaner page and prevents error messages from overwriting old results. Here's the code that clears the output text components. However, the more difficult question is: "Where should this code go and when should it be executed?"

```
timeCount.setValue("");
result.setValue("");
hyperlink1Text.setValue("");
```

The JavaServer Faces framework provides a life cycle for a JSP request. The six steps in this life cycle process are shown in Figure 6–5[2].

While the steps always occur in the same order, it is important to note that not all six steps will necessarily be processed for every page request. For example, validation rules are applied to the request during Step 3 (Process Validations). If a component fails a validation, the page is returned with an error message and the process skips directly to Step 6 (Render Response).

Creator provides hooks into this life cycle process for the application developer, but you have to know how to get at them. Once you have the hooks, you can write a method that clears the output text components before validation occurs. When errors occur, the previous requests' output does not appear on the page.

So how do you "hook into" the page request life cycle? You'll note that the Java page bean **Page1.java** extends class AbstractPageBean. As it turns out, AbstractPageBean (as well as AbstractSessionBean and AbstractApplicationBean) all extend from class FacesBean. There are twelve methods in FacesBean, each of which is called either before or after one of the six page request life cycle phases. Table 6.4 lists all twelve methods in the order that they're invoked in the page request life cycle.[3]

All methods have empty stubs, but they exist so that you can override them with your own versions in the page bean. Method `beforeRenderResponse()`, for example, is called before the Render Response phase. We've included the

---

2. This diagram is adapted from "JavaServer Faces Standard Request-Response Life Cycle," in the J2EE 1.4 Tutorial. See `http://java.sun.com/j2ee/1.4/docs/tutorial/doc/index.html` for more information.

3. Note that these methods are *protected*. This means you can call them from your page bean and any class derived from it.

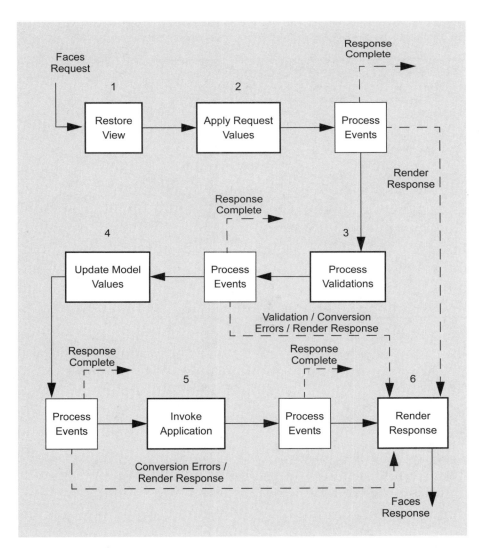

Figure 6–5 JSF Request-Response Life Cycle Process

code for the methods in **FieldGuide/Examples/WebServices/snippets/ life_cycle.txt** in case you want to use them in other projects.

Table 6.4 Page request life cycle methods

```
protected void beforeRestoreView();
protected void afterRestoreView();

protected void beforeApplyRequestValues();
protected void afterApplyRequestValues();

protected void beforeProcessValidations();
protected void afterProcessValidations();

protected void beforeUpdateModelValues();
protected void afterUpdateModelValues();

protected void beforeInvokeApplication();
protected void afterInvokeApplication();

protected void beforeRenderResponse();
protected void afterRenderResponse();
```

You'll need to call the `beforeProcessValidations()` method to clear the output text components in this project. If you include the code to clear the components at this point, the page will be blank and ready for either error messages (generated during the Process Validation phase) or output from the Google web search (displayed during the Render Response phase). This is what you need to do.

1. Inside the Java page bean **Page1.java**, add the following method. Copy and paste from the file **FieldGuide/Examples/WebServices/snippets/ google2_beforeProcessValidations.txt**.
2. Put this method after the `Page1()` constructor code.

```
public void beforeProcessValidations() {
    timeCount.setValue("");
    result.setValue("");
    hyperlink1Text.setValue("");
}
```

Now the previous page's results will be cleared from the current request's page, even if there is a validation error. Since you don't have to worry about validation error messages writing on top of previous results, move the inline message component on the design canvas so that it is directly below the text field (left aligned). You can experiment with its size and placement when you run and test the application.

Creator Tip

Method `afterRenderResponse()` *is particularly useful with "cleanup" duties since it's called at the very end of the page request cycle. This is a good place to make sure any state information is saved for the next page request cycle. Since the default scope for each page bean is request, the page bean's constructor will return all components to their initial states. If this behavior is not what you want, save the state in the SessionBean1 managed bean and retrieve it during construction.*

6.3 HTML with Output Text

The previous version of the application displays only the first result returned from a Google search. Most of the time, the Google search returns an array of 10 results. You get the first 10 results of the query if parameter `start` is set to zero and `maxResults` is set to 10, which is how you called `doGoogleSearch()`. To get the next set of 10 results, set `start` to 10 (instead of 0). For the third set of 10 results, set `start` to 20, and so on.

Google returns the total result count with method `getEstimatedTotalRe-sultsCount()`; you can easily determine the number of results returned by getting the `length` attribute of the `ResultElement` array. This will be at most 10. Furthermore, Google imposes a 1,000 count limit, so even if the query returns 30,000 hits, Google will give you at most 1,000 (in 10-count page increments).

In this version of our Google search application, you're going to display all (up to 10) elements of the `ResultElement` array (that is, the first *page*). You'll use an HTML table tag to display the results.

Copy a Project

As before, copy **Google2** and create a new project called **Google3**. This step is optional. If you don't want to copy the project, simply skip this section and continue making modifications to the previous project.

1. Bring up project **Google2** in Creator, if it's not already opened.
2. Click anywhere inside the design canvas.
3. From the File menu, select Save Project As and provide the new name **Google3**. You'll make changes to the **Google3** project.
4. Change the title to **Google Search 3**.

Modify the Components

To simplify our application, let's begin with the removal of the hyperlink component and its nested output text component. That is, you'll delete

```
hyperlink1
hperlink1Text
```

To do this:

1. Go to the Application Outline view and select `hyperlink1`. Right-click and from the context menu, select Delete. This automatically deletes the embedded output text component, `hyperlink1Text`, too.
2. Select component `result` in the design canvas and move it up so that it is directly under the `timeCount` component. Position it so that it is aligned on the left with the `timeCount` component.

    Instead of holding the result element's snippet only, you'll use the `result` output text component to display a table of result elements returned from the Google search.

3. Now go to the Java page bean file by right-clicking in the design canvas and selecting View Page1 Java Class. At the end of this file, you'll see syntax errors highlighted in red by the Java source editor.
4. In the `beforeProcessValidations()` method, remove the call to component `hyperlink1`. This clears the values of the two output text components, `timeCount` and `result` only. Here is the modified method.[4]

```
public void beforeProcessValidations() {
    timeCount.setValue("");
    result.setValue("");
}
```

There are still syntax errors in the `search_action()` method, but you'll fix them shortly.

Build HTML Output

An interesting feature of the output text component is that you can include HTML formatting tags in its `value` attribute along with plain text as long as the

---

4. If you didn't make the earlier life cycle modifications to project **Google2**, this method does not appear in the **Page1.java** source, so no modification is necessary here.

escape attribute is unchecked (false). The HTML tags will be rendered just as you'd expect. You've actually already seen this behavior when you assigned both the snippet string and the title string to output text components. You'll recall that the search query words appear in bold. If you leave the escape attribute *checked*, the search words are enclosed in HTML tags rather than appearing in bold. The following display shows the previous search snippet displayed with the escape attribute checked.

Sun Java Studio Creator brings together the power of the Java 2 Platform, Enterprise
 Edition, with the kind of simplified development model acknowledged by ...

This means the output text component can handle arbitrary HTML tags and text. Thus, you can programmatically build the output as an HTML table to display each result's title and snippet and use its URL as an href attribute. Since the result is an array, a for loop can easily build this output in a method and return it as a String.

1. In the Java page bean file, go to the search_action() method. Just before it, place the code for a new public method called buildTable() that will build the output string. Copy and paste file **FieldGuide/Examples/WebServices/snippets/google3_buildtable.txt**. Here is the code.

Listing 6.2 Method buildTable()

```
public String buildTable(webservice.
            googlesearchservice.ResultElement[] results) {
  String str = "<table border=\"2\" cellpadding=\"2\"" +
        " width=\"720\"><tbody>";

  // Set href to the url and the display text to the title
  // Include the index number
  // Place the snippet in the row underneath

  for (int i = 0; i < results.length; i++) {
    str = str + "<tr><td>" + (i) +
        "</td><td><a href=\"" + results[i].getURL() + "\">";
    str = str + results[i].getTitle() +
        "</a></td></tr><tr><td colspan=\"2\">";
    str = str + results[i].getSnippet() + "</td></tr>";
  }
```

Listing 6.2 Method `buildTable()` *(continued)*

```
// Close html table tag
str = str + "</tbody></table><p><p>";
return str;
}
```

Method `buildTable()` takes the `ResultElement[]` array and returns a
`String`. Note that you must precede embedded quotation marks in the Java
string with a backslash (\) character.

2. Now return to the `search_action()` method. You'll note that there are syntax errors highlighted in red squiggly underlines. That's because you still
have the previous version's code that accesses the `hyperlink1` and
`hyperlink1Text` components. Delete those statements now and replace the
previous `result.setValue()` call with a call to `buildTable()`. Here is the
new `search_action()` method (with the statement that calls `buildTable()`
in bold).

Listing 6.3 Method `search_action()`

```
public String search_action() {
  // User event code here...
  try {

    mySearchResult =
      googleSearchServiceClient1.
        googlesearchportDoGoogleSearch(
        "Your Google Key Here",(String)searchString.getValue(),
        0,10,true,"",true,"lang_en","","");
    timeCount.setValue("Search Time = " +
      mySearchResult.getSearchTime()
      + " Number of results returned = "
      + mySearchResult.getEstimatedTotalResultsCount());

    ResultElement[] myResults =
        mySearchResult.getResultElements();
    if (myResults.length > 0)
      result.setValue(buildTable(myResults));
  }
```

Listing 6.3 Method `search_action()` *(continued)*

```
catch (Exception e) {
    log("Remote Connect Failure", e);
    throw new FacesException(e);
}
return null;
}
```

Deploy and Run

- Deploy and run the **Google3** application. Depending on the input you provide for the search query, you should see up to 10 results displayed on the page. Figure 6–6 shows an example screen shot.

Figure 6–6 **Google Web Search application using HTML to build a results table**

6.4 Displaying Multiple Pages

Each Google request displays up to 10 results. It's time to add controls that move forward to retrieve additional results or move backward to display earlier results. You've seen how to use a button component to initiate an action. Now you'll use two button controls with "arrow" images and render them on the page in place of the default button look. This is quite easy to do and adds a nice touch to your web application.

The image files you'll need are in your Creator book's **FieldGuide** download bundle (**FieldGuide/Examples/WebServices/images**), but if you'd like to use arrow graphics of your own, simply substitute the appropriate **.gif** or **.jpg** file.

The modifications for this project include adding two new buttons and image files for their display. You'll also write action event methods for the buttons to page forward or backward through the Google search results. These additions are straightforward. What's a bit tricky is that you have to keep track of some of the parameters across page requests when you call Google. That means you can't use local variables with request scope inside **Page1.java**, since the Page1 bean is instantiated with each page request. Therefore, you'll need to save and restore these control variables in session scope. (You might want to review the discussion about the different types of scope for web application objects. See "Scope of Web Applications" on page 128.)

Remember, Google returns at most 10 results at once. So you'll need to access the subsequent pages by submitting a new call to the Google search method with a different starting index each time.

Copy a Project

Copy **Google3** and create a new project called **Google4**. This step is optional. If you don't want to copy the project, simply skip this section and continue making modifications to the previous project.

1. Bring up project **Google3** in Creator, if it's not already opened.
2. Click anywhere inside the design canvas.
3. From the File menu, select Save Project as . . . and provide the new name **Google4**. You'll make changes to the **Google4** project.
4. Change the project's title to **Google Search 4**.

Before you add components to project **Google4**, look at Figure 6–7, the design canvas for this project. You can see the placement of the buttons and the two output text components (faint dotted lines) below. Also, the web services component, `googleSearchServiceClient1`, appears in the nonvisual tray at the bottom.

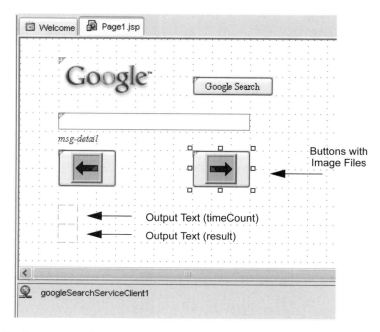

Figure 6–7 **Design canvas showing component layout for project Google4**

Add Button and Image File

1. Move the `timeCount` and `result` output text components down on the design canvas to make room for the arrow graphics components. (Leave the inline message component right below the text field.)
2. From the JSF Standard Components palette, select Button and drop it onto the design canvas. Place it under the inline message component off center to the left. Change its `id` attribute to **prev1** by selecting `id` in the Properties window.

Creator Tip

You're changing the standard `id` that Creator uses because it's easier to keep track of the components in the Java page bean file. By using meaningful `id` names (such as `prev1` and `next1`), the associated action methods that Creator generates will have meaningful names, too.

3. In the Properties window, set attribute `title` to **Get the previous set of results** for its tooltip.
4. In the Properties window under Appearance, click the small editing box opposite attribute `image`. Creator pops up an image selection dialog.
5. Select the File tab and browse to directory **FieldGuide/Examples/WebServices/images** in this book's download directory. Select file **arrow.blue.left.gif**. Click OK. Creator copies the image file to the Resources folder and the left-arrow image should now appear on the design canvas.
6. With the button still selected, click the small editing box next to the `value` attribute. When an editing box pops up, click the Reset to default button. This removes the `value` attribute from the generated JSF tags for the `prev1` button.

Here's the JSP code that Creator generates for the `prev1` button with the `image` attribute set to the **.gif** file in the project's resources folder.

```
<h:commandButton binding="#{Page1.prev1}" id="prev1"
image="resources/arrow.blue.left.gif"
style="position: absolute; left: 48px; top: 144px"/>
```

A Second Button and Image File

Follow the same procedure to add a second button and a second image to the page.

1. From the JSF Standard Components palette, select Button and drop it onto the design canvas. Place it under the inline message component off center to the right. Change its `id` attribute to **next1** by selecting `id` in the Properties window.
2. In the Properties window, set attribute `title` to **Get the next set of results** for its tooltip.
3. In the Properties window under Appearance, click the small editing box opposite attribute `image`. Creator pops up an image selection dialog.
4. Select the File tab and browse to directory **FieldGuide/Examples/WebServices/images** in this book's download directory. Select file **arrow.blue.right.gif**. Click OK. Creator copies the image file to the Resources folder and the right-arrow image should now appear on the design canvas.
5. With the button still selected, click the small editing box next to the `value` attribute. When an editing box pops up, click the Reset to default button.

Deploy and Run

You might want to experiment with the placement of these newly added graphic components. Deploy and run project **Google4**. (The arrow buttons won't do anything useful, but you should be able to display the 10 results as before.) Check the placement of the components and adjust them if necessary.

Creator Tip

Actually, the arrow buttons clear the page (why?). To see the search results again, click the Google Search button. The page is cleared because clicking an arrow button generates an action event, which initiates the JSF page life cycle process (see Figure 6–5 on page 185). You haven't specified any action, but the system proceeds through the different life cycle phases anyway. Before reaching the Process Validations phase, the system executes `beforeProcessValidations()`, *which clears the page.*

Add SessionBean1 Properties

You will soon add control variables to the **Page1.java** file. These values keep track of the current index and other controls you need for displaying more than the first page of results. To maintain these values across page requests, you add them to the SessionBean1 managed bean as *properties*. This automatically puts them in session scope. Here are the steps to add properties to SessionBean1.

Creator Tip

Creator allows you to interactively add properties to its managed beans (SessionBean1 for example). However, in this case, it's easier to simply copy and paste the code directly into the Java source file.

1. From the Project Navigator window, select Java Sources > google1.
2. Double-click file **SessionBean1.java**. This brings it up in the Java source editor.
3. Add instance variables with their setters and getters for the properties referenced in **Page1.java**. Copy and paste from file **FieldGuide/Examples/WebServices/snippets/google4_sessionbean.txt**.

Here's the **SessionBean1.java** source.

Listing 6.4 SessionBean1.java

```java
package google1;
import com.sun.jsfcl.app.*;

public class SessionBean1 extends AbstractSessionBean {

    // State variables saved in session scope
    private Integer startIndex = new Integer(0);
    public Integer getStartIndex() { return startIndex; }
    public void setStartIndex(Integer si) { startIndex = si; }

    private Integer currentCount = new Integer(0);
    public Integer getCurrentCount() { return currentCount; }
    public void setCurrentCount(Integer cc) {
            currentCount = cc; }

    private Integer totalCount = new Integer(0);
    public Integer getTotalCount() { return totalCount; }
    public void setTotalCount(Integer tc) { totalCount = tc; }
. . .
}
```

Specify the Action Code

When a user clicks the right-arrow button, the web application should display the next 10 results from the Google search. Conversely, clicking the left-arrow button displays the previous 10 results. Because you'll make similar calls to the Google search API, you should place this code in its own method. Furthermore, you need to keep track of the current start index and previous index so that you know how to access the results data when the user clicks right arrow or left arrow.

1. In the design canvas for Page1, select the right-arrow button, `next1`, and double-click.
2. Creator brings up the Java page bean file, **Page1.java**, and displays the generated event handler, `next1_action()`.
3. To keep track of the index variables and the result count information that Google returns, you'll need integer control variables. Scroll up the **Page1.java** file until you find the declaration for private variable `mySearchResult`. Immediately after this line (shown below), add the follow-

ing declarations. Copy and paste file **FieldGuide/Examples/WebServices/snippets/google4_variables.txt**.

```
private GoogleSearchResult mySearchResult;
private int startIndex = 0;
private int prevIndex = 0;
private int currentCount = 0;
private int totalCount = 0;
```

The `startIndex`, `currentCount`, and `totalCount` integer variables are saved and restored in session scope for the action handlers. To do this, you'll use methods `saveState()` and `restoreState()` and the SessionBean1 object that Creator generates for you from **SessionBean1.java**.

Let's look at the `saveState()` method first. This method calls setters to store `startIndex`, `currentCount`, and `totalCount` as equivalently named properties in the SessionBean1 object.

Listing 6.5 Method `saveState()`

```
private void saveState() {
    getSessionBean1().setStartIndex(new Integer(startIndex));
    getSessionBean1().setCurrentCount(
            new Integer(currentCount));
    getSessionBean1().setTotalCount(new Integer(totalCount));
}
```

Note that `getSessionBean1()` is what you use to access the session object in your page bean. You can use SessionBean1 to store your own data as needed in session scope.[5]

Next, let's look at `getState()`. This method calls getters to retrieve the equivalently named properties from the SessionBean1 object.

Listing 6.6 Method `getState()`

```
private void getState() {
    startIndex = getSessionBean1().getStartIndex().intValue();
    currentCount =
        getSessionBean1().getCurrentCount().intValue();
    totalCount = getSessionBean1().getTotalCount().intValue();
}
```

---

5. To store session data, be sure to use `Integer` (one of Java's wrapper classes) instead of an `int` primitive type. Integer allows property binding between components and JavaBeans properties.

1. Add the `saveState()` and `getState()` methods immediately after the variable declarations you just added in **Page1.java**. Copy and paste from **Field-Guide/Examples/WebServices/snippets/google4_save_restore.txt**.
2. Most of the code that resides in the `search_action()` event handler can be pulled out and placed in a method that all three action event handlers will call. Let's call this new method `doSearch()`. To create the `doSearch()` method, use **FieldGuide/Examples/WebServices/snippets/google4_doSearch.txt** and place it directly before the `search_action()` method (near the end of the Java page bean file).

Listing 6.7 Method `doSearch()`

```
public void doSearch(int start) {
  // Update control variables currentCount and totalCount
  // Display results (if there are any)
  try {

    mySearchResult =
        googleSearchServiceClient1.
          googlesearchportDoGoogleSearch(
            "Your Google Key Here",
            (String)searchString.getValue(),
            start,10,true,"",true,"lang_en","","");
    totalCount =
        mySearchResult.getEstimatedTotalResultsCount();

    timeCount.setValue("Search Time = " +
                    mySearchResult.getSearchTime()
                    + " Number of results returned = "
                    + totalCount);
    ResultElement[] myResults =
                    mySearchResult.getResultElements();

    currentCount = myResults.length;
    if (currentCount > 0) {
      result.setValue(buildTable(myResults));
    }
  }

  catch (Exception e) {
      log("Remote Connect Failure", e);
      throw new FacesException(e);
  }
}
```

(Remember, `Your Google Key Here` needs to be replaced by the licensed key supplied by Google when you register to access their service.)

3. The `search_action()` method is now simpler, since all that's required is to reset the index control variables and call `doSearch()`. Copy and paste from file **FieldGuide/Examples/WebServices/snippets/google4_search.txt** to modify this method. Here's the new code. Note the call to `saveState()` to save the index variables in the session object before returning.

Listing 6.8 Method `search_action()`

```
public String search_action() {
  // User event code here...
  startIndex = 0;
  prevIndex = 0;
  doSearch(startIndex);
  saveState();
  return null;
}
```

Clicking the right-arrow button returns the next set of results from Google. To effect this return, update the `start` parameter (see Table 6.1 on page 176) of the `doGoogleSearch()` method. Also note that the code in the action handler `next1_action()` is similar to the code in the above `search_action()`. You just need to check for upper limits in the index control variables.

4. Add code to the `next1_action()` event handler. Copy and paste from file **FieldGuide/Examples/WebServices/snippets/google4_next1.txt**. Here's the code. Note that in this method, it's necessary to call `getState()` to restore the index variables from the session object before using them. Likewise, `saveState()` saves the index variables in the session object before returning.

Listing 6.9 Method `next1_action()`

```
public String next1_action() {
  // User event code here...
  getState();
  prevIndex = startIndex;
  startIndex = startIndex + currentCount;

  if (startIndex >= totalCount || startIndex >= 1000) {
    startIndex = prevIndex;
    prevIndex -= currentCount;
  }
```

Listing 6.9 Method `next1_action()` *(continued)*

```
  doSearch(startIndex);
  saveState();
  return null;
}
```

Now let's add a `prev1_action()` method to handle action events associated with the left-arrow button.

5. Return to the design canvas by selecting the tab labeled **Page1.jsp** above the editor pane.
6. Select the left arrow button `prev1` and double click. This creates the event handler method in the Java page bean file for you and places the cursor at the beginning of the method.
7. Add the following code to the empty `prev1_action()` method. Copy and paste from file **FieldGuide/Examples/WebServices/snippets/google4_prev1.txt**.

Listing 6.10 Method `prev1_action()`

```
public String prev1_action() {
  // User event code here...
  getState();
  prevIndex = startIndex - currentCount;
  startIndex = prevIndex;

  if (startIndex <= 0) {
    startIndex = 0;
    prevIndex = 0;
  }

  doSearch(startIndex);
  saveState();
  return null;
}
```

You'll note that the structure of `prev1_action()` is similar to the `next1_action()` method.

One final modification is necessary in **Page1.java**. In method `buildTable()`, HTML tags produce the results table. Recall that you display the index number of the result. This index number starts at 0 and when there are 10 results continues through index 9. As you display other pages, this index number should reflect the number of the result.

8. Change variable `i` in the HTML tags (which is simply the index of the `results` array), to the expression `(i + startIndex)` for the correct result count. (So, for example, the second page of results will typically span indices 10 through 19.) To make this easy for you, here is the modified `build-Table()` method in its entirety with the modification in bold.

Listing 6.11 Method `buildTable()`

```
public String buildTable(ResultElement[] results) {
  String str = "<table border=\"2\" cellpadding=\"2\""
          + " width=\"720\"><tbody>";
  // Set href to the url and the display text to the title
  // Include the index number
  // Place the snippet in the row underneath

  for (int i = 0; i < results.length; i++) {
    str = str + "<tr><td>" + (i + startIndex) +
        "</td><td><a href=\"" + results[i].getURL() + "\">";
    str = str + results[i].getTitle() +
        "</a></td></tr><tr><td colspan=\"2\">";
    str = str + results[i].getSnippet() + "</td></tr>";
  }

  // Close html table tag
  str = str + "</tbody></table><p><p>";
  return str;
}
```

Deploy and Run

Deploy and run project **Google4**. You should be able to page through multiple result sets by using the arrow graphics "right" and "left." Figure 6–8 shows the third page of a result set. (Note that we moved the location of the arrows to get a bit more output into the screen shot. This is very easy to do with Creator's design canvas.)

Under the Hood

After running the project from Creator and testing the web application, you could easily assume that everything works. Another important test is to run more than one session concurrently, possibly from different machines. Once the web application is deployed, you can easily begin another session by specifying its URL from your browser, as follows.

```
http://localhost:18080/google4/faces/Page1.jsp
```

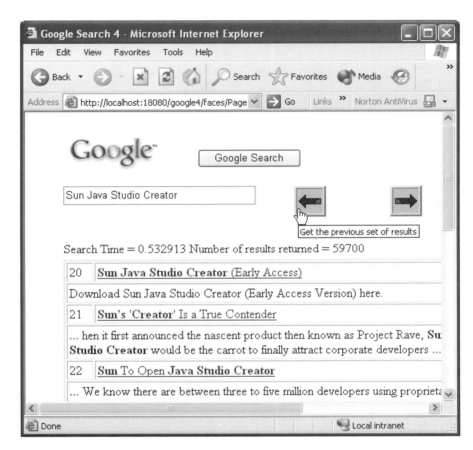

Figure 6–8 The Google Web Search application displaying the third page of results

To invoke the application from a remote machine, substitute the ISP or machine name for `localhost`. Once you have two or more applications running, perform different searches and page through the searches.

Each session is served by its own thread. This means that every session has its own copy of the control variables stored in session scope as properties of SessionBean1. The web form, Page1, is in request scope. It is created anew with each page request. What a jumbled mess there would be without each session having its own copy!

6.5 Key Point Summary

- Web services provide a standard way to access services over a network in a heterogeneous environment.
- The Google web service API provides a SOAP interface to search Google's index of pages.
- Initiate a search of the Google engine by invoking the `doGoogleSearch()` method in the Google web service API.
- Use image components to add graphics to your web pages.
- The text field component allows users to type in and edit textual information.
- The button component allows users to initiate an action. The action method associated with the component is called an event handler.
- You can access methods of a web service by dragging its node onto the design canvas. Web services appear in the nonvisual component tray at the bottom of the design canvas
- Use an output text component to display read-only text. Setting its `escape` attribute to false allows correct rendering of HTML formatting tags. JSF dynamically sizes the output text component for you.
- Use a hyperlink component for data-driven URLs. Clicking a hyperlink component does not generate an event.
- The length validator makes sure that input is within a certain range for length. It does not check for empty fields.
- The `required` attribute makes sure the field is not empty.
- Validators write error messages to the JSF context. Use an inline message component to display error messages generated by a specific component.
- The JSF framework provides a life cycle for a JSP page request.
- You can define methods to access the life cycle at its various phases.
- To display an image instead of the normal "button" graphic for a button component, specify an image file (attribute `image`) instead of a text value (attribute `value`) in Creator.
- Page1 lives in *request scope*. You can store information you need to access across page requests as properties in SessionBean1, which is defined in *session scope*.

ACCESSING DATABASES

Topics in This Chapter

- Database Basics
- JDBC RowSet Technology
- Data-Aware Components
- Master-Detail Relationship with Components
- Query Editor
- Converters
- Database Operations
- Cascading Deletes

Chapter 7

One of Creator's key goals is to simplify web application development with databases. To that end, Creator lets you add data sources to your projects and select them with the Server Navigator window. Once you add a data source to your project, you can select and view individual tables, including field names for each column.

Creator also gives you components that are data aware. Using the design canvas, you can select a number of different components and visually position them on your web page. You can select tables and add them to your application as rowsets, binding the components to the data from the rowsets. You can visually select or deselect columns to display, add tables to create database queries with "join" commands, and modify queries to include parameters. You can also modify transaction isolation levels and concurrency attributes through a rowset's Properties window.

Creator relies on multiple technologies to make this all happen. Besides using the JSF component and event models that we've already shown you, Creator makes use of JDBC and JDBC RowSet technology to simplify accessing the database.

In this chapter, we use a Music Collection Database for the project examples. Before we start, however, we review database and JDBC fundamentals and show you the organization of our Music database.

7.1 Database Fundamentals

We begin with an overview of databases and JDBC, discussing database tables and how to access data with JDBC. If you're already familiar with these subjects, you can skip to the next section.

A relational database consists of one or more tables, where each row in a table represents a database record and each column represents a field. Within each table, a record must have a unique key. This key, called a *primary key*, enables a database to distinguish one record from another. If a single field in a database table does not uniquely identify a record, a *composite primary key* can be used. A composite primary key combines more than one field to uniquely identify records in a database table. Each field of a composite primary key should be defined as a primary key.

A field within a table is either a primary key, a *foreign key* (used by the database to reference another table), or just plain data. To set up a database table, you must define fields so that the database software can maintain the integrity of the database. If a field is not "just data," then constraints are attached to the field. The description of the table's fields, data types, and constraints make up the metadata associated with the table. Creator uses metadata to help you configure your web application to access the database efficiently.

A very simple database consists of only a single table. However, many database schemata require multiple tables to efficiently represent related data. For example, our Music Collection database centralizes the information about each recording artist in one table. This table also cross-references a RecordingArtistID field in another table that stores data about a specific recording. Thus, if a recording artist has more than one recording, you don't have to duplicate the recording artist information.

To achieve cross-referencing and to avoid data duplication, you can mark a field in a database table as a foreign key. A foreign key in one table always matches either a primary or foreign key in another table. This is what helps you "relate" two or more tables.

Music Collection Database

The Music Collection database consists of four related tables. The database stores information about music recordings, a generic term we apply to music CDs and older LPs (long-playing records). Figure 7–1 shows the four tables, the fields in each table, and how they relate to each other through the foreign keys.

The Recordings table contains the bulk of the information about a recording. Its primary key (denoted PK) is the field RecordingID. It has two foreign key

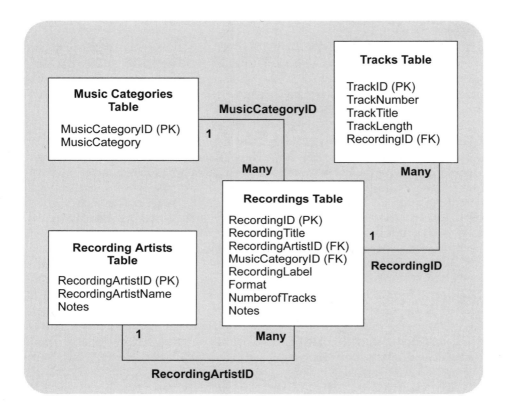

Figure 7–1 Music Collection Database Schema

fields (denoted FK): RecordingArtistID and MusicCategoryID. These foreign key fields refer to records in the Recording Artists table and the Music Categories table, respectively. For each row in the Music Categories table, there may be multiple rows in the Recordings table. (We indicate this relationship by placing the word **Many** next to the Recordings table and the numeral **1** next to the Music Categories table.) Similarly, for each row in the Recording Artists table, there may be multiple rows in the Recordings table. In the diagram, we show foreign key field names on the lines that relate two tables.

The Tracks table contains information about each track belonging to a recording. To determine which recording a track belongs to, we include the RecordingID as a foreign key in the Tracks table. Thus, for each row in the Recordings table, there are multiple rows in the Tracks table.

JDBC RowSets

Java DataBase Connectivity (or JDBC) evolved as a standard way for Java programs to perform relational database operations. The JDBC API is database independent and relies on a JDBC driver that translates standard JDBC calls into specific calls required by the database it supports. Different drivers provide access to different database products.

Before RowSets were added to JDBC, connecting to a database and performing queries was rather clumsy. The end result of a typical query was a ResultSet object. Basically, a ResultSet object is a table that consists of columns and rows. A cursor points to the current row, and you extract data from the columns as fields. Initially, the cursor is positioned before the first row, so you have to increment it before grabbing any data. Since the JDBC 2.0 specification, a ResultSet object includes methods to manipulate the cursor position, but not all JDBC drivers support this feature. For maximum portability, ResultSet objects should be read once in a forward direction only.

A JDBC RowSet object is a connected rowset that extends a ResultSet object. RowSet objects are structured to make the JDBC driver look like a JavaBeans component. Properties in RowSet objects may participate in event notification. RowSet listener methods include cursorMoved() (invoked when the RowSet's cursor moves), rowChanged() (invoked when one or more values in a row changes), and rowSetChanged() (invoked when the contents of the whole rowset change). JDBC RowSet objects are more flexible than ResultSets because they are scrollable and updatable.

When you select a data source from Creator's Server Navigator window, Creator generates code in the Java page bean file to access the data source through RowSet objects. To see how this works, here is some generated code that accesses the Recordings table of our Music Collection Database.

```
recordingsRowSet.setDataSourceName(
  "java:comp/env/jdbc/Music");
recordingsRowSet.setCommand("SELECT * FROM RECORDINGS");
```

First, we establish a connection to the JDBC Music database before creating a query command with setCommand(). Part of Creator's cleanup tasks includes closing the rowset inside method afterRenderResponse(). (Recall that in the JSF page request life cycle, method afterRenderResponse() is called at the very end after rendering the page.) Creator generates the following code for you.

```
protected void afterRenderResponse() {
  recordingsRowSet.close();
}
```

On the JSP side, when you select a data-aware JSF component and bind it to a rowset, Creator generates the JSP code for you. Here's an example that binds a dropdown list component to the `recordingsRowSet` object we just showed you (tag `selectOneMenu` is the dropdown list component).

```
<h:selectOneMenu binding="#{Page1.dropdown1}"
    converter="#{Page1.dropdown1Converter}"
    id="dropdown1" immediate="true"
    onchange="this.form.submit();"

    style="left: 48px; top: 72px; position: absolute"
    value="#{Page1.recordingsRowSet.currentRow.RECORDINGID}"
    valueChangeListener=
            "#{Page1.dropdown1_processValueChange}">
    <f:selectItems binding="#{Page1.dropdown1SelectItems}"
        id="dropdown1SelectItems"
        value="#{Page1.recordingsRowSet
            .selectItems['RECORDINGID,RECORDINGTITLE']}"/>
</h:selectOneMenu>
```

The embedded `selectItems` tag holds the selection choices for the dropdown list component. The displayed field is `RECORDINGTITLE` and the value field is `RECORDINGID` (which is returned from the dropdown list component's `getValue()` method). We show you how this all works later in the chapter.

Now let's build an application with Creator to access a database and dynamically update a data table component on the web page.

7.2 Data Sources

The first step in our application is to create a Music database and make it available to Creator. Creator is bundled with the PointBase database server and its JDBC driver for database access through Creator's IDE. Creator requires JDBC 3.0-compliant drivers. As of this writing, the Creator IDE includes drivers for DB2, Oracle, SQL Server, and Sybase. If you are using any of these database products, you should be able to configure Creator with the provided drivers to access your database.

Configuring for the PointBase Database

For our Music database example, we assume you're using the bundled PointBase database. Here are the steps to configure the Data Source in Creator for PointBase.

1. Exit Creator if you have it running.
2. Start up PointBase. In Windows, click the Start button. From All Programs, navigate to Sun Microsystems > J2EE 1.4 SDK and click Start PointBase. Creator also includes commands to start and stop PointBase.
3. Now start up Creator.
4. In the Creator Server Navigator window, make sure the Data Sources node is opened. Select the Travel Database.
5. Right-click and select Remove Data Source.
6. Repeat steps 4 and 5 for the Order Database.
7. Exit Creator.

For the following steps, use the files from your Creator book's download directory, **FieldGuide/Examples/Database/utils**.

1. Using a file copy utility, copy the following files to Creator's **startup/bin** directory. Copy

```
create-music-db.bat
create-music-db.sh
```

to directory

```
<Installation Directory>\Sun\Creator\startup\bin
```

2. Copy file

```
PBCreateMusicDB.class
```

to directory

```
<Installation Directory>\Sun\Creator\startup\samples
```

3. With PointBase running, execute the Windows script

```
create-music-db.bat        (Windows)
```

or the Unix script

```
create-music-db.sh         (UNIX)
```

When the script runs successfully, you will see the message

```
Music database was created.
```

4. Start up Creator, right-click Data Sources in the Server Navigator window, and select Add Data Source. The Add Data Source dialog appears.
5. Supply the values shown in Table 7.1. Click Test Connection to verify that all the values are correct. Click Add to finish.

Table 7.1 Add Data Source Dialog

Prompt	*Value*
Data Source Name	**Music**
Server Type	Pointbase Bundled
Database Name	(blank)
Host Name	(blank)
User ID	root
Password	admin
Database URL	jdbc:pointbase:server://localhost:19092/**Music**
Driver Class	com.pointbase.jdbc.jdbcUniversalDriver

Creator Tip

Make sure that Data Source Name is still set to Music after you select Pointbase Bundled from the dropdown menu and before clicking Add. Make sure that the Database URL includes the database name **Music** *as shown.*

Now when you open the Music and Tables node, you'll see four tables in the Music database: MUSICCATEGORIES, RECORDINGARTISTS, RECORD-INGS, and TRACKS.

Loading Other Data Sources

If you configure Creator to use a Data Source other than PointBase, see the **sql_readme.txt** file in your Creator book's examples (**FieldGuide/Examples/Database/utils**). We also provide an SQL script (**createMusicDB.sql**) that you can adapt to any SQL-compliant database. This script loads sample music data into a Music database. After the database tables and data have been built, you tell Creator how to access the database.

Here are the steps to configure a new (non-PointBase) Data Source in Creator.

1. In the Server Navigator window, right-click Data Sources and select Add Data Source from the menu.
2. Under Server Type, select the database product from the dropdown list.
3. Creator supplies default values for the Host Name (localhost), Database URL, and Driver Class. You'll need to supply values for the Data Source Name, Database Name, User ID (if applicable), and Password (if applicable). Figure 7–2 shows a screen shot of the Add Data Source window.

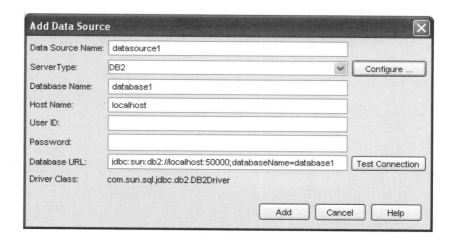

Figure 7–2 **Add Data Source window**

4. Use Test Connection to verify that Creator has all the information it needs to establish a connection to the database.
5. If the Test Connection succeeds, click Add. You should see the newly added Data Source under the Data Sources node in the Server Navigator window.

7.3 Accessing the Music Database

Now that you have a configured database, let's use Creator's data-aware components to build a master-detail relationship. You use a dropdown list component to hold the "master" information from which you select a single recording. You then use a data table component to display the recording's details.

Create a New Project

- In the Welcome Page, select button Create New Project. Specify project name as **Music1**. The selected project type is J2EE Web Application. Click OK.

Specify Title

After creating the project, Creator comes up in the design view of the editor pane. You can now set the title.

1. Click in the middle of the design canvas.
2. Select Title in the Properties window. This is the title displayed by the web application in the title bar in your browser.
3. Select the input field opposite the name `Title` and type the text **Music DB 1**. Finish by pressing **<Enter>**.

Add an Output Text Component

First, you'll add an output text component to place a heading title on the page.

1. From the JSF Standard Components palette, select Output Text. Drag it to the design canvas and place it near the top of the page. Don't resize it, and make sure that it's selected.
2. Type the text **Music Collection Database** followed by **<Enter>**. This is a Creator shortcut to modify the output text's `value` attribute. The component now displays the words you just entered.
3. In the Properties window under Appearance, edit the `style` attribute. After the `position` settings, add the following.

```
; font-family: Helvetica; font-size: 18pt
```

Press **<Enter>**. (You may find it easier to click the small rectangle that brings up an editing box. Click OK when you're done editing.) The output text should now display a bold heading in a larger font.

Add a Dropdown List Component

A dropdown list component creates a dropdown selection menu from a fixed list of choices. You can specify these choices directly by editing the Properties window, or you can bind this component to a data source and obtain the selection choices from a database (that is what you're going to do).

Creator Tip

Instead of a Dropdown List Component, you can also use a Listbox component here. The functionality is the same, but the listbox is rendered as a box with all of its choices displayed at once. If the selection list is too long, the component includes a vertical scrollbar. If you'd like to use a Listbox component, skip this section and follow the steps under "Add a Listbox Component" .

1. From the JSF Standard Components palette, select Dropdown List and drag it to the design canvas. Center it under the previously placed output text component.
2. Right-click inside the design canvas and choose View Page1 Java Class. This opens the Java page bean source file, **Page1.java**.

   For each component that you place on the page, Creator generates an associated object that is a property inside the JavaBeans component on your web page. You'll note that it currently contains the two objects from the components you just added to the design canvas: an `HtmlSelectOneMenu` (the dropdown list component named `dropdown1`) and the `HtmlOutputText` (the output text component named `outputText1`). In addition, the dropdown list component generates two supporting components: `dropdown1Default-Items` and `dropdown1SelectItems`.

3. Return to the design canvas (select the **Page1.jsp** tab at the top of the editor pane). Now select the Source tab at the bottom of the editor pane. This brings up the **Page1.jsp** source file. You'll see both the `<h:outputText>` and `<h:selectOneMenu>` tags. Note that the dropdown list component also has an embedded `<f:selectItems>` tag.

Skip over the next section "Add a Listbox Component" unless you've chosen to use a listbox in place of the dropdown list component.

Add a Listbox Component

Instead of using a dropdown list component to hold the data from the RECORDINGS table, let's use a listbox component. You can substitute the steps in this section for those outlined for the dropdown list component above. When you've finished the steps for adding a listbox component, continue to the next section ("Add a Data Source").

A listbox component creates a fixed list of choices that are all displayed. If the list is longer than the space allocated to the component, a vertical scrollbar provides access to the other choices. Just like the dropdown list component, you can specify the listbox choices directly by editing the Properties window, or you can bind this component to a data source.

1. From the JSF Standard Components palette, select Listbox and drag it to the design canvas. Center it under the previously placed output text component.
2. Resize it so that it is wider and longer. (You can experiment with its size by right-clicking in the design canvas and selecting Preview in Browser.)

The rest of the build steps assume you selected the dropdown list component, although the steps are the same for the listbox component.

Add a Data Source

1. Make sure the design canvas is visible by selecting the Design tab at the bottom of the editor pane.
2. From the Server Navigator window, expand the Data Sources, Music, and Tables nodes. Select the RECORDINGS table and drag it to the design view. Drop it on top of the dropdown list component.

   A dialog pops up and you see the `recordingsRowSet` component added to the nonvisual tray at the bottom of the editor pane.

3. In the dialog, select Fill the List. The text "abc" appears in the dropdown list component, signifying that the data is of type `VARCHAR` from the database.

Let's see what Creator knows about the database table at this point (these steps are for the curious-at-heart).

1. Right-click the dropdown list component. From the context menu, choose Fill List from Database. You have already completed the binding in the previous steps, but this step shows you the database table's metadata (its fields and table names). Creator displays a dialog with a database rowset, a Value field, and a Display field, as shown in Figure 7–3.

   The dropdown list component's `value` attribute is assigned field `RECORDINGID`, which is the primary key. Thus, when you invoke method

```
dropdown1.getValue();
```

   you'll get the value of the primary key for that selection.

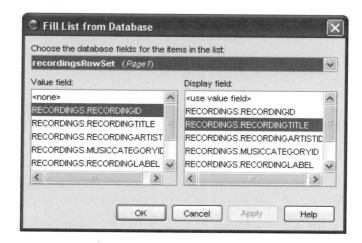

Figure 7–3 **Bind Display to Data dialog**

The text that's displayed in the dropdown list is the field selected in the Display field, which is set to RECORDINGTITLE.

2. Click OK to return to the design canvas.

As you saw from Chapter 2, you can view the actual data from a database table from Creator. Let's do that now.

1. From the Server Navigator window, select Data Sources > Music > Tables > RECORDINGS. Open the RECORDINGS node (click on '+') and Creator displays the field names.
2. Double-click the RECORDINGS node. Creator displays the table's data in the editor pane. We show this view in Figure 7–4.

Creator Tip

In general, it is easier to add a data-aware component to your design canvas before you add a database table from the selected data source. If the component is already on the design canvas, you can "drop" the database table directly on the component and Creator does the binding automatically. You can then modify the selected fields for the display or change the value attributes if necessary.

RECORDINGID	RECORDING...	RECORDING...	MUSICCATE...	RECORDING...	FORMAT	NUMBEROFT...	NOTES
1	Orff: Carmin...	1	1	Sony Classical		11	
2	Rites of Pas...	2	2	Epic		13	
3	Imagine	3	2	Warner Brot...		21	
4	Karla Bonoff	4	2	Columbia		10	
5	Graceland	5	2	Warner Brot...		11	
6	Congratulatio...	6	2	A&M Records		13	
7	Sgt. Pepper'...	7	2	EMI Records		12	

Figure 7–4 RECORDINGS Table View

Deploy and Run

Although we have only a page heading and a dropdown list, it's a good idea to deploy and run the application at this point. Go ahead and click the green chevron on the toolbar. A successful deployment is a significant milestone here because it shows you've successfully queried the database. It's also a good idea to look at the Java page bean to see how the JDBC RowSet objects are defined and how they are manipulated to obtain the data.

When you run the application, you'll see seven recording titles in the dropdown list. Right now, selecting one doesn't do anything other than display a different title.

Part of the power of data binding is that you can associate the component's value with a primary key. To *display* a field other than the primary key typically has more meaning, however. The component in this example displays the recording's title. When a user selects a specific title, you obtain the corresponding primary key through the component's `value` attribute. The primary key allows you to build additional queries to the database and obtain more details about the recording associated with that primary key. This is building a master-detail relationship, which is our next step.

Add a Data Table

Now you're ready to do something when the user selects a recording title in the dropdown list. In this section, you will display the recording's track information: the track number, its title, and its length. The track information is stored in the TRACKS table and is associated with the recording information through its foreign key, the RECORDINGID. In the Server Navigator window, expand the TRACKS table under the Data Sources > Music > Tables node (click on '+') to see the field names. TRACKID is the primary key for the TRACKS table, and

RECORDINGID is the foreign key (you may also want to refer to the diagram in Figure 7–1 on page 207 again).

1. Bring up the design canvas (**Page1.jsp**).
2. Select the Data Table component from the JSF Standard Components palette and drop it onto the design canvas under the dropdown list component that's already there.
3. Go to the Data Sources node in the Server Navigator window, choose the TRACKS table, and drop it onto the data table.
4. Drop the table directly onto the data table component. Creator will do the binding automatically. The data table should now have five columns (the fields in the TRACKS table).

Creator Tip

If you don't drop the table exactly onto the data table component in the design canvas, a Choose Target dialog pops up. If this happens, choose the dataTable1 *radio button and click OK. If you drop the TRACKS table onto the design canvas (but not onto the data table component), no binding occurs at all. You'll notice the* tracksRowSet *item added to the nonvisual component tray, but the data table is unchanged. In this case, right-click the data table and select Bind to Database. Select the* tracksRowSet *for binding. Auto-generate table columns should be enabled. Click OK. The data table component will reflect data binding and should now have five columns.*

The next step is to modify what the data table component displays.

1. Select the data table component. (If you have trouble selecting the entire table, position the mouse inside the data table component on the design canvas and issue successive clicks until Creator indicates that the data table component is selected.) Now right-click and choose Table Layout.

The Table Layout dialog appears. The Columns format should be selected. There are two lists: Available columns and Displayed columns.

2. Under the Displayed heading, remove columns TRACKS.TRACKID and TRACKS.RECORDINGID by selecting these columns and clicking the left arrow (<) button. There are now three columns in the Displayed list, as shown in Figure 7–5.
3. Select Apply, then OK. The data table component should now have only three columns.
4. Now select the data table component. In the Properties window, specify 3 for attribute border. (We like the look; you be the judge.)

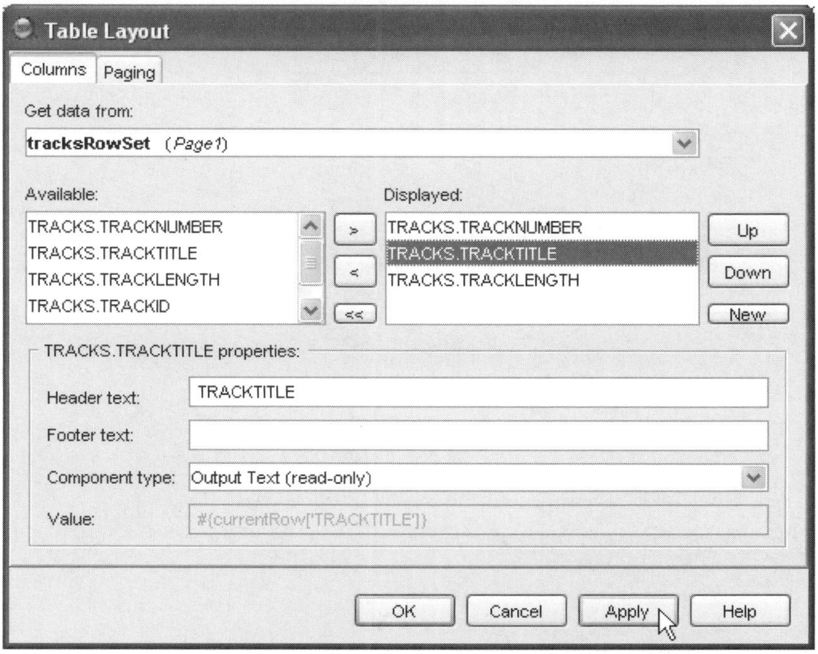

Figure 7–5 **Table Layout dialog**

Congratulations, you've just created a table with a data-aware component. You've also manipulated the component by telling it what columns from the rowset you want displayed. Creator generates code to populate the data table component and builds headers in the table with the column names. Figure 7–6 shows the design canvas with the data table component configured for the TRACKS table.

You might want to look at the JSP source Creator generates for the data table component. The data table contains an embedded column component (for each of its columns), and a column can be rendered by one of several JSF components. The default is an output text component. Creator uses a JSF `<f:facet>` tag to render the column headers.

The column's embedded output text component is resized dynamically to fit the data. You can change the look of the data table's display by modifying its properties in the Properties view. For example, you can change property values for `bgcolor` (Background Color), `cellpadding`, `cellspacing`, and `border`.

You can also choose a different embedded component to hold the data. Another popular component to use here is a text field component, which allows editing. If you select a text field component, you will need to approxi-

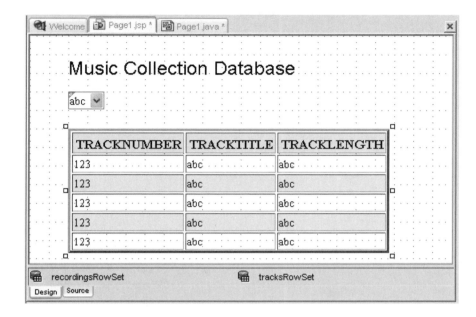

Figure 7–6 **Data-aware table component bound to TRACKS table**

mate its size (it won't be sized dynamically). The two components (text field and output text) give different looks. Experiment with this to get the look you want.

Modify the SQL Query

The modifications you've just performed affect the data table component and its binding to the `tracksRowSet` component. The `tracksRowSet` object includes an SQL query that reads the database. Now you'll use the Query Editor to modify the default query.

- Double-click the `tracksRowSet` component (select it at the bottom of the editor pane in the nonvisual component tray). This opens the Query Editor for the `tracksRowSet` object, as shown in Figure 7–7.

The Query Editor has several views. The top portion (the table view) is a visual view of the data table (or tables) involved in the query. Here the query references one table, the TRACKS table. Note that all five fields are displayed and that the primary and foreign keys are marked with key icons. Only the

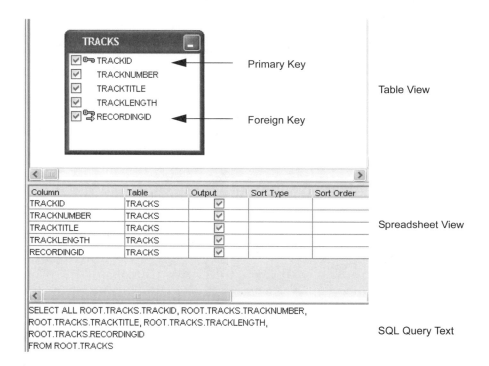

Figure 7–7 **Query Editor for TRACKS table**

fields that are selected (checked) will be returned in the query. Here, all fields are checked.

Below the table view is the spreadsheet view of the fields that are returned in the query. Only the fields selected (checked) in the Output column appear in this view.

At the bottom of the Query Editor is the actual SQL query. As you make modifications to the query, the Query Editor updates this text.

Add Query Criteria

When the user selects a recording title from the dropdown list component, you want to display only those tracks that belong to the selected recording. You identify these tracks by matching the track's RECORDINGID foreign key with the dropdown list component's `value` attribute, the primary key of the RECORDINGS database table. Let's do this now.

1. In the Query Editor, make sure that the RECORDINGID foreign key in the TRACKS table is checked.
2. In the spreadsheet view, right-click the RECORDINGID field and choose Add Query Criteria from the context menu.
3. The Add Query Criteria dialog appears. Select radio button Parameter. Figure 7–8 shows the Add Query Criteria dialog at this point. Leave the Comparison at the default (= Equals), and click OK. These steps add a WHERE clause to the query.

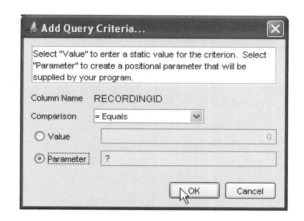

Figure 7–8 **Add Query Criteria dialog**

You're almost done, but we have another modification to make to the query. Recall that the TRACKS table contains all the tracks of all the recordings. In addition, each row contains a track number, which refers to the order in which that track appears on the recording. This may or may not correspond to the actual order of the information in the database. We'd like to order the track display (from lowest to highest) in the data table component. To do this, we'll modify the query so that it sorts the results by track number in ascending order.

1. Locate the TRACKNUMBER field in the spreadsheet view of the Query Editor. Opposite this field, select the Sort Type cell. A dropdown menu appears.
2. Select Ascending. This step adds an ORDER BY clause to the query. Since this is the only field involved in the ordering criteria, the TRACKNUMBER Sort Order cell is set to 1.
3. In the table view of the Query Editor, uncheck the RECORDINGID and TRACKID fields. (Although the RECORDINGID field participates in the selection criteria of the query, we don't include this field in the data that are returned in the RowSet object.)

Here is your modified query, shown at the bottom of the Query Editor.

```
SELECT ALL ROOT.TRACKS.TRACKNUMBER, ROOT.TRACKS.TRACKTITLE,
ROOT.TRACKS.TRACKLENGTH FROM ROOT.TRACKS WHERE
ROOT.TRACKS.RECORDINGID=? ORDER BY ROOT.TRACKS.TRACKNUMBER ASC
```

The WHERE clause expects a parameter to match with the RECORDINGID field, and the results will be ordered (in ascending order) by the TRACKNUMBER field.

4. Return to the design canvas by selecting the **Page1.jsp** tab. Right-click in the design canvas and select View Page1 Java Class. Inside the `Page1()` constructor (unfold the Creator-managed Component Initialization box), you'll see the updated query appear in the call to `tracksRowSet.setCommand()`.

```
tracksRowSet.setCommand("SELECT ALL ROOT.TRACKS.TRACKNUMBER,
    ROOT.TRACKS.TRACKTITLE, ROOT.TRACKS.TRACKLENGTH \n
    FROM ROOT.TRACKS\n
    WHERE ROOT.TRACKS.RECORDINGID=?\n
    ORDER BY ROOT.TRACKS.TRACKNUMBER ASC");
```

Add a SessionBean1 Property

In the previous chapter, you learned how to save control variables in session scope to maintain data across page requests (see "Add SessionBean1 Properties" on page 195). In this project, you will save the dropdown list's current selection in session scope. Without this step, the dropdown list returns to its initial state at each page request, since it exists in request scope. As in the previous chapter, you will add information to the SessionBean1 managed bean as a *property*. Call the property `recordingID`; it will be type Integer. Here are the steps to add property `recordingID` to SessionBean1.

1. In the Project Navigator window, expand Java Sources > music1.
2. Right-click on **SessionBean1.java** and select Add > Property. Creator displays the New Property Pattern dialog, as shown in Figure 7–9.
3. Fill in the fields as shown above. Specify **recordingID** for Name. Select **Integer** in the dropdown list for Type. Select **Read/Write** for Mode. Make sure the options Generate Field, Generate Return Statement, and Generate Set Statement are all checked.
4. Click OK.

Now you need to provide the instantiation with operator `new` for property `recordingID` in **SessionBean1.java**.

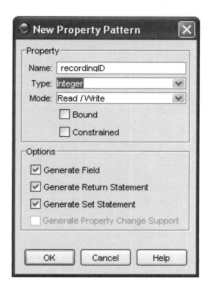

Figure 7–9 **Adding a property to SessionBean1**

1. From the Project Navigator window, double-click file **SessionBean1.java**. This brings it up in the Java source editor.
2. Add instantiation with operator `new` for property `recordingID` inside the `SessionBean1()` constructor. Place it after the comment, as follows.

```
// Additional user provided initialization code
recordingID = new Integer(0);
```

Connect Dropdown List to Query

All that's left is to detect the change in the dropdown list component's selection and use it to set the parameter for the query with the `tracksRowSet` object.

1. In the design canvas, select the dropdown list component, right-click, and select Edit Event Handler > processValueChange. This brings up the Page1 Java class source and places the cursor in the `dropdown1_process-ValueChange()` method. This is the event handler for processing the change in the dropdown list's value. Creator creates the stub for this event handler for you.

2. Add the code to the `dropdown1_processValueChange()` method. Copy and paste from your Creator book's file **FieldGuide/Examples/Database/snippets/Music1Dropdown.txt**. (The added code is bold).

```
public void dropdown1_processValueChange(ValueChangeEvent vce)
{
    // User event code here...
    getSessionBean1().setRecordingID(
              (Integer)dropdown1.getValue());
    try {
        dataTable1Model.setObject(1,
                getSessionBean1().getRecordingID());
        dataTable1Model.execute();
    } catch (SQLException e) {
        error("Music: Master Detail " + e);
        log("Music: Master Detail " + e);
    }
}
```

Use Creator's shortcut **<Alt-Shift-I>** to add the import statement for SQLException. This code sets the parameter of the `tracksRowSet` query (the `dataTabel1Model` object) to the `value` attribute of the `dropdown1` component (the primary key of the specific record in the RECORDINGS table). The `execute()` method executes the query. The selected primary key is saved in session scope.

3. Return to the design canvas. From the JSF Standard Components palette, select Message List and place it on the page next to the dropdown list.

Important Creator Tips

*You must **not** throw an exception from any event handler. Instead, use `log()` (to record the error in the server log) and `error()` (to report status to the user). Throughout this chapter, we use a message list component for all messages (error and general feedback) to the user. Methods `info()`, `warn()`, `error()` (shown above), and `fatal()` all write to the faces context. You need a message list to display these messages. These methods are all inherited from class FacesBean. When you bind a data source to a data table component, you manipulate the associated `dataTableNModel` object. With all other components, however, you make calls to the rowset object.*

4. Add initialization statements to the `Page1()` constructor. This code initializes the data table to hold the track information from the `recordingsRowSet`'s first row. Copy and paste from your Creator book's file

FieldGuide/Examples/Database/snippets/Music1Init.txt. (The added code is bold.)

```
public Page1() {
  // code omitted . . .
  // Additional user provided initialization code
  try {
    if (getSessionBean1().getRecordingID().intValue() == 0) {
      recordingsRowSet.execute();
      recordingsRowSet.next();
      getSessionBean1().setRecordingID(new Integer(
                recordingsRowSet.getInt("RECORDINGID")));
      recordingsRowSet.previous();
    }
    dataTable1Model.setObject(1,
          getSessionBean1().getRecordingID());
  } catch (SQLException e) {
      throw new FacesException(e);
  }
}
```

5. Return to the design canvas (select the **Page1.jsp** tab).
6. Right-click the dropdown list component and check the Auto-submit on change option. This adds the JavaScript

```
this.form.submit();
```

to the dropdown list component's JavaScript Events onchange attribute in the Properties window. Now when a user selects a new title from the menu, the system resubmits and updates the page with the new track list.

Deploy and Run

It's time to deploy and run this web application. Figure 7–10 shows what the page looks like as the user is selecting a title in the dropdown list. Note that as the user selects different recording titles, the data table is updated with the corresponding track information. The number of rows as well as the width of the columns changes with the new data. You also see that the track numbers appear in ascending order. (Some of the recordings do not have track lengths.)

Under the Hood

Besides the code that Creator generates for you in the page bean constructor to initialize the RowSet objects, Creator also generates code to clean up. Specifi-

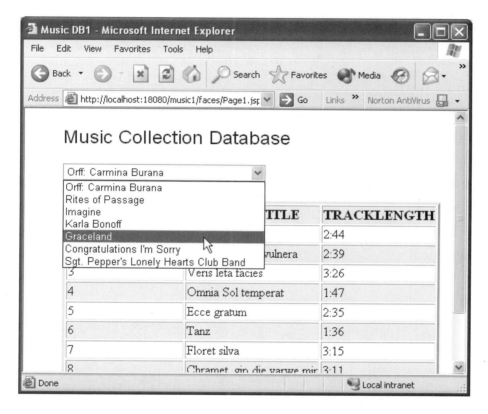

Figure 7–10 The Music Collection Database application: selecting title Graceland

cally, it closes the database connections with the RowSet's `close()` method. Creator uses life cycle method `afterRenderResponse()`, as follows.

```
protected void afterRenderResponse() {
  recordingsRowSet.close();
  tracksRowSet.close();
}
```

This ensures that the database will be in a valid, known state at the beginning of each page request cycle. For more information on the life cycle methods, see "JSF Request-Response Life Cycle Process" on page 185 (Figure 6–5) and "Page request life cycle methods" on page 186 (Table 6.4).

7.4 Database Joins

Both of the data-aware components we've configured are bound to data that originate from a single database table. In this section, we'll add a second data table component to the page. Its data will be bound to a rowset that is a result of a query "joining" multiple tables.

Copy the Project

To avoid starting from scratch, copy the **Music1** project to a new project called **Music2**. This step is optional. If you don't want to copy the project, simply skip this section and continue making modifications to the **Music1** project.

1. Bring up project **Music1** in Creator, if it's not already opened.
2. Click anywhere inside the design canvas.
3. From the File menu, select Save Project As and provide the new name **Music2**. You'll make changes to the **Music2** project.
4. Click anywhere in the design canvas of the **Music2** project. In the Properties window, change the page's `Title` attribute to **Music DB 2**.

Add a Second Data Table

1. From the design canvas view of the editor pane, select component `dataTable1` and move it down on the page so that there is room for a one-row data table to fit above it on the page.
2. Select Data Table from the JSF Standard Components palette and drag it onto the web page.
3. Position the component so that it is below the dropdown list component and above the first data table component you added in the previous section.
4. In the Properties window for `dataTable2`, change attribute `border` to **3**.

You have added component `dataTable2`, giving you two data table components on the page. Don't worry about the tables overlapping each other.

Select a Data Source

1. In the Server Navigator window, select the Data Sources > Music > Tables > RECORDINGARTISTS node and drop it onto the data table that you just added.
2. If you drop the database source directly on top of the data table, Creator performs the binding automatically. Otherwise, a Choose Target dialog appears. If this happens, select `dataTable2` and click OK.

On the design canvas, the data table contains three columns that correspond to the three fields in the RECORDINGARTISTS table: RECORDINGARTISTSID, RECORDINGARTISTNAME, and NOTES. You'll also see the component `recordingartistsRowSet` added to the nonvisual component tray. Figure 7–11 shows the design canvas with the two (somewhat overlapping) data table components.

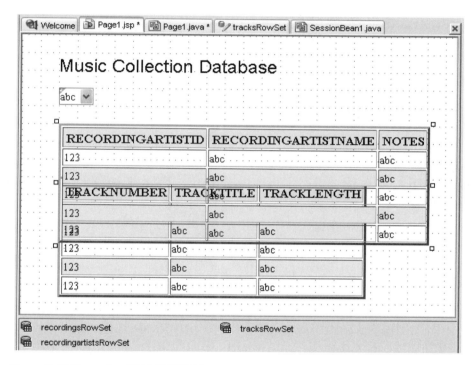

Figure 7–11 Dropping RECORDINGARTIST table on dataTable2

Modify the SQL Query

1. In the nonvisual component tray, double-click the `recordingartistsRowSet` component. This brings up the Query Editor for the selected RowSet object.
2. In the table view (which shows the RECORDINGARTISTS table), uncheck all fields except the RECORDINGARTISTNAME field.
3. Right-click anywhere in the table view and select Add Table from the context menu. Choose table RECORDINGS. Click OK.

This step adds an INNER JOIN statement to the SQL query. Note that Creator has modified the query in the Query View. The Creator SQL code generation figures out which keys are required in order to join the two tables.

4. The Recordings table is the same one we used with the dropdown list component. Uncheck all fields except RECORDINGID and RECORDINGLABEL. You'll note that this table contains two foreign keys, RECORDINGARTISTID (linking it to the RECORDINGARTISTS table) and MUSICCATEGORYID (linking it to the MUSICCATEGORIES table).
5. Right-click in the table view and again select Add Table from the context menu. This time choose table MUSICCATEGORIES. Click OK. This step adds another INNER JOIN statement to the SQL query.
6. Uncheck the MUSICCATEGORYID field in the MUSICCATEGORIES table. Figure 7–12 shows the Query Editor's table view after two tables were added to the query.

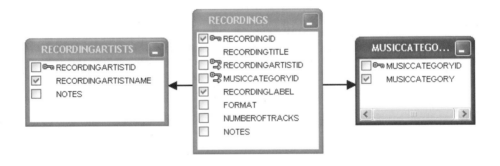

Figure 7–12 **Table view in Creator's Query Editor after addition of two tables**

Add Query Criteria

1. In the spreadsheet view of the Query Editor, right-click RECORDINGID and choose Add Query Criteria. Select = Equals criterion and the Parameter radio button. Click OK.
2. Uncheck the RECORDINGID for output (in the spreadsheet view) or uncheck it in the table view.
3. You've now added a parameter to limit the rows returned from the database query based on the value of the RECORDINGID field. This should return at

most one row since there is one recording artist and one music category for each row in the RECORDINGS table. Here is the modified query.

```
SELECT ALL ROOT.RECORDINGARTISTS.RECORDINGARTISTNAME,
    ROOT.RECORDINGS.RECORDINGLABEL,
    ROOT.MUSICCATEGORIES.MUSICCATEGORY
    FROM ROOT.RECORDINGARTISTS

INNER JOIN ROOT.RECORDINGS ON
    ROOT.RECORDINGS.RECORDINGARTISTID=
    ROOT.RECORDINGARTISTS.RECORDINGARTISTID

INNER JOIN ROOT.MUSICCATEGORIES ON
    ROOT.RECORDINGS.MUSICCATEGORYID=
    ROOT.MUSICCATEGORIES.MUSICCATEGORYID
WHERE ROOT.RECORDINGS.RECORDINGID=?
```

Table Layout

1. Return to the design canvas by selecting the **Page1.jsp** tab at the top of the editor pane.
2. Select the `dataTable2` component (use the Application Outline view or click inside the table until the top-level component appears in the Properties window). Right-click and choose Table Layout.
3. Choose the following fields from the left window (Available fields). Select the right-arrow symbol (>) and copy the field name to the Displayed fields window. The Displayed fields should look like this.

```
RECORDINGARTISTS.RECORDINGARTISTNAME
MUSICCATEGORIES.MUSICCATEGORY
RECORDINGS.RECORDINGLABEL
```

4. (Get rid of any spurious columns by selecting them and clicking the left-arrow symbol (<).) Select Apply and OK. Figure 7–13 shows the Table Layout dialog with the fields you want in the Displayed list.

Java Class Modifications

1. Bring up the Java page bean by selecting the **Page1.java** tab at the top of the editor pane (or right-click in the design canvas and select View Page1 Java Class).
2. In the dropdown menu at the top of the Java editor pane, select the event handler method, `dropdown1_processValueChange`. In the editor, the cursor is placed at this method for you.

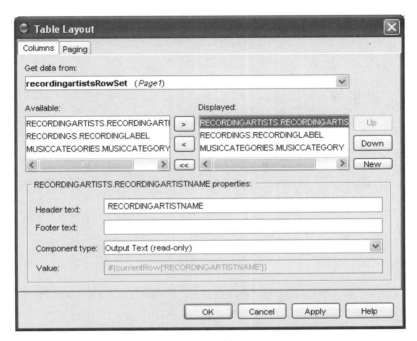

Figure 7–13 Table Layout dialog for dataTable2 component

3. First, add code to the event handler. Use file **FieldGuide/Examples/Database/snippets/Music2Dropdown.txt**, and add the code where indicated. The added code is bold.

```
public void dropdown1_processValueChange(ValueChangeEvent vce)
{
    // User event code here...
    getSessionBean1().setRecordingID(
            (Integer)dropdown1.getValue());
    try {
        dataTable1Model.setObject(1,
                getSessionBean1().getRecordingID());
        dataTable1Model.execute();
        dataTable2Model.setObject(1,
                getSessionBean1().getRecordingID());
        dataTable2Model.execute();
    } catch (SQLException e) {
        error("Music: Master Detail " + e);
        log("Music: Master Detail " + e);
    }
}
```

4. Add code to the `Page1()` constructor after the `dataTable1Model` initialization code you added in the previous section. This is initialization code to grab the database records corresponding to the RECORDINGID returned in the first row from the `recordingsRowSet` component. Some code in the constructor is omitted below. Copy and paste from your Creator book's file **FieldGuide/Examples/Database/snippets/Music2Init.txt**. (The added code is in bold.)

```
public Page1() {
    // code omitted . . .
    // Additional user provided initialization code
    try {
        if (getSessionBean1().getRecordingID().intValue() == 0) {
            recordingsRowSet.execute();
            recordingsRowSet.next();
            getSessionBean1().setRecordingID(new Integer(
                    recordingsRowSet.getInt("RECORDINGID")));
            recordingsRowSet.previous();
        }
        dataTable1Model.setObject(1,
                getSessionBean1().getRecordingID());
        dataTable2Model.setObject(1,
                getSessionBean1().getRecordingID());
    } catch (SQLException e) {
        throw new FacesException(e);
    }
}
```

Deploy and Run

It's time to deploy and run the application. Figure 7–14 shows a screen shot of the page after selection of the recording title **Imagine**. Now when you select different titles, you'll see the artist's name, recording label, music category, and the tracks for the selected title.

7.5 Database Updates

The previous example accessed the Music Collection database in a read-only mode. When you add a data table to your project and bind it to a data source, Creator assumes that the access will be read-only. Furthermore, the embedded

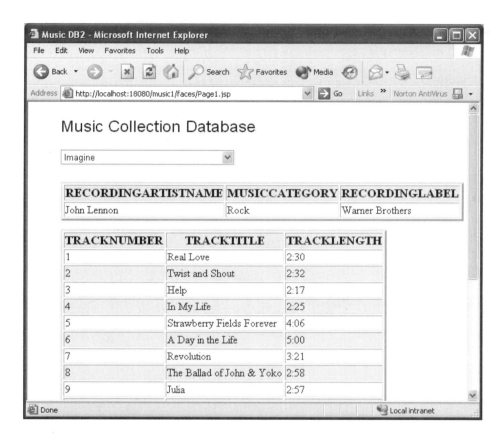

Figure 7–14 The Music Collection Database after selection of title Imagine

components of the data table component are output text components, which are read-only components.

In this section you'll create a project that allows a user to modify data fields in the database. Many of the steps are similar to those you've just worked through, but some code changes and some Properties window attributes require different settings. Let's begin by creating a new project.

Create a New Project

- In the Welcome Page, select button Create New Project. Specify project name as **MusicUpdate**. The selected project type is J2EE Web Application. Click OK.

Specify Title

After creating the project, Creator comes up in the design view of the editor pane. You can now set the title.

1. Click in the middle of the design canvas.
2. Select `Title` in the Properties window and type the text **Music DB Update**. Finish by pressing **<Enter>**.

Add an Output Text Component

Place a heading title on the page with an output text component.

1. From the JSF Standard Components palette, select Output Text. Drag it to the design canvas and place it near the top of the page. Don't resize it, and make sure it's selected.
2. Type the text **Update Music Category** followed by **<Enter>**. The component now displays the words you just entered.
3. In the Properties window under Appearance, edit the `style` attribute. Add the following after the `position` settings.

```
; font-family: Helvetica; font-size: 18pt
```

4. Press **<Enter>**. (You may find it easier to click the small rectangle that brings up an editing box. Click OK when you're done editing.) The output text should now display a bold heading in a larger font.

Add a Button Component

A button component allows the user to initiate a command. In this project, a button will indicate when a user finishes editing so that the database can be updated with all of the displayed rows' changes.

1. From the JSF Standard Components palette, select Button and drag it to the design canvas. Position it under the previously placed output text component. Creator assigns the default identifier name `button1`.
2. Make sure the button is still selected and type **Update Music Database** followed by **<Enter>**. Creator updates the `value` attribute in the Properties window. The button's label should now display the words you just entered.

Add a Data Table Component

To display data from the MUSICCATEGORIES table, you need a data table component. The component allows users to edit and update the data.

1. From the JSF Standard Components palette, select Data Table and drop it onto the design canvas under the button component that's already there.
2. Go to the Data Sources node in the Server Navigator window. Under Music > Tables, choose the MUSICCATEGORIES table and drop it onto the data table.
3. Drop the table directly onto the data table component. Creator automatically binds the data to the data table component. The data table should now have two columns (the fields in the MUSICCATEGORIES table).

Creator Tip

If you don't drop the table exactly onto the data table component in the design canvas, a Choose Target dialog pops up. If this happens, choose the dataTable1 *radio button and click OK. If you drop the* MUSICCATETORIES *table onto the design canvas (but not onto the data table component), no binding occurs at all. You'll notice the* musiccategoriesRowSet *item added to the nonvisual component tray, but the data table is unchanged. In this case, right-click the data table and select Bind to Database. Select the* musiccategoriesRowSet *for binding. Auto-generate table columns should be enabled. Click OK. The data table component will reflect data binding and should now have two columns.*

4. Select the data table and modify its attributes in the Properties window. (Click inside the data table component successive times until the data table appears in the Properties window.) Under category Appearance, make bgcolor **lightcyan,** border **2,** and cellpadding **6.** You should see the appearance of the table change in the design canvas.

Creator Tip

This step is optional, but it helps bring contrast to the data table and will emphasize the appearance difference between read-only and editable table cells.

Modify the Table Layout

Now let's modify the data table's layout.

1. Select the data table component, right-click, and choose Table Layout.

   The Table Layout dialog appears. The Columns format should be selected. There are two lists: the Available columns and Displayed columns. You should see both column names in both of these lists.

2. Under the Displayed fields window, select the MUSICCATEGORYID column. In the view underneath you'll see the column name, Header and Footer fields, and the column's component type. The default component type is Output Text (read-only). Leave the default setting unchanged.
3. Select the MUSICCATEGORY column in the Displayed fields window. Change the default component type to Input Text (editable).
4. Click Apply, then OK. Figure 7–15 shows the Table Layout dialog for this step.

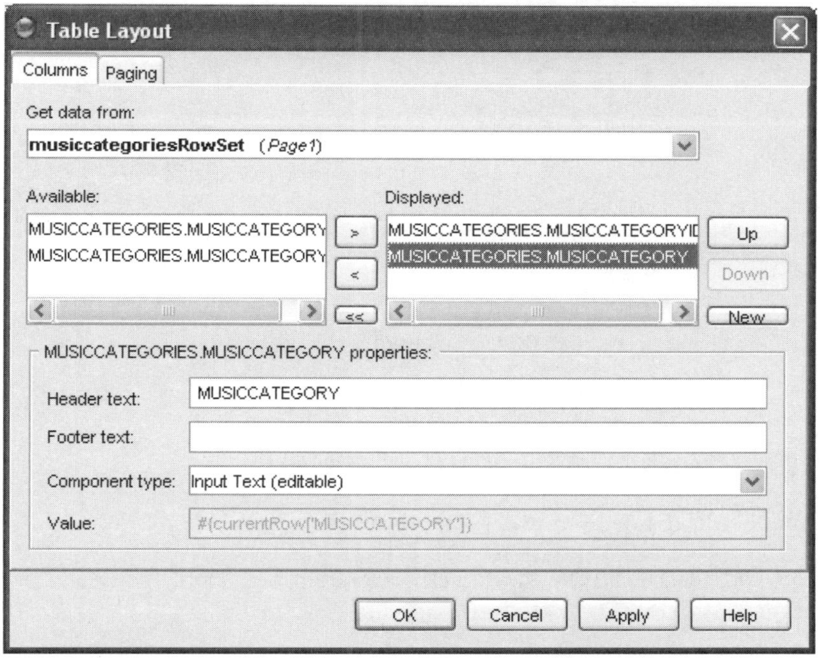

Figure 7–15 **Table Layout dialog: changing the component type**

Figure 7–16 shows the design view after changing the table layout. The data table component displays two columns. The first column holds the primary key, and it retains the default display component, output text. The second column uses a text field component, which enables editing. If you changed the table's `bgcolor` attribute to lightcyan, you'll see the text field component is white against the table's cyan background.

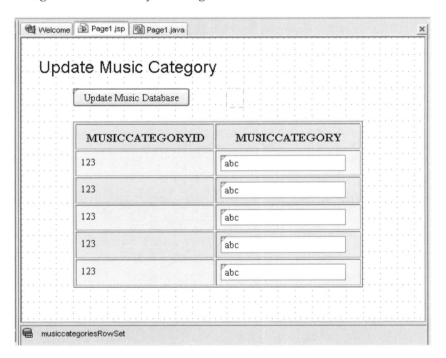

Figure 7–16 Design canvas view after changing the table layout

Add the Button Event Handler

It's time to add the code to process the button's action event.

1. From the design canvas, double-click the button component you added earlier.

   Creator brings up the Java source editor with the cursor at the `button1_action()` method.

2. Add code to the event handler. Copy and paste from your Creator book's file **FieldGuide/Examples/Database/snippets/MusicUpdate_button1.txt**. (The added code is bold.)

```
public String button1_action() {
// User event code here...
   try {
     dataTable1Model.commit();
     dataTable1Model.execute();
     info("Update Successful");
   } catch (SQLException e) {
     log("Music Update: " + e);
     error("Music Update: " + e);
   }

   return null;
}
```

To add the import statement for SQLException, click inside the word SQLException. Press **<Alt-Shift-I>** and click OK.

Add a Message List Component

The event handler code in the above `buttton1_action()` method uses the page bean's `info()` and `error()` methods. These methods create a FacesMessages. By placing a message list component on the page, the messages are displayed to the user.

- From the JSF Standard Components palette, select Message List and drag it to the design canvas. Place it next to the button component. (This component will display messages written to the faces context by methods `info()` and `error()`.)

Deploy and Run

Deploy and run the application. Figure 7–17 shows you what the page looks like after the user changes several of the music categories from the original text. Note that you can make changes to more than one row before updating the database. Also, note that you can't edit the primary key field. To see the music category data changes, select Data Sources from the Server Navigator window.

Expand Music > Tables. Double-click table MUSICCATEGORIES, and Creator displays the table's data (including the changed fields) in the editor pane.

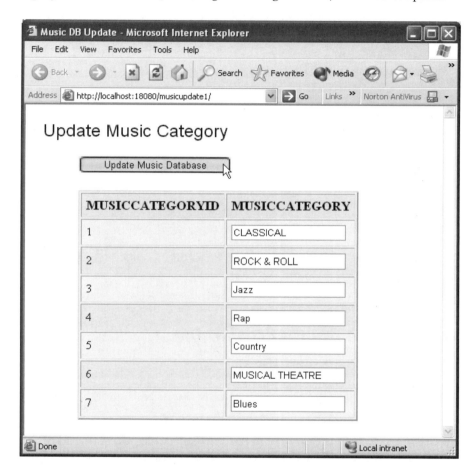

Figure 7–17 **The Music Collection Database: updating the Music Categories table**

Under the Hood

Creator helps out with the database updates by providing a data table model component that is bound to the JSF data table component. When you invoke

```
dataTable1Model.commit();
```

in the button event handler, all of the table's rows are written to the database. There's a few items of interest about the JSF data table and Creator database operations.

- The JSF data table is the only component that has a special, built-in connection to Creator's data table model. (Note how simple the event handler is in this application.)
- If you write an application that updates a database (such as this example), and you use the JSF data table's paging mechanism, you must issue the commit for the current page before navigating to view the next page's data.

7.6   Database Row Inserts

The previous sections showed you how to read a database, create a master-detail database display, perform join operations with more than one database table, and edit and update a database table. Now you'll create an application that inserts new data into the database table. This operation is called a row insert.

This application will come up with a data input page to collect data for the row insert operation. It consists of text fields, labels, and inline message components to collect the data. A button issues the row insert command.

Create a New Project

- In the Welcome Page, select button Create New Project. Specify project name as **MusicInsert**. The selected project type is J2EE Web Application. Click OK.

Specify Title

After creating the project, Creator comes up in the design view of the editor pane. You can now set the title and components to the first page.

1. Click in the middle of the design canvas.
2. Select Title in the Properties window and type in the text **Music DB Insert**. Finish by pressing **<Enter>**.

Add an Output Text Component

Place a heading title on the page with an output text component.

1. From the JSF Standard Components palette, select Output Text. Drag it to the design canvas and place it near the top of the page. Don't resize it, and make sure it's selected.
2. Type the text **Music Collection Database - Add Data** followed by **<Enter>**. The component now displays the words you just typed in.
3. In the Properties window under Appearance, edit the `style` attribute. Add the following after the `position` settings.

```
; font-family: Helvetica; font-size: 18pt
```

Finish with **<Enter>**. The output text should now display a bold heading in a larger font.

Create the Form's Input Components

The next set of components you'll place on the page will gather text for a new database row. A row in the RECORDINGARTISTS table consist of a primary key (an integer), an artist name (text), and notes (also text). The artist name field is a VARCHAR field up to 36 characters in length and is required. The optional notes field is a VARCHAR field up to 200 characters. In our example, the primary key is an integer and must be unique. Many database systems generate primary keys for you, but we'll have the user supply one here. If an input key number is already in the database, an `SQLException` is thrown from the database, allowing the user to choose another key.

For the artist name field, you'll add a component label, a text field to gather data, and a validator to make sure that the input is valid. You'll also need an inline message component to display error validation messages. Figure 7–18 shows what the design canvas looks like after the page is populated with these components. We've labeled the component for the primary key input; you'll use the same components for the artist name and artist notes input. You may find it helpful to refer to this diagram as you add components to your project.

Components for Artist Name

1. From the JSF Standard Components palette, select Component Label and drag it to the design canvas. Place it below the output text component on the left side of the page.
2. In the Application Outline view, select the embedded output text component, `componentLabel1Text`, and change its `value` attribute to **Artist Name**.
3. From the JSF Standard Components palette, select Text Field and drag it to the design canvas directly below the component label.
4. In the Properties window, change its `id` attribute to **artistName**.
5. Set its `title` attribute to **Type in the artist's name**. This sets the component's tooltip.

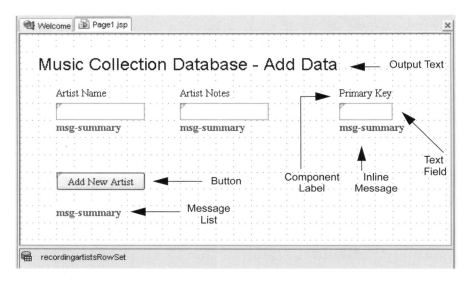

Figure 7–18 **Design canvas view with components on page**

6. Under Data in the Properties window, select attribute `required` (make sure it's *checked*).

The database expects a character string, so you'll use a length validator to make sure it doesn't exceed the maximum length.

1. Select the JSF Validators/Converters bar on the palette. From the JSF Validators/Converters palette, select Length Validator and drop it directly on top of the text field `artistName`. This sets the validator attribute of the `artistName` component to `lengthValidator1`.
2. Using the Application Outline view, select the validator component (`lengthValidator1`). In the Properties window, set its minimum to **1** and its maximum to **36**.
3. From the JSF Standard Components palette, select Inline Message and place it on the design canvas directly under the text field component.
4. In the Properties window attribute, `showSummary` should be checked.
5. Under Appearance and after the position values in its `style` attribute, add the following.

```
; font-style: italic
```

6. In the Properties window for the inline message component, click the editing box opposite attribute for. Select artistName from the pop-up dialog and click OK. This tells the message component to display error messages generated on behalf of component artistName.
7. Now select the component label (componentLabel) in the Application Outline view. In its Properties window, click the editing box opposite attribute for. Select artistName from the pop-up dialog and click OK.

Components for Artist Notes

For the Artist Notes field, you'll need the same components. Place them to the right of the artist name components, directly below each other, as follows.

1. Add a component label and change its embedded output text component's value attribute to **Artist Notes**.
2. Below this add a text field. Change its id attribute to **artistNotes**.
3. Set its title attribute to **Type in notes about the artist**. This sets the component's tooltip.
4. Under Data in the Properties window, select attribute required (make sure it's *checked*).

The database expects a character string, so you'll use a length validator to make sure it doesn't exceed the maximum length.

1. From the JSF Validators/Converters palette, select Length Validator and drop it directly on top of component artistNotes. This sets the validator attribute of the artistNotes component to lengthValidator2.

Creator Tip

Note that you must use a new length validator here. You can't reuse the validator you applied to the artistName component, since you have to specify different minimum and maximum values.

2. Using the Application Outline view, select the validator component (lengthValidator2). In the Properties window, set its minimum to **1** and its maximum to **200**.
3. From the JSF Standard Components palette, select Inline Message and place it on the design canvas directly under the text field component you just added.
4. In the Properties window, attribute showSummary should be checked.
5. Add the following after the position values in its style attribute.

```
; font-style: italic
```

6. In the Properties window for the inline message component, click the editing box opposite attribute `for`. Select `artistNotes` from the pop-up dialog and click OK. This tells the message component to display error messages generated on behalf of component `artistNotes`.
7. Select the component label (`componentLabel2`) from the Application Outline view. In its Properties window, click the editing box opposite attribute `for`. Select `artistNotes` from the pop-up dialog and click OK.

Components for Primary Key

For the primary key field, you'll need the same components. Place them to the right of the artist notes components, directly below each other, as before. Because the primary key is an integer field, you'll also need an integer converter for the text field component.

1. Add a component label and change its embedded output text component's `value` attribute to **Primary Key**.
2. Below this add a text field. Change its `id` attribute to **pkfield**.
3. Set its `title` attribute to **Type in an integer-value primary key**. This sets the component's tooltip.
4. Check attribute `required`.

The database expects an integer value for the primary key, so you'll use an integer converter to convert the user's input.

1. From the JSF Validators/Converters palette, select Integer Converter and drop it directly on top of component `pkfield`. In the `converter` field under Data, you should see `integerConverter1`.
2. From the JSF Standard Components palette, select Inline Message and place it on the design canvas directly under the text field component you just added.
3. In the Properties window, attribute `showSummary` should be checked.
4. Add the following after the position values in its `style` attribute.

```
; font-style: italic
```

5. In the Properties window for the inline message component, click the editing box opposite attribute `for`. Select `pkfield` from the pop-up dialog and click OK. This tells the message component to display error messages generated on behalf of component `pkfield`.
6. Now select the component label (`componentLabel3`) from the Application Outline view. In its Properties window, click the editing box opposite attribute `for`. Select `pkfield` from the pop-up dialog and click OK.

Add a Button, Message List, and a Data Source

1. From the JSF Standard Components palette, select Button and drag it to the design canvas. Position it under the inline message component for the artist name.
2. Make sure it's selected and type **Add New Artist** followed by **<Enter>**. The button's label should now display these words.
3. From the JSF Standard Components palette, select Message List and drag it to the design canvas. Place it under the button component. (This component will display messages written to the faces context by methods `info()` and `error()`.)
4. From the Data Sources > Music > Tables node in the Server Navigator view, select the RECORDINGARTISTS table and drag it anywhere in the open design canvas. You are *not* binding it to any components. The `recording-artistsRowSet` component appears in the nonvisual component tray at the bottom of the design canvas.
5. Select the `recordingartistsRowSet` component. In the Properties window, change attribute `concurrency` to CONCUR_UPDATABLE.

Add Initialization Code

First, right-click in the design canvas and select View Page1 Java Class to bring up **Page1.java**. Go to the `Page1()` constructor. Add initialization statements after the Creator-generated code inside its own `try` block. The initialization code includes calls to invoke the `execute()` and `next()` methods for the `recordingartistsRowSet` object. This executes the query and puts the rowset cursor at the first record. Should the user want to insert more than one row, this ensures that the rowset is in a valid state.

Copy and paste from your Creator book's file **FieldGuide/Examples/Database/snippets/MusicInsert_init.txt**. (The added code is bold.).

```java
public Page1() {
// Creator-managed initialization code
 . . . code omitted . . .
  // Additional user provided initialization code

  try {
    recordingartistsRowSet.execute();
    recordingartistsRowSet.next();

  } catch (Exception ex) {
      throw new FacesException(ex);
  } // end try catch
}
```

Add Button Event Handler Code

Your one remaining task is to the add the code in the button1's event handler to update the RECORDINGARTISTS table.

1. From the design canvas, double-click the Add New Artist button. This brings up the Java page bean, **Page1.java** and places the cursor at the button1_action() event handler.
2. Add the following code to the button1_action() method. Copy and paste from your Creator book's file **FieldGuide/Examples/Database/snippets/ MusicInsert_button1.txt**. (The added code is bold).

```java
public String button1_action() {
    // User event code here...
    try {
        recordingartistsRowSet.moveToInsertRow();
        recordingartistsRowSet.updateInt("RECORDINGARTISTID",
            ((Integer)pkfield.getValue()).intValue());
        recordingartistsRowSet.updateString(
                "RECORDINGARTISTNAME",
                artistName.getValue().toString());
        recordingartistsRowSet.updateString("NOTES",
            artistNotes.getValue().toString());
        recordingartistsRowSet.insertRow();
        recordingartistsRowSet.moveToCurrentRow();
        recordingartistsRowSet.commit();
        info("Successful Add to RecordingArtists Table");
    } catch (SQLException ex) {
        error("MusicInsert: " + ex);
        log("MusicInsert: " + ex);
        try {
            recordingartistsRowSet.rollback();
        } catch (SQLException f) {
            log("MusicInsert: " + f);
        }
    }
    return null;
}
```

(We'll fix the red underline syntax error shortly.) When the user clicks the Add New Artist button, the action event handler prepares the rowset for insertion and fetches the data from the text fields. At this point we know there are no conversion or validation errors, but it's possible that the primary key provided by the user is not unique within the table. If this happens, we catch the

SQLException error thrown by the database software. The error message is displayed in the message list component, and the user gets to try again.

Primary Keys

You might want to have your own method that generates unique primary keys instead of requesting a key from the user. This would eliminate the problem of duplicate primary keys.

To insert a new row of data, you must invoke method `moveToInsertRow()` and then update each field. After the fields have been updated, you call `insertRow()`.

Note the event handler contains nested catch handlers at the end of the try block. The first catch handler accepts an SQLException thrown from the database. If this happens, the exception's message is displayed in the message list component (using method `error()`). The second catch handler catches possible errors from the call to `rollback()`. If no exceptions occur, the database was updated and a success message is shown to the user (using method `info()`).

To fix the syntax error in the event handler, use Creator's fast import shortcut to have the necessary import statements included.

1. Click inside the word SQLException in the code you just added.
2. Press **<Alt-Shift-I>**. In the Import Class dialog, choose the Import Class radio button.
3. Click OK. Creator adds this import statement to your file.

```
import java.sql.SQLException;
```

Deploy and Run

Deploy and run the application. Figure 7–19 shows how recording artist ISAM Band is added to the database.

After running the **MusicInsert** web application, you can check the status of the database by inspecting the tables with Creator's Server Navigator window. Select Data Sources > Music > Tables > RECORDINGARTISTS. Double-click the RECORDINGARTISTS table. Creator displays the data in the Table View window of the editor pane.

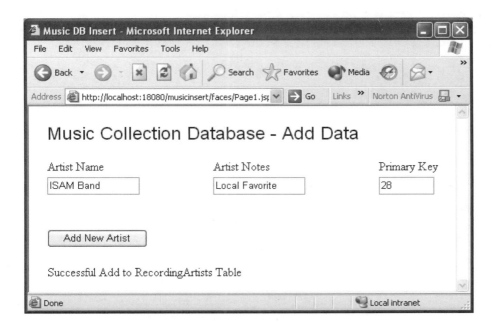

Figure 7–19 **After the insert row operation to the RecordingArtists table**

7.7 Database Deletions

Four database operations are represented by the acronym CRUD: Create (insert), Read, Update, and Delete. The previous sections have shown you all these operations except delete.

Deleting is not that different from the other operations. To demonstrate, we'll build a two-page web application that deletes a database row as dictated by the selection of a listbox component. The listbox is similar to a dropdown list component because it displays one field and returns another in its getValue() method. We'll work with the RECORDINGARTISTS table. The listbox will display RECORDINGARTISTNAME and return the primary key field, RECORDINGARTISTID. The primary key field will determine the row to delete.

Handle Cascading Deletes

When you target a row for deletion that is referenced with a foreign key in another (related) table, you will have to delete the related records first. For example, to delete a record in the RECORDINGARTISTS table that is referenced in the RECORDINGS table, you must first delete the related row in the RECORDINGS table. You can locate the row by matching its foreign key value for RECORDINGARTISTID.

Furthermore, to delete the row in the RECORDINGS table, you'll also have to delete the related rows in the TRACKS table. These you find by locating all tracks with a foreign key that matches the RECORDINGSID. This "cascading" effect that trickles through the database is called *cascading deletes*.

The database enforces data integrity by preventing deletes on rows referenced by other tables. In our example, deleting a row in the RECORDING-ARTIST table means we have to find and delete the related records in the RECORDINGS table and TRACKS table. This is not difficult to do, but it does require careful coding.

Create a New Project

- In the Welcome Page, select button Create New Project. Specify project name as **MusicDelete**. The selected project type is J2EE Web Application. Click OK.

Specify Title

After creating the project, Creator comes up in the design view of the editor pane. You can now set the title and components to the first page.

1. Click in the middle of the design canvas.
2. Select `Title` in the Properties window and type in the text **Music DB Delete**. Finish by pressing **<Enter>**.

Add an Output Text Component

Place a heading title on the page with an output text component.

1. From the JSF Standard Components palette, select Output Text. Drag it over to the design canvas and place it near the top of the page. Don't resize it and make sure it's selected.
2. Type the text **Music Database - Delete Recording Artist** followed by **<Enter>**. The component now displays these words.

3. In the Properties window under Appearance edit the `style` attribute. After
   the `position` settings, add the following.

```
; font-family: Helvetica; font-size: 18pt
```

Finish with **<Enter>**. The output text should now display a bold heading in a
larger font.

Create the Form's Components

The set of components that you'll place on this page will display records from
the RECORDINGARTISTS table. You'll use a listbox to display the recording
artist name, and you'll provide a button to delete the selection from the database table. You'll also have an output text component to display errors.

When the user successfully deletes an artist, a second web page comes up.
The user can return to the original page by clicking the Back arrow on the
browser to perform another delete.

Figure 7–20 shows the first page's design canvas with all the components
added.

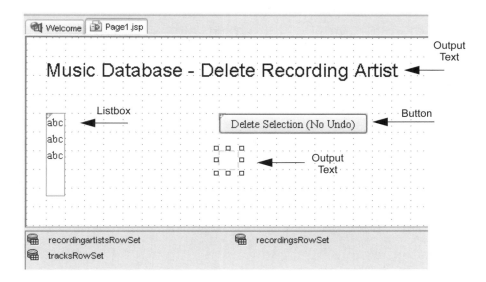

Figure 7–20 **Design canvas view with components on page**

1. From the JSF Standard Components palette, select Listbox and drag it to the design canvas. Place it below the output text component on the left side of the page. You don't need to resize it.
2. From the Data Sources > Music > Tables node in the Server Navigator view, select the RECORDINGARTISTS table and drop it directly on top of the list-box component. A dialog appears.
3. In the dialog, select Fill the List. The text "abc" appears in the listbox indicating that the data is of type VARCHAR from the database.
4. The `recordingartistsRowSet` component appears in the nonvisual component tray.

Let's see what assumptions Creator has made about the database table.

1. Right-click the listbox component. From the context menu, choose Fill List from Database. You have already completed the binding in the previous steps, but this action enables you to view the database table's metadata (its fields and table names). Creator displays a dialog with a database rowset, a Value field, and a Display field, as shown in Figure 7–21.

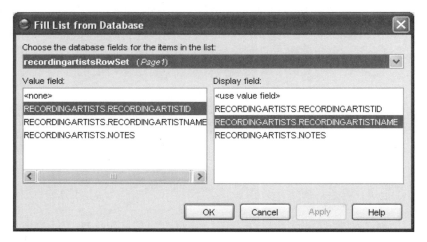

Figure 7–21 **Bind Display to Data dialog**

The database rowset is `recordingartistsRowSet`.

The listbox component's `value` attribute is assigned field RECORDING-ARTISTID, which is the primary key. Thus, you'll get the value of the primary key for the selection when you invoke method

```
listbox1.getValue();
```

The listbox's displayed text is the field highlighted under Display field, which is set to RECORDINGARTISTNAME.

2. Click OK to return to the design canvas.

You'll now add a button component.

1. From the JSF Standard Components palette, select component Button and place it under the title on the right side of the page. Leave plenty of room since you don't know exactly how much space the listbox will consume when populated with data.

2. With the button still selected, type the label **Delete Selection (No Undo)** followed by **<Enter>**.

Include Additional RowSets

Figure 7–20 on page 251 shows the rowset components for both the RECORDINGS and TRACKS tables (as well as the RECORDINGARTISTS table you just added). Let's add these two rowset components now.

1. From the Data Sources > Music > Tables node in the Server Navigator view, select the RECORDINGS table and drop it directly on top of the design canvas. (Don't drop it on any components.)

The `recordingsRowSet` component appears in the nonvisual component tray.

2. Again from the Data Sources > Music > Tables node in the Server Navigator view, select the TRACKS table and drop it directly on top of the design canvas.

The `tracksRowSet` component appears in the nonvisual component tray.

Modify the SQL Queries

When you access these tables from the application, you'll perform a query to select only those rows that have matching foreign keys for the target row deletion in the RECORDINGARTISTS table (for the recordingsRowSet object) or the target row deletion in the RECORDINGS table (for the tracksRowSet object). Therefore, you'll need to modify the default query for both of these objects to add query criteria. This is the same type of master-detail relationship you built in the **Music1** and **Music2** projects. Let's modify the recordingsRowSet's query first.

1. Double-click the recordingsRowSet object in the nonvisual tray at the bottom of the editor pane. This brings up the Query Editor.
2. In the spreadsheet view, right-click the RECORDINGARTISTID field and choose Add Query Criteria from the context menu.
3. The Add Query Criteria dialog appears. Select radio button Parameter and leave the Comparison at the default (= Equals). Click OK.

   This adds a WHERE clause to the query. Here is the modified query as shown at the bottom of the Query Editor.

```
SELECT ALL ROOT.RECORDINGS.RECORDINGID,
ROOT.RECORDINGS.RECORDINGTITLE,
ROOT.RECORDINGS.RECORDINGARTISTID,
ROOT.RECORDINGS.MUSICCATEGORYID,
ROOT.RECORDINGS.RECORDINGLABEL, ROOT.RECORDINGS.FORMAT,
ROOT.RECORDINGS.NUMBEROFTRACKS, ROOT.RECORDINGS.NOTES
FROM ROOT.RECORDINGS WHERE ROOT.RECORDINGS.RECORDINGARTISTID=?
```

4. Now click the tab labeled **Page1.jsp** at the top of the editor pane to return to the design canvas.
5. Double-click the tracksRowSet object to modify the tracksRowSet query.
6. In the spreadsheet view, right-click the RECORDINGID field and choose Add Query Criteria.
7. In the Add Query Criteria dialog, select radio button Parameter and click OK.

   Here is the modified query for the tracksRowSet.

```
SELECT ALL ROOT.TRACKS.TRACKID, ROOT.TRACKS.TRACKNUMBER,
ROOT.TRACKS.TRACKTITLE, ROOT.TRACKS.TRACKLENGTH,
ROOT.TRACKS.RECORDINGID FROM ROOT.TRACKS
WHERE ROOT.TRACKS.RECORDINGID=?
```

Add Initialization Code

You'll need to add initialization code to the end of the Page1() constructor.

1. Return to the design canvas by selecting the **Page1.jsp** tab. Right-click in the design canvas to bring up **Page1.java** in the Java editor.
2. Select the Page1() constructor from the dropdown menu at the top left of the editor pane. Creator puts the cursor at the beginning of the constructor.
3. Add the following statements after the Creator-generated code. Copy and paste from your Creator book's file **FieldGuide/Examples/Database/snippets/MusicDelete_init.txt**. (Added code is bold).

```
public Page1() {
// Creator-managed initialization code
. . . code omitted . . .
// Additional user provided initialization code
   try {
     recordingartistsRowSet.execute();
     recordingartistsRowSet.next();
   } catch (Exception ex) {
       throw new FacesException(ex);
   } // end try catch
}
```

4. Return to the design canvas by selecting the tab labeled **Page1.jsp**.
5. Select the recordingartistsRowSet component. In the Properties window, change attribute concurrency to CONCUR_UPDATABLE.
6. Select the recordingsRowSet component. In the Properties window, change attribute concurrency to CONCUR_UPDATABLE.
7. Select the tracksRowSet component. In the Properties window, change attribute concurrency to CONCUR_UPDATABLE.
8. From the JSF Standard Components palette, select Message List and place it on the page underneath the button.

Add Button Event Handler Code

You'll now add the button event handler code. Return to the design canvas by selecting the tab labeled **Page1.jsp** at the top of the editor pane.

1. From the **Page1.jsp** design canvas, double-click the Delete Selection button. This brings up the Java page bean, **Page1.java** and places you at the button1_action() event handler.
2. Add the following code to the button1_action() method. Copy and paste from your Creator book's file **FieldGuide/Examples/Database/snippets/**

MusicDelete_button1.txt. (The added code is bold). Make sure you delete the `return null` statement at the end of the method.

```java
public String button1_action() {
  // User event code here...
  int pK = ((Integer)listbox1.getValue()).intValue();
  try {
    recordingartistsRowSet.execute();
    while (recordingartistsRowSet.next()) {
      if (pK == recordingartistsRowSet.getInt(
                      "RECORDINGARTISTID")) {
        cascadeDelete(pK);
        recordingartistsRowSet.deleteRow();
        recordingartistsRowSet.commit();
        break;
      }
    }
  } catch (SQLException ex) {
      log("MusicDelete: " + ex);
      error("MusicDelete: " + ex);
      try {
        tracksRowSet.rollback();
        recordingsRowSet.rollback();
        recordingartistsRowSet.rollback();
      } catch (SQLException f) {
        log("MusicDelete: rollback exception " + f);
      }
      return null;
  }
  return "deleteOK";
}
```

(We'll fix the red underline syntax errors shortly.) When the user clicks the Delete Selection button, the action event handler prepares the rowset for the delete operation. The `while` loop gets the value from the listbox and compares it to the primary key in the rowset's current row. When a match is found, the code inside the `while` loop calls method `cascadeDelete(pK)`, deletes the row, and breaks out of the loop. If there are no errors, the method returns string `"deleteOK"`.

After you add the code for method `cascadeDelete()`, the red underlines will disappear. Let's fix the error with SQLException first. You'll use Creator's fast import shortcut to add the necessary import statement.

1. Click inside the word SQLException in the code you just added.
2. Press **<Alt-Shift-I>**. In the Import Class dialog, choose the Import Class radio button.

3. Click OK. Creator adds this import statement to your file.

```
import java.sql.SQLException;
```

Add Method Cascade Delete

Now let's look at the cascadeDelete() method. Its argument is a key, specifically, the RECORDINGARTISTID corresponding to the selected row in the RECORDINGARTISTS table. This method finds the related records in both the RECORDINGS and TRACKS tables.

Creator Tip

Method cascadeDelete() *may not be necessary for some database configurations. Check with your database software.*

Method cascadeDelete() has a throws clause. This allows you to call RowSet object methods without creating a new try block. Since the button event handler calls cascadeDelete() within its own try block, it will catch any thrown exceptions from cascadeDelete(). Inside the method, nested while loops iterate through the data. The outer while loop steps through the recordingsRowSet object and finds the related records in the TRACKS table. The inner while loop steps through the tracksRowSet.

Here is the code for the cascadeDelete() method, which you can place in front of or after the button handler. Copy and paste your Creator book's file **FieldGuide/Examples/Database/snippets/MusicDelete_cascade.txt**.

```
private void cascadeDelete(int foreignKey) throws SQLException
{
  recordingsRowSet.setInt(1, foreignKey);
  recordingsRowSet.execute();
  while (recordingsRowSet.next()) {
    tracksRowSet.setInt(1, recordingsRowSet.getInt(
          "RECORDINGID"));
    tracksRowSet.execute();
    while (tracksRowSet.next()) {
      tracksRowSet.deleteRow();
      tracksRowSet.commit();
    }
    // delete matching recording
    recordingsRowSet.deleteRow();
    recordingsRowSet.commit();
  }
}
```

Set Up the Second Page

Let's create the second page, add a navigation rule, and add an output text component to the page.

1. From the design canvas, right-click anywhere in the background and choose Page Navigation.
2. The Page Navigation editor comes up and displays **Page1.jsp**. Click anywhere in the background and choose New Page. Accept the default name, Page2.
3. Click inside **Page1.jsp** and draw a navigation arrow to **Page2.jsp**. Specify case label **deleteOK** (the string that matches the button event handler return value). This is the only navigation rule you'll define for this project.
4. Now double-click inside **Page2.jsp**. Creator brings up the design canvas for Page2.
5. Select Output Text from the palette and drop it onto the design canvas. Type the text **Record was successfully deleted from the database table** followed by **<Enter>**. The text will appear on the page.
6. In the Properties window under Appearance, edit the `style` attribute. After the `position` settings, add the following.

```
; font-family: Helvetica; font-size: 14pt
```

7. Press **<Enter>**. The output text now displays a bold heading in a larger font.

Deploy and Run

From the main menu bar, select Build > Run Project to deploy project MusicDelete. Figure 7–22 shows the application as the user is about to remove Steely Dan from the database by clicking the Delete Selection button.

After running the **MusicDelete** web application, you can check the status of the database by inspecting the tables with Creator's Server Navigator window. Select Data Sources > Music > Tables > RECORDINGARTISTS. Double-click the RECORDINGARTISTS table. Creator displays the data in the Table View window of the editor pane. Inspect tables RECORDINGS and TRACKS using the same key strokes.

7.8 Key Point Summary

- The Java Database Connectivity (JDBC) and JDBC RowSets technology provide a portable way to access a relational database using SQL.
- A JDBC RowSet object is a connected rowset that extends a ResultSet object.

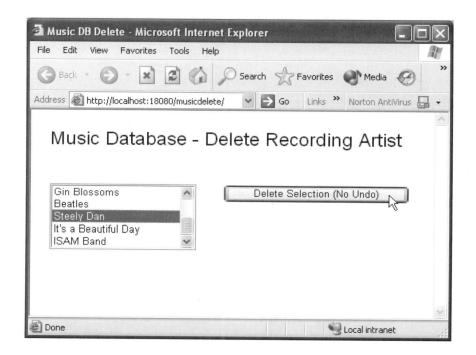

Figure 7–22 MusicDelete application's initial page

- When you select a data source from Creator's Server Navigator window, Creator generates code in the Java page bean to access this data through RowSet objects. The default access is read-only.
- The Music Collection Database consists of four related tables, as diagrammed in Figure 7–1 on page 207. Relational databases use foreign keys to relate records from one table to records of another table.
- A dropdown list creates a selection menu from a fixed list of choices. You can bind the component to a rowset to obtain the selection choices from a database.
- A listbox component creates a fixed list of choices that are all displayed. You can also bind this component to a rowset.
- Selection components (such as dropdown and listbox) let you specify a database field for display and a different database field for its value. This allows meaningful text to be displayed to the user and at the same time the selection is automatically tied to a row's primary key.
- Adding a data table (a Data Source) to your Creator project creates a rowset, which is a nonvisual component.

- Creator generates code in the page bean constructor to initialize the database rowset object. Creator also generates `close()` statements in the `afterRenderResponse()` method to close the connection to the database.
- You can add a data table component and bind it to a database rowset. You can modify which columns are displayed and the embedded component to use with the data table (output text is the default). You can also apply data converters to a column.
- You can control the data that is returned by invoking the Query Editor.
- You can use the Query Editor to sort the rowset, add a criterion based on a parameter or a fixed value, or create a JOIN by adding additional database tables.
- You can edit and update data in your underlying database when you bind a data table component to a rowset and edit the fields in the component.
- You can insert or delete rows in a database by manipulating the data's RowSet object.
- Database applications that perform delete operations must handle cascading delete situations when the database contains related tables.

CUSTOMIZING APPLICATIONS WITH CREATOR

Topics in This Chapter

- Localizing and Internationalizing Applications
- Setting Up Properties Files
- Locales and Languages
- Configuring Your Browser
- Setting a Locale from Your Application
- Creating Custom Validation
- Accessing a Custom Validation Method
- Using Localized Error Messages

Chapter 8

An IDE like Creator is only as good as its supporting technology. Fortunately, Creator is built on the solid foundation of JSF, and under that, live a host of other Java technologies that we've touched upon. One area that you'll explore in this chapter is the duo of localization and internationalization.

Another important facet of web application design is providing custom validation. We show you how to write a custom validator method for your Creator project. You'll be able to validate a component's input, control error message display with a message component, and use localized error messages.

8.1 Localizing an Application

Localization means that you customize an application to a given locale. The Java programming language has the concept of a locale that affects many objects. For example, the String class has a version of `toLowerCase()` that takes a Locale object as its argument. When you supply this argument, `toLowerCase()` uses the Locale's idea of translating a String to lowercase letters. More commonly, you use Locale to control the format of a Date object or a monetary amount, using the local currency symbol.

Consider the following Java code fragment.

```
import java.util.*;
import java.text.*;
. . .

Locale currentLocale = new Locale("en", "US");
Date myDate = new Date();

DateFormat df = DateFormat.getDateInstance(
    DateFormat.LONG, currentLocale);
System.out.println(df.format(myDate));
```

The DateFormat class uses the locale argument (if provided) to determine how to format the date. Here we provide a locale language ("en" for English) and country ("US" for the United States). The println statement produces

```
April 2, 2004
```

But if we change the country locale to "GB" for Great Britain, the output becomes

```
02 April 2004
```

to reflect the customary British date format. Furthermore, if we use Spanish and Spain ("es" and "ES" for español and España, respectively), we get

```
2 de abril de 2004
```

However, it's not good enough to simply customize an application for a specific locale. You also need to make your application language independent. To accomplish this task, you gather all the text messages, error messages, and labels from your web page and put them in a "properties" file. Each properties file isolates messages for a specific Locale. To run a program, you "bundle" those messages that are specific to the user's Locale. This creates a Resource-Bundle containing locale-specific objects.

The project example in this section shows you how to

- create the property file that holds localized messages;
- configure your application to accept localized messages;
- create and load the resource bundle that makes the localized messages available to the pages in your application; and
- allow the user to dynamically change the locale.

A Word About Locales

Locales designate both a language and a country (or region). Many readers are aware of the differences between British English and American English, for example, so specifying just a language isn't always good enough. The Spanish spoken in Mexico is different from that spoken in Spain. Similarly, the French spoken in Montreal is distinct from the French spoken in Paris.

On the other hand, specifying a generic language (without a country) may be just fine. A locale may represent just a language or a language and a country.

You can learn more about internationalization[1] from the following tutorial.

```
http://java.sun.com/docs/books/tutorial/i18n/index.html
```

To learn about internationalization support in Java, visit

```
http://java.sun.com/j2se/corejava/intl/index.jsp
```

Localize Application Labels and Text

Much of the time we forget to plan ahead for localization and are therefore forced to localize an application after it's already written. For our first example, let's localize project **Login2** from Chapter 5. Then we'll internationalize it and provide a way for the user to select the application's language.

Localizing an application means that the messages and labels on the page are determined by the locale. When there are no explicit instructions to use a particular locale, a properly localized application simply uses the default locale.

Let's start with opening up project **Login2** from Chapter 5.

Copy the Project

To avoid starting from scratch, copy project **Login2** to a new project called **Login3**. This step is optional. If you don't want to copy the project, simply skip this section and continue making modifications to the **Login2** project.

1. Bring up Creator and open project **Login2** from Chapter 5.
2. From the File menu, select Save Project As and provide the new name **Login3**. You'll make changes to the **Login3** project.

---

1. The term "i18n" refers to the word internationalization: the 18 letters sandwiched between the initial i and the final n.

Specify Title

In the design view of the editor pane, change the title.

1. Click in the middle of the design canvas.
2. Select `Title` in the Properties window and type in the new title **Login 3**. Finish with **<Enter>**.

Isolate Labels and Text Messages

Go ahead and deploy project **Login3** unchanged. Recall that the project consists of three pages: the initial page (**Page1.jsp**), the page you get when you successfully login (**LoginGood.jsp**), and the login failure page (**LoginBad.jsp**). Provide input for a successful login as well as errors. (For a successful login, type "rave4u" for both the username and password fields.) Note that you get validation errors when you fail to provide any input. (Fortunately, the JSF validators are already localized components. You'll notice that when you provide support for different locales, these components automatically provide locale-specific text.)

To isolate the text in a web page, you must extract each label or message and put it in a property file. Let's look at the localized property file in English for this application.

Listing 8.1 asg.messages.login3.properties

```
welcomeGreeting = Welcome
loginPageTitle = Members Login Page
usernameLabel = Username
passwordLabel = Password
usernameTip = Please type in your username

passwordTip = Please type in your password
loginButtonLabel = Login
resetButtonLabel = Reset
badLogin = Invalid username or password. To try again click
hereHyperlink = HERE
```

Fortunately, there are not many messages and component labels to extract, but the format is important. The format is a *key* (for example, `welcomeGreeting` listed above), an equal sign (=), followed by the message or label *text*. Spaces around the equal sign are optional. You place these key/value pairs in a text file and give it a name with a **.properties** extension. If the file represents the default locale, the name doesn't need a locale identifier. Otherwise, append **_LOCALE** to the base filename.

With English as the default locale, the name of this file is **login3.properties** (with no locale designation) in package **asg.messages**. Later, you'll implement translations to German and Spanish. These files will have the names **login3_de.properties** (for German) and **login3_es.properties** (for Spanish).

With country codes as well as language codes, use **login3_es_ES.properties** (for Spanish in Spain) and **login3_de_DE.properties** for German in Germany. (By the way, American English is **login3_en_US.properties** and British English is **login3_en_GB.properties**.) Adding country-specific translations involves creating additional translations with the country-specific filename. You can easily add these to your application later.

Accessing the login3.properties File

The **login3.properties** file is in the JAR file you added as a Library Reference during the building of project **Login2** (see "Add a Library Reference to Your Project" on page 133). Creator lets you view the file as a key-value database in the editor pane, showing all of the locales. Here's how you can view it.

1. In the Project Navigator window under Library References, expand the Bean_Examples > asg.jar > asg > messages nodes.
2. Under folder messages, select **login3.properties** file and double-click. Creator displays the key-value data in the editor as shown in Figure 8–1.

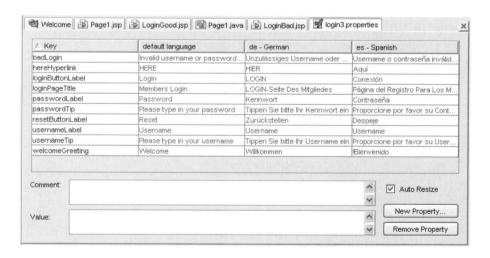

Figure 8–1 **Viewing the properties file in Creator's editor pane**

You can use the editor to modify any of the key-value entries, as well as add or remove entries. To add a new key-value pair, click button New Property and fill in the New Property's dialog, as shown in Figure 8–2. Click OK.

Figure 8–2 **New Property dialog for properties files**

Create a New Properties File

You can also create a new properties file and add it to your project. Here's how (you don't need to create a properties file for this project since you imported it using the library reference).

1. In the Project Navigator window, expand Java Sources and select your project's default package name.
2. Right-click on the package name and select New > All Templates.
3. Expand the Java Classes option and select **properties.properties**. Click Next.
4. Specify a name (**mybundle**, for example) and click Finish. Creator creates file **mybundle.properties** and brings it up in the properties file editor. From the editor, you can add key/value pairs, as shown in Figure 8–2 on page 268

Localize the JSF Source

Once you've created a properties file for at least one locale, you must tell your program where to access these messages. JSF has a `loadBundle` tag that accomplishes this. Let's put a `<f:loadBundle/>` tag in each of your page's JSF source files, as follows.

1. Bring up the **Page1.jsp** page in the design editor.
2. Click the Source tab at the bottom of the editor pane. This brings up the JSF source tags for this page.

3. Directly after the `<f:view/>` tag, open a new line and add the following `loadBundle` tag. (Put the tag all on one line.)

```
<f:loadBundle basename="asg.messages.login3"
    var="messages"/>
```

The `loadBundle` tag appears in the Application Outline view under Page1.

With the `loadBundle` tag, JSF loads the resource bundle from the properties file with basename **login3** in package **asg.messages**. This selects the properties file that corresponds to the current locale. If no locale is specified, JSF loads resource property file **login3.properties**.

The `var` property specifies how you'll refer to the message text in the rest of the JSF source. Here you've set `var` to "messages," so the JSF EL that grabs the text corresponding to the key `welcomeGreeting` is

```
#{messages.welcomeGreeting}
```

Note that `messages` is the value of the `var` property and `welcomeGreeting` is the key in the properties file that corresponds to the text you want.

Creator Tip

There is a big advantage to having a distinct `var` *property specify a "handle" to the properties file. If the properties file name changes, you only have to modify the* `basename` *attribute of the* `loadBundle` *tag. All of the JSF EL expressions for your application's components remain unaffected, since they reference the* `var` *property.*

Now add the same `loadBundle` tag to the pages **LoginGood.jsp** and **Login-Bad.jsp**. Go to the Project Navigator window, double-click the filename, and click the Source tab at the bottom of the editor pane. Copy and paste the `load-Bundle` tag into each JSP source file at the same spot.

Modify JSF Components for Localized Text

You've created the properties file with the localized text. Next, you'll modify the project's components to use it.

1. Bring up the design canvas for the initial page, **Page1.jsp**.
2. Select the component that displays the page's title, `outputText1`.[2] Bring up the Property window. Its `value` is set to Members Login. Select the small

editing square to bring up the dialog box. In the field labeled Current value setting, change the `value` to

```
#{messages.loginPageTitle}
```

Click OK. (Note that the label is removed from the design pane and replaced with the italicized word *Text*.)

3. Select the component that displays the label for username input, `componentLabel1Text`. Its `value` is currently Username. Change it to

```
#{messages.usernameLabel}
```

4. Repeat this process for the component that displays the label for password input (`componentLabel2Text`), the login button component (`login`), and the reset button (`reset`). Use the following JSF EL expressions for their values.

```
#{messages.passwordLabel}
#{messages.loginButtonLabel}
#{messages.resetButtonLabel}
```

5. The two input components have tooltips. Change the `title` attribute for components `userName` and `password` to the following.

```
#{messages.usernameTip}
#{messages.passwordTip}
```

Each of the other two pages contains components as well.

6. Bring up the design canvas for page **LoginGood.jsp**. Select the output component that's on the page (there's only one) and change its `value` to (keep it on a single line)

```
#{messages.welcomeGreeting},
#{SessionBean1.loginBean.username}!
```

---

2. For each of these steps, you can also use the Property Bindings dialog. Select the component in the design canvas, right-click, and select Property Bindings. Choose the property you want bind to in the Select bindable property window. Under New binding expression, specify the binding as indicated. Click Apply, then Close.

This expression concatenates the welcome greeting text with the user's login name. Figure 8–3 shows the modified design canvas for page **Login-Good.jsp**.

Figure 8–3 **Using localized messages and property binding**

7. Bring up the design canvas for page **LoginBad.jsp**. There are two components: an output text component and a link action component.
8. Change the `value` attribute of the output text component to

```
#{messages.badLogin}
```

9. Change the `value` attribute of the nested output text component (it's under the link action component) to

```
#{messages.hereHyperlink}
```

Deploy and Run

Ok, you've completed the steps for localization, so now it's time to deploy and run the application. If you've done everything right, you should not see any changes from the **Login2** application. The messages are still in English and the login procedure is unchanged. Underneath, however, there is a big difference. No hard-wired English labels or messages appear on the page. Everything is read from the properties file you reference for the default locale. The next step is internationalization.

Creator Tip

If you're having trouble with your application working correctly, here are some things to check. First, if deploying throws an exception, open the **Page1.jsp** *file in source mode and make sure you have the* **asg.messages.login3** *properties file spelled correctly in the* `<f:loadBundle>` *tag. Check the other pages, too. If the application deploys but doesn't work properly, use the Properties window or the JSP source in Creator to check that all the JSF EL expressions are correct.*

8.2   Internationalizing an Application

A localized application is much easier to internationalize than one that is not localized. Since you've already extracted the messages and labels, it won't be difficult to configure your application to access translated versions of the text.

Provide Translations

Fortunately, you can provide translations at any time once you've isolated the text that requires translation. (This is when you hire a bank of native speakers who can translate your English language text into the target languages.) Here is our translation for Spanish, in file **login3_es.properties**.

Listing 8.2 asg.messages.login3_es.properties

```
welcomeGreeting = ¡Bienvenido
loginPageTitle = Página del Registro Para Los Miembros
usernameLabel = Username
passwordLabel = Contraseña
usernameTip = Proporcione por favor su Username
passwordTip = Proporcione por favor su Contraseña

loginButtonLabel = Conexión
resetButtonLabel = Despeje
badLogin = Username o contraseña inválido. Para tratar otra
vez escoge
hereHyperlink = Aquí
```

Here is the translation for German, in file **login3_de.properties**.

Listing 8.3 asg.messages.login3_de.properties

```
welcomeGreeting = Willkommen
loginPageTitle = LOGIN-Seite Des Mitgliedes
usernameLabel = Username
passwordLabel = Kennwort
usernameTip = Tippen Sie bitte Ihr Username ein
passwordTip = Tippen Sie bitte Ihr Kennwort ein

loginButtonLabel = LOGIN
resetButtonLabel = Zurückstellen
badLogin = Unzulässiges Username oder Kennwort. Um es erneut
zu versuchen klicken Sie
hereHyperlink = HIER
```

Note that the text *keys* are unchanged from the original version. In any properties file, the keys remain consistent across all translations. With Spanish and German text isolated into properties files (they're already installed in our JAR file, **asg.jar**), the only step left is to tell JSF which locales the application supports.

Specify Supported Locales

Once your configuration is done, you can set up your browser for one of the supported locales. To do this, use an XML configuration file called **faces-config.xml** and install it in the same directory as the other configuration files that Creator generates. Here are the contents. We've included the source in **Field-Guide/Examples/Custom/login3_faces-config.xml** (note the different file name here).

Listing 8.4 faces-config.xml

```
<faces-config>
   <application>
      <locale-config>
       <default-locale>en</default-locale>
         <supported-locale>es</supported-locale>
         <supported-locale>de</supported-locale>
      </locale-config>
   </application>
</faces-config>
```

Here, the default locale is English (**en**), and Spanish (**es**) and German (**de**) are supported locales.

To install file **faces-config.xml** in your project, follow these steps.

1. In the Project Navigator window, select the top node **Login3**, right-click, and select New Item . . . ; Creator brings up the New Wizard dialog.
2. Under Select a Template, expand node Resources and select XML Document. Click Next.
3. For Target Location, expand path **<...>Projects/Login3/src/web** and select **Web-INF**. (Scroll down to the end of the file list.)
4. At the top of the dialog, specify **faces-config** for Name. Click Next.
5. Under Select Document Type, choose radio button Well-formed Document and click Finish.

Creator brings up the XML editor for you. Open the **login3_faces-config.xml** file in your Creator book's download directory **FieldGuide/Examples/Custom** and copy and paste the contents into the XML editor pane. Paste over any XML tags that are already there (use **<Ctrl-V>**). When you build your project, Creator makes this configuration file available to JSF.

Configure Your Browser

If you use Internet Explorer, do this:

1. Select Tools > Internet Options > Languages. Click the Add button and select the following lines in the supported languages box.

```
Spanish [es]
English [en]
German [de]
```

2. Click OK.
3. To change your locale, select the target language and move it to the top with the Move Up button.

If you use Netscape Navigator as your browser, do this:

- Select Edit > Preferences > Languages. Provide the same locale specifications as for Internet Explorer. Select the target locale and move it to the top with the Move Up button.

Deploy and Run

With the preceding changes, you can run the application in either English, Spanish, or German by configuring your browser for these different locales. Note that if you don't supply a username or password, the application displays the error message in the selected language. This is because the JSF validator is already configured to get its text from locale-specific messages.

Figure 8–4 shows a successful login page in the Spanish version.

Figure 8–4 **A successful login with the Spanish version**

8.3 Controlling the Locale from the Application

You may want users of your web application to select a language directly without having to modify browser configurations or change default locale settings. In this example (still **Login3**), you'll add a dropdown list component to the initial page that offers language selection for the application. Since the web application has already been internationalized (for three languages, at least), these modifications are minor.

Here's the approach. You'll use a dropdown list to hold the locale choices. When the user changes the locale, you save the choice as a property in session scope. Then, when the user returns to the application's initial page, you make sure that the language choice is still selected in the dropdown component. This save-restore step is similar to the save-restore you coded in projects **Music1** and **Music2**. Your first step, then, is to add a property to session scope.

Add a SessionBean1 Property

In this project, you will save the dropdown list's current selection in session scope. Call the property myLocale; it will be type String. Here are the steps to add property myLocale to SessionBean1.

1. In the Project Navigator window, expand Java Sources > login1 (the package name).
2. Right-click on **SessionBean1.java** and select Add > Property. Creator displays the New Property Pattern dialog.
3. Fill in the fields as follows. Specify **myLocale** for Name. Select **String** from the dropdown list for Type. Select **Read/Write** for Mode. Make sure the options Generate Field, Generate Return Statement, and Generate Set Statement are all checked.
4. Click OK.

Now you need to provide the instantiation with operator new for property myLocale in **SessionBean1.java**.

1. From the Project Navigator window, double-click file **SessionBean1.java** to bring it up in the Java source editor.
2. Add instantiation with operator new for property myLocale inside the SessionBean1() constructor, as follows.

```
// Additional user provided initialization code
myLocale = new String();
```

This instantiates an empty String.

Add a Dropdown List Component

Now, let's add a dropdown list component with three language choices.

1. Bring up **Page1.jsp** in the design canvas.
2. From the JSF Standard Components palette, select component Dropdown List and drag it onto the design canvas of page **Page1.jsp**. Place it under the inline message component.
3. In the Application Outline view, select item dropdown1DefaultItems (it's at the bottom of the Application Outline view).

4. In the Properties window, select the small editing box under `items`. A dialog pops up. Add the following.

```
English [en]
Deutsch [de]
Español [es]
```

5. Remove the default items in the list and click OK.
6. Select the dropdown list component. Right-click and select Edit Event Handler > processValueChange from the context menu. This action generates a `processValueChange()` method for the dropdown list component in the Java page bean, **Page1.java**.

> **Creator Tip**
>
> *The code you are about to add will cause the Java source editor to complain because it doesn't have all of the necessary import statements. After you add the code, we'll show you how to make Creator generate the import statements for you.*

7. Add the following code to method `dropdown1_processValueChange()`. Copy and paste from file **FieldGuide/Examples/Custom/snippets/ Login3_dropdown.txt**. The added code is bold.

```
public void dropdown1_processValueChange(ValueChangeEvent vce)
{
    // User event code here...
    FacesContext context = FacesContext.getCurrentInstance();
    UIViewRoot viewRoot = context.getViewRoot();
    String loc = dropdown1.getValue().toString();
    viewRoot.setLocale(new Locale(
        loc.substring(loc.indexOf('[')+ 1,loc.indexOf(']'))));
    getSessionBean1().setMyLocale(
        (String)dropdown1.getValue());
}
```

This method retrieves the faces context and the root view (the top level for all the components on the page). From the dropdown list's value, it parses the String to extract the locale designation that's between the square brackets (`[de]` for German, for example). After setting the locale, the method saves the dropdown list's value in session scope using property `myLocale`.

The code you just added is underlined in red because the Java page bean file is lacking three import statements. Here's how to fix them.

1. First, click anywhere inside the word `FacesContext` and press **<Alt-Shift-I>**. Creator pops up the Import Class dialog and displays `javax.faces.context.FacesContext`. Choose radio button Import Package and click OK.
2. Repeat this step with the class `UIVewRoot`. Press **<Alt-Shift-I>**, and choose Import Package for `javax.faces.component`.
3. Choose class `Locale` and choose Import Package for `java.util`.

Creator adds the following import statements along with the others in file **Page1.java**. The red underlines in your code should go away now.

```
import java.util.*;
import javax.faces.component.*;
import javax.faces.context.*;
```

Method `dropdown1_processValueChange()` saves the new locale selection in session scope as property `myLocale`. It's the constructor's job to make sure the dropdown list's selection is initialized to the requested locale. Place this code in the `Page1()` constructor after the comment as indicated. Here's the code. Copy and paste from file **FieldGuide/Examples/Custom/snippets/Login3_init.txt**. The added code is bold.

```
public Page1() {
// omitted code . . .
  // Additional user provided initialization code
  if (getSessionBean1().getMyLocale().length() != 0) {
    dropdown1.setValue(getSessionBean1().getMyLocale());
  }
}
```

Make the following final modifications to your project.

1. Return to the design canvas and select the dropdown list component.
2. Right-click and check Auto-submit on change (it is currently *unchecked*). This submits the page when the dropdown list selection changes.
3. Select the secret text component, `password`.
4. In the Properties window, make sure that the `required` attribute is unchecked. (Because a dropdown list component was added, you don't want the validator to flag an error when the password field is empty. An empty password is still an invalid password submission, so if the user leaves the field blank, the application behaves properly. You then don't need to supply a password before selecting the target language.)

Delete file **faces-config.xml** from your project. This is to prevent the locale settings performed by the event handler from interfering with the settings indicated by your browser. Without the configuration information in **faces-config.xml**, the dropdown component's event handler will determine the current locale.

1. In the Server Navigator window, right-click **Login3**, the top node. Select Show File System View.
2. Expand nodes **src** > **web** > **WEB-INF**. Under **WEB-INF**, right-click file **faces-config.xml** and select Delete. (Click OK to the confirmation.)
3. Right-click **Login3** again and now select Clean Project (this removes **faces-config.xml** from the project's build).

Deploy and Run

Deploy and run the application. You can now select the target language without configuring your browser. Figure 8–5 shows the initial page (still in English) as the user is about to select German.

8.4 Creating Custom Validation

Sometimes you need to provide your own validation for input. There are two approaches to take here. One is to write your own custom validator that you can use with other projects. Writing your own validator is a lot more work, but it does give you a reusable component. The other approach is to write a validation method and add it to your page bean. This is appropriate for input validation that you don't expect to use with other pages or other applications. It's the easier of the two approaches and a good first step if you're thinking about creating your own custom validator.

Let's see how you can write your own validation method. It's not difficult to do and it gets you up and running quickly. You can convert it to a validation component later if you want.

You've just learned about localization and internationalization in the previous sections. We're also going to show you how to make your validation method access the current locale for error messages and post messages to the faces context. Using the current locale allows you to provide international support for your validator error messages. By posting error messages to the faces context you can use message components to report validation errors generated by your custom validation method.

You'll accomplish all this with a simple application that uses a JavaBeans component called ColorBean to store red-green-blue (RGB) color values. Each color property of ColorBean stores its value as a two-digit hexadecimal string.

Figure 8–5 Setting the locale from the application

A `getColor()` method returns a String that sets HTML colors. The String's format is `#rrggbb`, where `rr` is a two-digit hex value for red, `gg` is a two-digit hex value for green, and `bb` is a two-digit hex value for blue.

The user can modify the two-digit value of any color, but a custom validator makes sure that the user's input is only two digits and that the digits are valid. The validator also allows upper- and lowercase input for the hex digits `a` through `f`.

This application comes up with all color properties set to the String `"ff"` (white). See Figure 8–6 for the page layout. When the user modifies an RGB color value, the background color of the enclosing Grid Panel changes to the new color.

Figure 8–6 **Using custom validation**

Create a Project

Let's start by creating a project called **Color1**. When the design canvas comes up, change the **Page1.jsp**'s page title to **Color1**.

Add a Library Reference to Your Project

Before you add components, configure properties files, and create a **faces-config.xml** file, add a library reference to your project. You'll use the same JAR file from the previous project. This JAR file contains **ColorBean.java** (the source for your JavaBeans component), **ColorBean.class** (the compiled class file), and the **.properties** files you'll need to internationalize the application.

1. Open up the Project Navigator window. This window displays all the resources, pages, Java sources, and references used by your project.

2. Expand the Library References node (if it's not already expanded). Creator lists several different libraries used by your project. You're going to add the **asg.jar** file as a new library reference.

3. Right-click the Library References node and select Create New Library Reference. Creator pops up the Create New Library Reference dialog. (See Figure 8–7.)

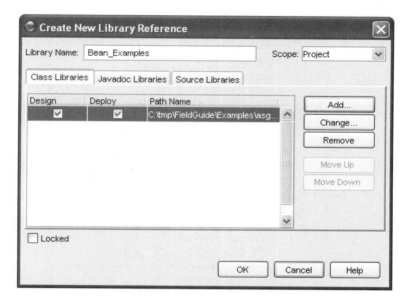

Figure 8–7 **Create New Library Reference dialog**

4. For Library Name, specify **Bean_Examples**. Scope should be set to Project.
5. Select tab Class Libraries and click Add. The Open dialog is displayed.
6. Browse to the location of your Creator book's examples. Under directory **FieldGuide/Examples** select **asg.jar** and click Open. Creator adds the JAR file path to the Path Name field. Click OK.

Bean_Examples now appears under the Library References node. If you expand it, you'll see the added JAR file, **asg.jar**.

Add a ColorBean Property to SessionBean1

Now that you've added the library reference containing the ColorBean class file, you'll need to make it accessible within your project. Since you want Color-Bean to have session scope, let's add it to the managed bean SessionBean1 as a property. This enables JSF to automatically instantiate the bean when it instan-

tiates SessionBean1. The bean will also become available to the GUI components as a SessionBean1 property.

Creator Tip

*Why put ColorBean in session scope? Although the web project we are
building is a single page application, users will submit the page multiple
times. If we want the previous settings to carry over to each new rendering of
the page, then ColorBean's state must be saved in session scope.*

1. In the Project Navigator window, expand the Java Sources folder and then
   the `color1` folder. You'll see the Java page bean source for your project,
   Page1.java.
2. You'll also see "template" beans **ApplicationBean1.java** and
   SessionBean1.java for beans at application and session scope, respectively.
3. Right-click the file node **SessionBean1.java** and select Add > Property. Creator pops up the New Property Pattern dialog (see Figure 8–8).

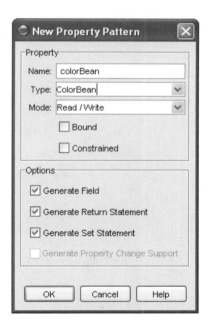

Figure 8–8 **New Property Pattern dialog**

4. Fill in the dialog as follows. Under Name specify **colorBean**, under Type specify **ColorBean**, and under Mode, select **Read/Write**.

Creator Tip

Since Name and Type are case sensitive, make sure you copy the capitalizations exactly.

5. Options Generate Field, Generate Return Statement, and Generate Set Statement should all be checked. Click OK to add property `colorBean` to SessionBean1.

6. Still in the Project Navigator window, double-click the file node **SessionBean1.java**. This brings up the file in the Java source editor. Here are the getter /setter methods Creator generated.

```java
/**
 * Getter for property colorBean.
 * @return Value of property colorBean.
 */
public ColorBean getColorBean() {
  return this.colorBean;
}
/**
 * Setter for property colorBean.
 * @param colorBean New value of property colorBean.
 */
public void setColorBean(ColorBean colorBean) {
  this.colorBean = colorBean;
}
```

You'll note that the code is marked with syntax errors because type ColorBean is unknown in the current compilation scope. Here's how to fix the errors.

1. In the Java source editor for file **SessionBean1.java**, click the cursor in the ColorBean class reference.

2. Press the shortcut keys **<Alt-Shift-I>**. Creator's Java source editor displays the Import Class dialog box as shown in Figure 8–9.

3. Make sure that `asg.bean_examples.ColorBean` and radio button Import Class are selected. Click OK.

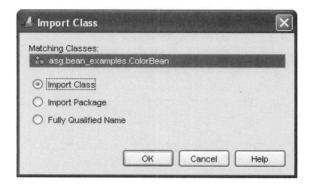

Figure 8–9 **Import Class dialog box**

This adds an import statement for the ColorBean class near the top of source file **SessionBean1.java**, as shown below. The added import statement is bold. The red underlines should disappear.

```
package color1;

import asg.bean_examples.ColorBean;
. . .
```

Now you'll add the Java code that instantiates (with operator new) the Color-Bean object.

1. Still editing file **SessionBean1.java**, place the cursor after the comment line in the SessionBean1() constructor.
2. Add instantiation with operator new for property colorBean, as follows.

```
// Additional user provided initialization code
colorBean = new ColorBean();
```

The code that you added to **SessionBean1.java** makes the colorBean object a property of SessionBean1. Thus, to access the redColor property of color-Bean (for example), use the following JSF EL expression.

```
#{SessionBean1.colorBean.redColor}
```

This is how you'll bind ColorBean's properties with the GUI components on your web page. Before you specify binding for the components, however, let's look at the source code for **ColorBean.java**.

ColorBean.java Code

The source for **ColorBean.java** is included in the **asg.jar** JAR file. Since the JAR file is installed in your project as a library reference, you can easily view the file in Creator's Java source editor.

1. In the Project Navigator window under Library References, expand nodes Bean_Examples > asg.jar > asg > bean_examples.
2. Double-click file **ColorBean.java**. Creator brings it up in the Java source editor as a read-only file for you.

Listing 8.5 shows the source for **ColorBean.java**.

Listing 8.5 ColorBean.java

```java
// ColorBean.java

package asg.bean_examples;

public class ColorBean {
    private String redColor;
    private String greenColor;
    private String blueColor;

  /** Creates a new instance of ColorBean */
    public ColorBean() {
        redColor = "ff";
        greenColor = "ff";
        blueColor = "ff";
    }

// Setters
    public void setRedColor(String c) { redColor = c; }
    public void setGreenColor(String c) { greenColor = c; }
    public void setBlueColor(String c) { blueColor = c; }
```

Listing 8.5 ColorBean.java *(continued)*

```
// Getters
   public String getRedColor() { return redColor; }
   public String getGreenColor() { return greenColor; }
   public String getBlueColor() { return blueColor; }
   public String getColor() {
       return "#" + redColor + greenColor + blueColor;
   }
}
```

ColorBean has four properties: three are read/write and the fourth is a read-only property (color). All properties have String values. You will bind three text field components to the properties redColor, greenColor, and blueColor. You'll also bind the background color of a grid panel to the color property.

Isolate Localized Text

This time you're going to plan ahead for localization. Your application will have a page title, labels for three text field components, a button label, and two different error messages that result from validation. The properties file will contain the labels and error messages in English. The name of this file is **color1.properties**, and it lives in the **asg.jar** library under package **asg.messages**. (You can also find it in your Creator book's download at **FieldGuide/ Examples/asg/messages/color1.properties**.) The code for this file is shown in Listing 8.6.

Listing 8.6 asg.messages.color1.properties

```
pageTitleLabel = Color Fun
redValueLabel = Red Value
greenValueLabel = Green Value
blueValueLabel = Blue Value
updateButtonLabel = Update Color
lengthError = Hex numbers must be two digits exactly.
digitError = Hex characters must be [0-9][A-F][a-f] only.
```

Creator Tip

*You can also view the properties file with Creator. In the Project Navigator window under Library References, expand the asg.jar > asg > messages folders. Double-click file **color1.properties**. Creator displays each key-value pair for both the default locale and the Spanish locale in the editor pane.*

Let's add the JSF `loadBundle` tag to your **Page1.jsp** source page. This tells JSF to use the resource bundle from the current locale. Here are the steps.

1. Bring up **Page1.jsp** in the design canvas.
2. Select the tab labeled Source at the bottom of the design window.
3. Add the `<f:loadBundle>` tag after the `<f:view>` tag in the JSP source. Here's the JSF tag. (Put the tag all on one line.)

```
<f:loadBundle basename="asg.messages.color1"
    var="messages"/>
```

Now you'll be able to bind the text messages in the **.properties** file to the components that you place on the page.

Adding Components to the Page

With all the setup work complete, it's time to add the components, event handling code, and validation method to the page bean. To help you add components to the page, Figure 8–10 shows the design canvas with the components you need.

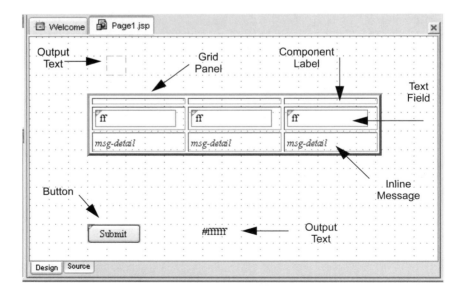

Figure 8–10 **Design canvas with components added to Page1.jsp for project Color1**

1. Bring up the design canvas for the project.
2. From the JSF Standard Components palette, select Output Text and drag the component to the canvas.
3. Change the component's `id` attribute to **pageTitle**.
4. Add the following to its `style` attribute.

```
; font-family: Helvetica; font-size: 24pt
```

5. Bind its `value` attribute to the localized messages, using

```
#{messages.pageTitleLabel}
```

(Select the small editing square opposite attribute `value`. Click OK when finished.)

6. Add component Grid Panel to the page. This component lets you format components within a grid.
7. In the Properties window, change `cellpadding` to 3, `border` to 3, and `columns` to 3.
8. Bind the grid panel's `bgcolor` attribute to the ColorBean `color` property. Select the grid panel component, right-click, and choose Property Bindings. Use the dialog box to select the `bgcolor` property in component `gridpanel1` and bind it to the `colorBean.color` property under SessionBean1. (See Figure 8–11 for the Property Bindings dialog box.) Click Apply and Close. The JSF EL expression should be the following.

```
#{SessionBean1.colorBean.color}
```

Add Components for Input

For each of the three color values (red, green, and blue) you'll need a component label, a text field component to gather input, and an inline message component for validation. Each color will occupy a column in the grid panel you placed on the page.

There are a lot of components to add here, so it's best to place all three labels on the page first, followed by all three text field components, and finally all three inline message components. As you add the components, check the Application Outline view to make sure you're not nesting components inappropriately.

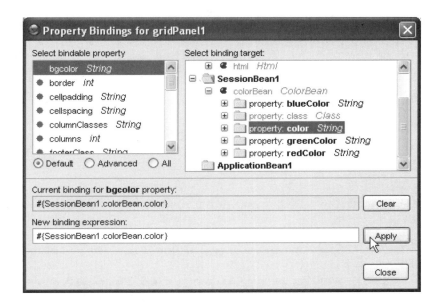

Figure 8–11 Property Bindings dialog

Creator Tip

Drag each JSF component from the Design Palette and drop it directly onto gridPanel1 in the Application Outline window. This is much safer than dropping the components onto the grid in the design pane, since with the latter technique you can't control their placement as easily. When you're finished, all the components should be at the same "level" under the grid panel component (except for the component label's embedded output text components). Figure 8–12 shows the Application Outline view after all the components have been added.

Table 8.1 shows the component labels, their properties, and the embedded output text component used to display the label's text.

With the component labels, you'll need to specify the setting of property `for` *after* you've added the text field components from Table 8.2. When you set the values for the embedded output text components (`componentLabel1Text`, for instance), select the component first in the Application Outline view and then set the value property in the Properties window. Note that the `value` attribute

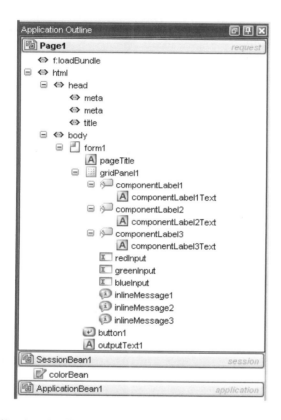

Figure 8–12 Application Outline view for project Color1

for each component matches the associated key from the **color1.properties** file (see Listing 8.6 on page 287.)

Table 8.2 shows the text field components and settings you'll use for gathering color value input. All text field components specify validators, but the validator specification is not one of the standard JSF validators. Instead, the `validator` property references custom method `validateHexString()`.

Creator Tip

The Properties window assumes that you will use one of the standard validators. For custom validators, set the property manually in the JSP source file. Click the Source tab at the bottom of the editor pane and add the tag `validator="#{Page1.validateHexString}"` *to each text field.*

Table 8.1 Component labels

Component	Property	Setting
component label (componentLabel1)	for	redInput
embedded output text (componentLabel1Text)	value	#{messages.redValueLabel}
component label (componentLabel2)	for	greenInput
embedded output text (componentLabel2Text)	value	#{messages.greenValueLabel}
component label (componentLabel3)	for	blueInput
embedded output text (componentLabel3Text)	value	#{messages.blueValueLabel}

Table 8.2 Text field components for color input

Component	Property	Setting
text field	id	redInput
	required	true (checked)
	validator	#{Page1.validateHexString}
	value	#{SessionBean1.colorBean. redColor}
text field	id	greenInput
	required	true (checked)
	validator	#{Page1.validateHexString}
	value	#{SessionBean1.colorBean. greenColor}
text field	id	blueInput
	required	true (checked)
	validator	#{Page1.validateHexString}
	value	#{SessionBean1.colorBean. blueColor}

To bind the value attribute of the text field components to the color properties of ColorBean, select the text field component and right-click. Select Property Bindings. Creator displays the Property Bindings dialog. Expand the colorBean property under SessionBean1 and select the desired property as shown in Figure 8–13 (here we show component `blueInput`). Make sure you click Apply followed by Close.

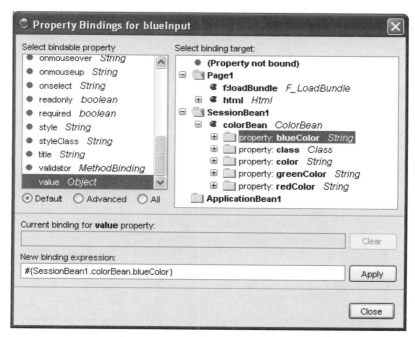

Figure 8–13 Property Bindings dialog to specify binding for text field blueInput

For the third row in the grid panel, Table 8.3 shows the inline message components and settings to report validation errors. Each of the three text field components has an associated inline message component.

The grid panel is now set. It has three component labels, three text fields, and three inline messages.

Add a Button and an Output Text Component

Now let's add a button component and an output text component to the page. Place these components below the grid panel. Allow plenty of space between the grid panel and the button since the grid panel's size changes dynamically, depending on its embedded components. For example, if the validator detects an error, the error message appears in the grid panel, expanding its size. Table 8.4 shows the button and output text components. Note that the button's label is bound to the localized messages file and the output text's label is bound to ColorBean's `color` property.

Table 8.3 Inline message components

Component	Property	Setting
inline message	for	redInput
(inlineMessage1)	style	font-style: italic
	showSummary	checked (true)
inline message	for	greenInput
(inlineMessage2)	style	font-style: italic
	showSummary	checked (true)
inline message	for	blueInput
(inlineMessage3)	style	font-style: italic
	showSummary	checked (true)

This example does not require an action method associated with the button component. That's because we just want the page to be submitted when the user clicks the button. All the work is done by input validation and component binding.

Table 8.4 Button and output text components

Component	Property	Setting
button (button1)	value	#{messages. updateButtonLabel}
output text (outputText1)	value	#{SessionBean1. colorBean.color}

Add a Validation Method

To "hook" into JSF's component validation process, all custom validation methods must conform to the correct format. Specifically, they must accept arguments that include the faces context, the input component that's being validated, and the input string that's being validated.

Furthermore, to keep with the stipulation that all messages are localized, you'll have to access the resource bundle from the current context to build the error message. Once the error message is formed, we add the message to the faces context and mark the component "not valid."

Custom method `validateHexString()` calls `toLowerCase()` to convert possible uppercase values to lower case. Note that we supply the optional Locale argument to the call.

Listing 8.7 shows the source to add to the Java page bean, **Page1.java**. (Copy and paste from file **FieldGuide/Examples/Custom/snippets/Color1_validate-Hex.txt**.) Open the **Page1.java** file and place this method at the end of the page bean file after the `Page1()` constructor.

Listing 8.7 Method `validateHexString()`

```
public void validateHexString(FacesContext context,
              UIComponent toValidate, Object value) {
  String hexString = value.toString().toLowerCase(
        context.getViewRoot().getLocale());
  boolean valid = true;
  String message = "";

  if (hexString.length() != 2) {
    valid = false;
    message = hexString + ": " +
        lookup_message(context, "lengthError");
  }

  else {
    for (int i = 0; i < 2; i++) {
      char hd = hexString.charAt(i);
      int v = Character.digit(hd, 16);

      if (v < 0 || v > 15) {
        valid = false;
        message = hexString + ": " +
            lookup_message(context, "digitError");
        break;
      }
    }
  }

  if (!valid) {
    ((UIInput)toValidate).setValid(false);
    context.addMessage(toValidate.getClientId(context),
        new FacesMessage(message));
  }
}
```

After you paste in the method code, the Java source editor will show red underlines for any unknown classes. We'll show you how to fix this after you add the code for the `lookup_message()` method.

Method `lookup_message()` is a private helper function that looks up the resource bundle associated with this context and locale. It finds the message text with the key from the resource bundle.

Listing 8.8 shows the source to add to the Java page bean, **Page1.java**. (Use file **FieldGuide/Examples/Custom/snippets/Color1_lookup.txt**).

Listing 8.8 Method `lookup_message()`

```
private String lookup_message(
       FacesContext context, String key) {
  String text = null;

  try {
    ResourceBundle bundle =
        ResourceBundle.getBundle("asg.messages.color1",
           context.getViewRoot().getLocale());
    text = bundle.getString(key);

  } catch (Exception e) {
    text = "???" + key + "???";
  }
  return text;
}
```

Next, you'll add import statements to the **Page1.java** source file. These imports will eliminate the editor's unresolved symbol errors. (Use the Java Source editor shortcut **<Alt-Shift-I>** to make Creator generate the import statements for you.) Here are the imports you need.

```
import java.util.ResourceBundle;
import javax.faces.application.FacesMessage;
import javax.faces.component.*;
import javax.faces.context.FacesContext;
import javax.faces.validator.*;
```

Deploy and Run

Deploy and run the application by clicking the green chevron on the toolbar. Figure 8–14 shows the page after the user changes the color to yellow (`#ffff00`) and then supplies invalid input for the red color value.

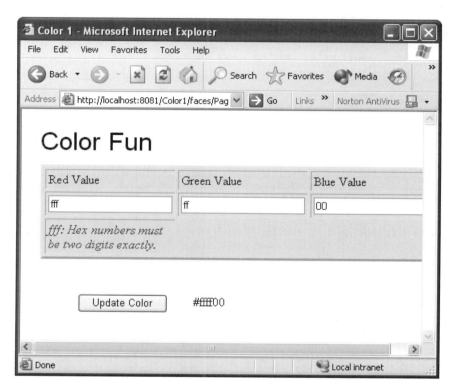

Figure 8–14 **Custom validation with localized error messages in English**

Creator Tip

If you're having trouble with your application working correctly, here are some things to check. First, if deploying throws an exception, open the **Page1.jsp** *file in source mode and make sure you have the* **asg.messages.color1** *properties file spelled correctly in the* `<f:loadBundle>` *tag. If the application deploys but doesn't work properly, use the Properties window in Creator to check that all the property bindings are correct. Make sure you click Apply when using the Property Bindings dialog.*

Internationalize for Spanish

In keeping with our two-step process for internationalization (localization being the first step), let's look at the Spanish text for the keys we already created in the default **color1.properties** file. We'll call this file **color1_es_ES.properties** (for Spanish as it's spoken in Spain). The file is already in the **asg.jar** file installed in your project. You can view it at **FieldGuide/Examples/asg/messages/color1_es_ES.properties**. Here is the properties file. (You can also view it in the editor pane by expanding the **asg.jar** library reference in the Project Navigator window. Double-click the **color1.properties** file to bring it up in the editor.)

Listing 8.9 asg.messages.color1_es_ES.properties

```
pageTitleLabel = Diversión con color
redValueLabel = Valor Rojo
greenValueLabel = Valor Verde
blueValueLabel = Valor Azul
updateButtonLabel = Fije el Color
lengthError = Los números hexadecimales deben ser dos dígitos
   exactamente.
digitError = Los caracteres hexadecimales deben ser
   [0-9][A-F][a-f] solamente.
```

Specify Supported Locales

You'll need to specify which locale you want since your project has multiple **color1.properties** files. This step isn't necessary with just a default locale, but if you want to configure your browser to use a different locale, you'll have to tell the application which locales are supported.

You'll also need to install a **faces-config.xml** file in your project directory. Here is the **FieldGuide/Examples/Custom/color1_faces-config.xml** file from your Creator book download. (Note the different file names.)

Listing 8.10 faces-config.xml

```
<faces-config>
   <application>
    <locale-config>
       <default-locale>en_US</default-locale>
       <supported-locale>es_ES</supported-locale>
    </locale-config>
   </application>
</faces-config>
```

To install the **faces-config.xml** file in your project, follow these steps.

1. In the Project Navigator window, select the top node **Color1**, right-click, and select New Item . . . ; Creator brings up the New Wizard dialog.
2. Under Select a Template, expand node Resources and select XML Document. Click Next.
3. For Target Location, expand path **<...>Projects/Color1/src/web** and select **Web-INF**.
4. At the top of the dialog, specify **faces-config** for Name. Click Next.
5. Under Select Document Type, choose radio button Well-formed Document and click Finish.

Creator brings up the XML editor for you. Open the **color1_faces-config.xml** file in your Creator book's download directory **FieldGuide/Examples/Custom** and copy and paste the contents into the XML editor pane. Paste over any XML tags that are already there (use **<Ctrl-V>**). When you build your project, Creator makes this configuration file available to JSF.

Configure Your Browser

If you use Internet Explorer as your browser, follow these steps.

1. Select Tools > Internet Options > Languages.
2. In the Language Preference window, click the Add button and type the following lines in the User defined box.

```
es-ES
en-US
```

3. Make sure you use a hyphen (-) and not an underline (_) here. Click OK.
4. To change your locale, select the target language you want and move it to the top with the Move Up button.

If you use Netscape Navigator, follow these steps.

1. Select Edit > Preferences > Languages.
2. Provide the same locale specifications as above.
3. Select the target locale and move it to the top with the Move Up button.

Deploy and Run

Deploy and run the application by clicking the green chevron on the toolbar. Figure 8–15 shows the page after the user changes the color to yellow (#ffff00) and then supplies invalid input for the red color value. When you configure your browser for Spanish, the custom validator displays the messages you supplied for the Spanish locale.

Figure 8–15 Custom validation with localized error messages in Spanish

8.5 Key Point Summary

- Localization and internationalization enable your applications to run in a global environment.
- Java uses a Locale to customize an application for a target language and country.
- To localize an application, first isolate all textual labels and messages and organize them into key-value pairs.
- Java uses a properties file to hold key-value pairs of text to identify text data.
- Use the `loadBundle` JSF tag to identify the resource bundle of the current locale.

- To internationalize an application, translate the messages and labels in the properties file to the target languages you intend to support.
- Each supported locale has its own properties file.
- Components access message keys in the properties file instead of using literal text. JSF uses value binding for this.
- When you want to support more than one locale by configuring your browser, specify the supported locales in an XML configuration file.
- You can also control the locale programmatically by invoking the `setLocale()` method of `UIViewRoot`.
- You can provide custom validation by writing a validation method in your Java page bean.
- You must modify a component's `validator` attribute to use a custom validator method.
- The custom validator method should access the current locale to obtain localized error messages.
- The custom validator should add error messages to the faces context so that you can use message components to display them.

DEBUGGING WITH CREATOR

Topics in This Chapter

- Planning for Debugging
- Running the Debugger
- Setting Breakpoints
- Stepping Through Your Code
- Tracking Variables
- Setting Watches
- Using the Call Stack
- Detecting Exceptions
- Using Log Files

Chapter 9

L et's face it, everyone makes mistakes. Designing and coding a web application is certainly no exception. Even simple web applications can be complex to work with, and there are lots of things to keep track of. As a programmer you have to be conversant with Java programming as well as XML. If all goes well, there's no problem. But when things don't work right, you can use all the help you can get.

Fortunately, Creator has a built-in debugger that can assist you in troubleshooting your web applications. The debugger is smart, includes lots of features, and has a user-friendly interface. You can use the debugger to monitor program flow, find out why variables aren't set to proper values, and help decipher why you're getting a Java exception. All this is not difficult if you know what to do. This chapter shows you how. And if you haven't used a debugger before, don't worry, we take it one step at a time.

This chapter shows you the different features of the Creator debugger as we look at an application that you've already seen. We'll examine breakpoints, watches, call stacks, variable tracking and show you how to apply the debugging features of Creator while your web application is running. To make it easier to follow, we include lots of screen shots so you can see what's going on. You are also welcome to perform each step as you read along, too.

Before we begin, however, let's talk about debugging in general.

9.1   Planning for Debugging

Unless you are very bold and confident, it's best to plan ahead for debugging. This mode of operation is often called *defensive programming*. Although this is a broad topic that covers many things, the main philosophy here is to simply plan ahead. Don't be too fancy with your code and follow some simple rules. Here are some of ours.

- Keep methods short in size. Call other methods as needed (this practice is often called *stepwise refinement*).
- Use local variables to store important data so that it's easier to track the data with a debugger.
- Use assertions in your program at places where disaster can occur if something goes wrong.
- Use log files to store important data, monitor program flow, and document the capture of a critical exception in a catch handler.
- Provide catch handlers to capture uncaught or unexpected exceptions early in your designs.

Although we won't show you all these suggestions in this chapter, here are several to look at.

Local Variables

```
public double getPayment() {
    double monthly_interest = this.rate / 1200;
    int months = this.years * 12;
    return this.amount * (monthly_interest /
      (1-Math.pow(1+monthly_interest,-1*months)));
}
```

In the above method, the calculation of a monthly interest payment is performed in the return statement. This approach makes it difficult to access the payment amount in a debugger. A better approach for debugging is to store the payment in a local variable before returning its value.

```
public double getPayment() { {
    double monthly_interest = this.rate / 1200;
    int months = this.years * 12;
    double pmt = this.amount * (monthly_interest /
      (1-Math.pow(1+monthly_interest,-1*months)));
    return pmt;
}
```

Now you can track the pmt variable in memory as you test out the algorithm with different input values. A class field, rather than a local variable, can also be used here.

Assertions

Another programming technique for debugging is a Java assertion.[1] There are two formats.

```
assert expression1;
assert expression1 : expression2;
```

An assertion is a boolean expression that is expected to be true at run time. In the first format, an AssertionError is thrown if *expression1* evaluates to false. The second format customizes the message for AssertionError from *expression2*, which is typically a String.

There are many ways to use assertions in Java. Here's an example with a private class method that tests a precondition.

```
private void myMethod(int arg) {
    assert arg >=0 && arg <= 100 : "Bad argument: " + arg;
    // rest of code here...
}
```

Log Files

The last example of defensive programming is a simple output print statement, strategically placed where it might be important to see in a log file or in a message window. To do this, use System.out.println(). Here's an example.

```
System.out.println("button was clicked");
```

Creator also provides a log() method.

```
log("button was clicked");
```

We show both methods in "Using Log Files" on page 321.

---

1. Java assertions were introduced in JDK 1.4.

9.2   Running the Debugger

Before you run your project with the debugger, let's show you the debugging commands in Creator and what they mean. We'll also discuss the contents of the Debugger Window, which gives you a visual look at your running program.

Debugging Commands

The **Debug** menu on the Creator menu bar lists the following debugging commands. Most of these commands also have hotkeys listed in the menu.

> Debug Project
> Finish Sessions
> Pause
> Continue
> Step Into
> Step Over
> Step Out
> Run to Cursor
> Fix
> Stack
> New Breakpoint
> New Watch

Debug Project runs Creator in debugging mode, and **Finish Sessions** stops the debugging session. Most of the other commands deal with *breakpoints*, a central concept in a debugger. A breakpoint is a spot in your program at which you can stop the execution of your program. Once you're at a breakpoint, you can examine the values of program variables or monitor program flow by means of a call stack of method calls. Breakpoints allow you to use other debugging commands to find out why your code is not working correctly. Here is a description of the debugging commands that affect breakpoints.

- **Pause** – Temporarily halt the execution of your program.
- **Continue** – Execute to the next breakpoint or if there are no more breakpoints, run until the program completes.
- **Step Into** – Execute only the next statement, but if it's a method, pause before executing the first statement in the method.
- **Step Over** – Execute only the next statement, then pause again. If the statement is a method call, execute the entire method code and pause after returning from it.

- **Step Out** – Execute the rest of the current method and pause in the method that called it.
- **Run to Cursor** – Execute up to the point where the cursor is positioned.

We'll show you later how to set breakpoints and use these debugging commands.

Open Project and Files

Let's start our tour of the Creator Debugger with the Monthly Payment Calculator program from Chapter 5 (see "LoanBean Component" on page 144). Here's what you do.

1. In the Welcome Page, open project **Payment1** from the list of projects.
2. You should see the **Page1.jsp** page appear.
3. In the design view, right-click the page and select View Page1 Java Class.
4. In the Project Navigator window, click the '+' for Java Sources, the '+' for **asg**, and the '+' for **bean_examples**. Double-click **LoanBean.java** to see the Java code for this file.
5. You'll need to see line numbers in both Java files, so right-click anywhere in the left margin column of the Java source file window and select Show Line Numbers.

Run and Deploy in Debug Mode

Now let's run the Payment program in debug mode with Creator.

- In the Creator toolbar, select Debug, then Debug Project.

Creator will compile and deploy the system. If the server is already running, Creator will stop the server and restart it in debug mode. After deployment, the Calculator page appears in the browser window. You can execute the program by typing in various input values for the loan amount, interest rate, and loan term (in years).

Open the Debugger Window

Click the **Page1.jsp** tab to the see the design canvas for the Calculator application. A debugger window should be at the bottom of your screen. If it's not there, go to View in the Creator toolbar and select Debugger Window. Or, click the Debugger icon at the bottom of your screen.

At the far left of the Debugger window, you will see three columns of icons. The first column contains shortcut icons for Creator's debugging commands. The second column shows icons for the various displays that are available in the Debugger window. The last column is a list of class visibility icons. If you place the cursor over any icon, Creator tells you what it means.

The display icons (second column) control what you see in the Debugger window. Let's show you the list of display icons now. (You may have to make the Debugger window larger to see them all.)

> Sessions
> Threads
> Call Stack
> Local Variables
> All in One
> Watches
> Classes
> Breakpoints

We show you how to use most of these features shortly, but for now let's just learn how to manipulate the display. If you hold your mouse over any of the icons, a pop-up will tell you what they are. Clicking the icon is a toggle to display or not display. If you click the Watches display icon, for instance, the Watches display disappears. Clicking the icon again brings it back.

You can also change the display format of the Debugger window. The top right corner of the Debugger window has several icons. The red X removes the debugger window (you can always get it back with View on the Creator toolbar). The other icons widen the Debugger window and display it vertically or horizontally. Figure 9–1 shows the Debugger window as a horizontal display with only the Call Stack and Local Variables.

Now you are ready to work with the Debugger window and learn its features. Let's start with breakpoints.

9.3   Setting Breakpoints

Go to the Calculator Page and exit the browser to end the current session. Switch back to Creator. The first thing you'll do now is set a *breakpoint*. Recall that a breakpoint is a place in your program at which the debugger stops the

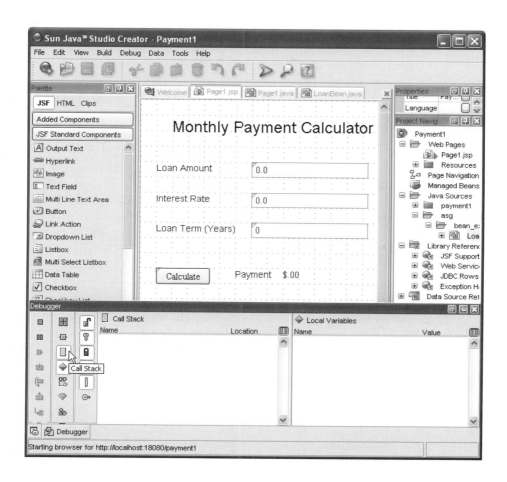

Figure 9–1 **The Debugger window**

execution of your program. In Creator, you can set a breakpoint for any of the following.

> Line
> Method
> Exception
> Variable
> Thread
> Class

With any breakpoint, the program stops *before* the breakpoint is executed (in other words, before a line is reached, a method is called, an exception is thrown, etc.)

Let's set breakpoints for a line[2] and a method in our Java code. Here's what you do.

1. Click the **LoanBean.java** tab to open the window with the Java code.
2. Set a breakpoint at the line where the amount field is initialized. Right-click Line 46 and select Toggle Breakpoint. Creator will highlight Line 46 in red for you, showing that a breakpoint has been set.
3. Move the cursor down to the getPayment() method at line 107. Put the cursor on the line and click the left button of the mouse.
4. Select Debug on the Creator toolbar and choose New Breakpoint.
5. You will see a Breakpoint Type selection menu at the top of the New Breakpoint window. Select **Method** from this list. This is how you set a breakpoint to a Java method. This means that the Creator debugger will stop the execution of your program when the method is called, as shown in Figure 9–2.

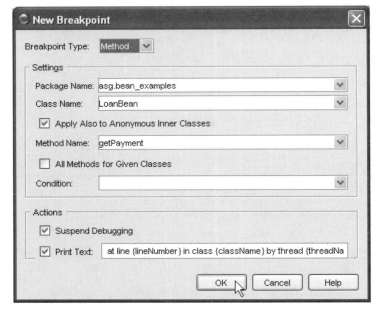

Figure 9–2 **New Breakpoint dialog**

---

2. The format of your program may be slightly different than ours. If so, use your line numbers from the same spots in the program.

6. Click the OK button to finish setting your breakpoint.
7. Right-click the line number at the getPayment() method and select Toggle Breakpoint. Creator will highlight the line in red for you. (This step is optional, but we're doing it so you can see where all the breakpoints are set.)

Figure 9–3 shows you the **LoanBean.java** code with the breakpoints. Note that the breakpoints at Lines 46 and 107 are marked in red (shown as dark lines in the figure) for you.

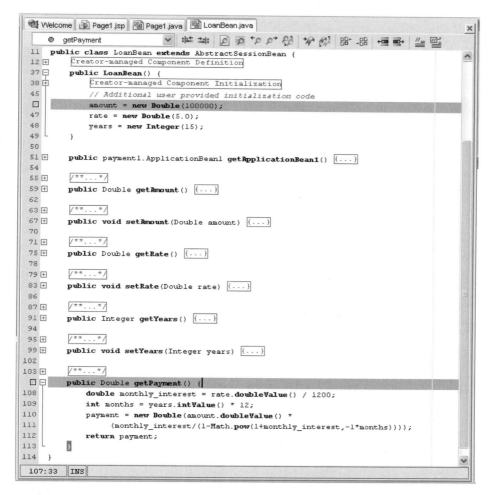

Figure 9–3 Setting breakpoints

You are now ready to run and deploy the program again, so click Debug Project in the Debug toolbar of Creator. Several things will happen. First, a

Start New Session Dialog appears. This gives you several choices. You can restart the current debugging session, start up an additional one, or cancel and continue debugging the current session. Choose Finish & Start to restart your debugging session.

Next, Line 46 changes color from red to green in the **LoanBean.java** window. This means that the first breakpoint was reached and the program has been stopped. Since we are inside the LoanBean constructor at this point and Creator has not finished initializing the LoanBean object, the Calculator JSP page cannot be rendered. Hence, your browser window is empty.

9.4   Stepping Through the Code

Debuggers typically allow you to execute your code one line at a time as it executes. This is called *stepping*. Let's step through the LoanBean constructor code now with the Creator debugger to initialize the LoanBean's fields. This is where we'll use the Debugger window, so make sure you have that window open. Here's what this window displays for you.

> Call Stack
> Local Variables
> Watches
> Classes
> Breakpoints

Click the Call Stack icon in the left column of the Debugger window to make the Call Stack display go away. We'll just look at the Local Variables display for now. Here's what you do.

1. Click the '+' for the `this` reference. Underneath this name, you will see the fields for the LoanBean constructor: `amount`, `rate`, `years`, and `payment`.
2. From the Debug toolbar, select Step Over (you may also hit the F10 key). This makes the Creator debugger execute Line 46 and stop at Line 47, which will now be green in color.

In the Local Variables display, the `amount` field should be set to 100000.0.

3. Now Step Over Line 47 to Line 48, and then Step Over again to Line 49.
4. In the Local Variables display, the `rate` field should now be 5.0 and the `years` field should be 15.

Figure 9–4 shows you what the screen looks like after the LoanBean constructor has finished executing.

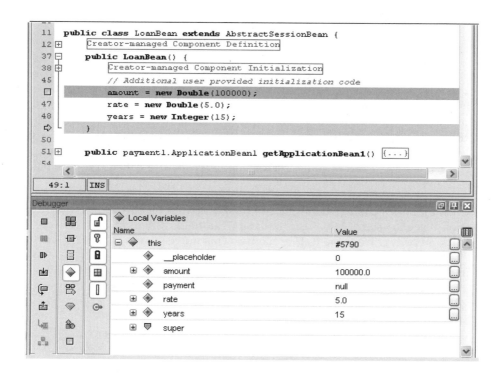

```
11   public class LoanBean extends AbstractSessionBean {
12 ⊞     Creator-managed Component Definition
37 ⊟     public LoanBean() {
38 ⊞         Creator-managed Component Initialization
45           // Additional user provided initialization code
□            amount = new Double(100000);
47           rate = new Double(5.0);
48           years = new Integer(15);
⇨         }
50
51 ⊞     public payment1.ApplicationBean1 getApplicationBean1() {...}
54
```

```
49:1    INS
```

Debugger			
Local Variables			
Name		Value	
⊟ this		#5790	
__placeholder		0	
⊞ amount		100000.0	
payment		null	
⊞ rate		5.0	
⊞ years		15	
⊞ super			

Figure 9–4 Displaying LoanBean fields

Creator Tip

It's easy to change the value of a local variable in memory with Creator. Just click the '+' on any variable, then click the rounded box. Use the custom editor to modify the value. This feature can be very handy for checking out boundary conditions and algorithm correctness during debugging.

Creator Tip

There are other ways to step through your code in Creator. You can, for instance, Step Into a method or Step Out of a method. You can also move the cursor to a line and select Run to Cursor.

9.5 Tracking Variables

Now let's make Creator execute our program to the next breakpoint. To do this, click Continue from the Debug menu. The Continue command makes the Creator debugger continue execution from the current breakpoint to the next one.

Inside the **LoanBean.java** window, you'll see that Creator has stopped execution at the second breakpoint. This is the first statement in the getPayment() method (Line 108), and is highlighted in green. Note that this method calculates the loan payment, using local variables to store data. Let's see how to monitor these variables with a Creator debugger feature called *tracking*. Here are the steps.

1. Click the '+' for the this reference in the Local Variables window. You should see the same values for the LoanBean fields as before.
2. Click Step Over from the Debug toolbar. This moves the focus to Line 109.

   In the Local Variables display of the Debugger window, a new entry appears above the this reference. The local variable monthly_interest shows up with a value of 0.00416666.

3. Click Step Over from the Debug toolbar. This moves the focus to Line 110.

   The local variable months appears in the Local Variables display with a value of 180.

4. Click Step Over one more time. The LoanBean payment field changes to a value of 790.79362. Figure 9–5 shows the result.
5. Click Continue from the Debug toolbar and switch to the Calculator page in your browser. You will see a Loan Payment of $790.79 displayed on the page.

TroubleShooting Tip

You can repeat this whole exercise again by changing any of the input fields on the Calculator page. When you click the Calculate button and return to the Creator screen, you will see the program stop at the same breakpoint. By stepping through getPayment() as before, you can see the changed values in the Local Variables display. When you click Continue in the debugger, the Calculator page will show the new payment. This is a handy way to test an algorithm and see whether a method is working correctly for a wide range of input test values.

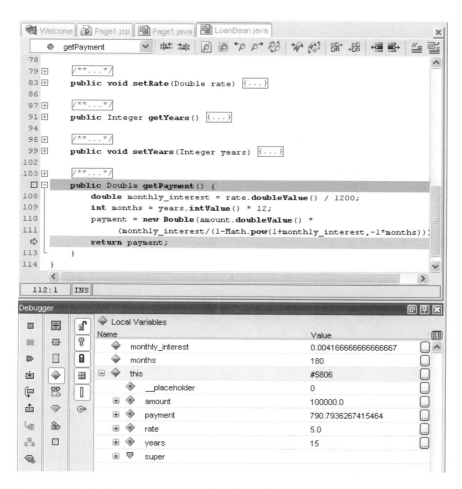

Figure 9–5 Displaying **getPayment()** local variables

9.6 Setting Watches

There are several local variables inside the getPayment() method, but the LoanBean payment field is the most important. Since this field holds the payment amount that will be displayed on our web page, let's use another feature of the Creator debugger called a *watch*. With watches, you can monitor key variables as they change values during the execution of a program. Whereas the Local Variables window shows values for variables in the currently executing method, the Watch window monitors values of variables selected by you (including class fields). Here's how to set a watch.

1. In the second column of the Debugger window, click the Local Variables icon to make the display go away.
2. Now click the Watches icon to make this display show up.
3. Click the Breakpoints icon to show the current list of breakpoints. (You may have to make the Debugger window larger.)
4. In the Breakpoints display, disable all the breakpoints by clicking the check-boxes underneath the Enabled heading. (Alternatively, you can right-click in the Breakpoints display and select Disable All.)
5. Put a new breakpoint at line 112 in **LoanBean.java** where `payment` is set to the new calculated amount. To do this, place the cursor at the line, right-click, and choose Toggle Breakpoint. Line 112 should now be highlighted in red.
6. Right-click line 112 on the `payment` variable and select New Watch. The Watch Expression dialog should display the `payment` variable.
7. Click OK to make `payment` a watch variable.

The `payment` variable should appear in the Watches display of the Debugger window. Note that its value is not defined at this point.

Now return to your browser to interact with the Calculator page. Supply the following input: **100000** for Loan Amount, **5.0** for Interest Rate, and **30** for Loan Term. Click the Calculate button and switch back to the Creator screen. Figure 9–6 shows the result for the Watches and Breakpoints display. In the Watches display, the value of the `payment` field is now set to the current payment. (If you didn't supply the same input fields on the Calculator page, your `payment` variable will have a different value from ours.)

Click Continue on the Creator toolbar. When you go back to the Calculator page, you will see the same loan payment amount displayed. Now type in various input values for the amount, interest rate, and loan term. Click the Calculate button again and switch back to the Creator screen. Click Continue when the breakpoint at line 112 is reached and is highlighted in green. Each time you do this, the `payment` watch variable displays the new loan payment. This is the same value that is printed on the Calculator web page in your browser.

TroubleShooting Tip

Watches are a handy way to monitor how a variable changes during the execution of a program. Use Continue in Creator to step through the breakpoints as you do this.

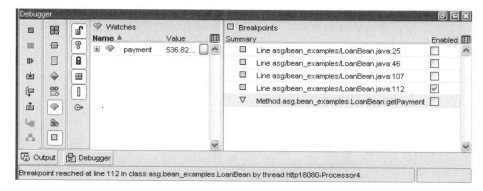

Figure 9–6 **Monitoring watches**

9.7   Using the Call Stack

The Java Virtual Machine executes your Java code and maintains a call stack list. This list shows the order of method calls that have been invoked but have not yet returned (this type of list is often called a *call chain*). The current method is at the top of the list, and the invocations of each parent method appears below it as you work down the call list.

To see the Call Stack in action, click the Calculate button on the Calculator web page in your browser. Now switch back to Creator and make sure line 112 is highlighted in green. Click the Call Stack icon in the second column of the Debugger window and remove the other displays (click the Watches and Breakpoints icons). Figure 9–7 shows the result. At the top of the Call Stack is the current method LoanBean.getPayment(), which was called from a series of native methods in the underlying system. If you scroll through this display, you'll see various calls to binder methods, UI components, and servlets. At the very bottom of the Call Stack is Thread.run(), which starts it all.

Creator also lets you manipulate the Call Stack. When you click **Debug** on the Creator menu bar, you'll see a choice called **Stack** on the dropdown list. With the Call Stack, you can select from any of the following.

> Make Callee Current
> Make Caller Current
> Pop Topmost Call

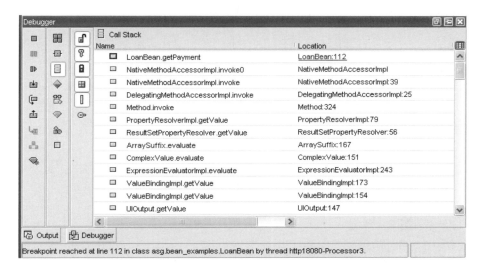

Figure 9–7 Displaying the Call Stack

The first two commands let you change the current method of the call stack. The pop command removes the current method from the top of the stack.

TroubleShooting Tip

The Call Stack display is useful when your program calls a method and you aren't sure why. When you set a breakpoint at a method and run your program, the Call Stack tells you the call chain of methods up to and including the breakpoint. You can learn a lot about how things happen by taking a closer look at the Call Stack. Call stacks are also handy when you need to determine which method threw an exception.

9.8 Detecting Exceptions

When using Creator's debugger, you can detect and track thrown exceptions. We'll show you how to do this now.

Our working Calculator program doesn't throw any exceptions directly, but it does generate an internal exception that is handled by JSF. This happens when you don't type anything in one of the input text fields and click the Calculate button. In this case, an error message appears on the Calculator page, because an exception was thrown and handled.

Here are the steps for detecting an exception with the debugger.

1. Remove all breakpoints. To do this, open the Debugger window and bring up the Breakpoint display. Right-click anywhere in the Breakpoint display, and select Delete All. A pop-up window appears to prompt you for the deletion. Answer Yes.
2. Click on the Debug toolbar and select New Breakpoint.
3. In the dropdown list for Breakpoint Type, select Exception.
4. In the dropdown list for Package Name, select `java.util`. (If the package name does not appear in the list, type it in.)
5. In the dropdown list for Exception Class Name, choose MissingResourceException. (Again, type in the name if it doesn't appear in the dropdown list.)
6. In the dropdown list for Stop On, choose Exception Caught, as shown in Figure 9–8.

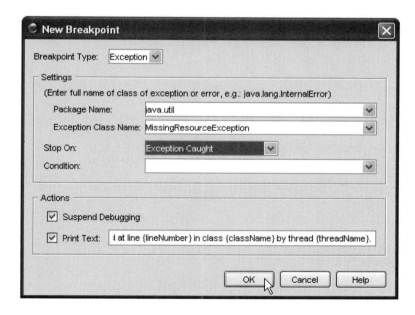

Figure 9–8 **Setting a breakpoint on a caught exception**

7. Click the OK button. In the Breakpoint display of the Debugger window, you should see the exception enabled.
8. If line 112 is still highlighted in green, click Continue from the Debug toolbar.
9. Switch to the Calculator page and clear the input for the Interest Rate field. Click the Calculate button.

Figure 9–9 shows you what the Call Stack in the Debugger window looks like when you switch back to Creator. At the bottom of the screen, you see this error message.

```
Exception java.util.MissingResourceException reached at line ?
in class java.util.ResourceBundle . . .
```

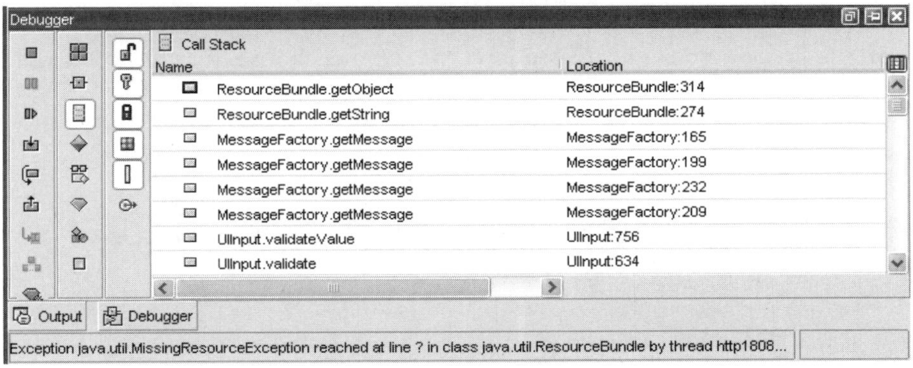

Figure 9–9 **Exception caught**

Because you did not type anything into the interest rate input field, a `MissingResourceException` was caught by the `ResourceBundle()` method. The line number appears as ? in the error message because the source code for this method is not available to Creator. At the top of the Call Stack, you will see `ResourceBundle.getObject()` as the current method.

Go to the Breakpoint display in the Debugger window and disable the Exception breakpoint by unchecking the Enabled checkbox. Now click Continue from the Debug toolbar and execution resumes. In the Calculator page, the following error message appears from the Validator since the exception was handled.

```
Validation Error: "interestRate": Value is required.
```

Creator Tip

In Creator, click New Breakpoint again from the Debug toolbar. In the dialog box, choose Exception at the top and then peruse the choices in the checkbox for Package Name. Note that there are lots of choices. If you scroll down and select javax.faces, *for instance, you'll see the choices for Exception Class Name change, too. (The only choice here is* FacesException.*) If you examine the checkbox for Stop On, you'll notice that you can monitor uncaught exceptions as well as caught exceptions, or both. All this gives you a variety of ways to track exceptions as you debug your applications with Creator.*

9.9   Using Log Files

There are two ways to write debugging information to your application server's log file. You can use a Java System.out.println() statement or Creator's log() method. Let's look at Java print statements first, since they can be used in any Java source file (including your own JavaBeans components, such as LoanBean).

Method System.out.println()

It's easy to write to a Creator log file with simple Java print statements. Here are some examples.

```
System.out.println("amount = " + this.amount);
System.out.println("button1_action called");
System.out.println("input: " + (Double)inputText1.getValue());
```

Let's assume that Creator is installed on the C: drive. If you are using the J2EE application server, the log file is

C:\Sun\Creator\SunAppServer8\domains\creator\logs\server.log

On our system, we use the following commands to examine the output from Java `println()` statements.

```
$ cd C:\Sun\Creator\SunAppServer8\domains\creator\logs
$ tail -30 server.log
. . .
...amount = 120000
...button1_action called
...input: 4.5
```

The Unix `tail` command displays the last 30 lines of the log file.

Creator Tip

The server log file is also accessible from the Server Navigator window in Creator. In the Server Navigator window, right-click Deployment Server and select View Server Log. The server log is displayed at the bottom of your screen in its own Output window.

Let's write to the log file now from the application to show you how it works. Here's what you need to do.

1. Bring up the **Page1.jsp** screen in Creator.
2. Double-click the Calculate button. This makes Creator write Java code for the button action method.

   Creator opens the **Page1.java** file and puts the cursor in the `calculate_action()` method.

3. Add the following `println()` statement to the button handler.

```
public java.lang.String calculate_action() {
    System.out.println("button clicked");
    return null;
}
```

You don't need a button handler in this program, but we include it to show you how to write to log files. All the `println()` statement does is write to the log file. When the user clicks the Calculate button, JSF submits the page. If no validation errors occur, JSF invokes the button handler method. The `println()` output tells us that the `calculate_action()` method was invoked.

Recompile and redeploy the program. Click the Calculate button with *valid entries* for the amount, interest rate, and loan term.[3] The loan payment should appear on the Calculator page. When you examine the log file, the last line in the file should contain

```
button clicked
```

Method log()

The `log()` method, defined in FacesBean, is another way to write debugging information to the server log file. This method, however, can only be called from Creator's preconfigured managed bean files, since they extend the Faces-Bean class. Calls to `log()`, therefore, are valid only in **Page1.java**, **SessionBean1.java**, **ApplicationBean1.java**, or other page beans that you create in your project.

The `log()` method has two formats.

```
void log(java.lang.String);
void log(java.lang.String, java.lang.Throwable);
```

The first format is handy for printing event information (such as "button clicked"). The second format is useful in catch handlers with thrown exceptions.

```
catch (Exception e) {
    log("SQL ROWSET UPDATE ERROR", e);
    throw new FacesException(e);
}
```

Note that this form of the `log()` method uses the `Exception` object with the textual message you want to use.

The information from the `log()` method is available in Creator's output window. To see what this looks like, replace the `System.out.println()` statement in your button handler with a call to `log()`, as follows.

```
public java.lang.String calculate_action() {
    log("button clicked");
    return null;
}
```

---

3. Remember that validation errors cause the life cycle process to skip some of life cycle stages and `calculate_action()` won't be called (see "JSF Request-Response Life Cycle Process" on page 185).

Now deploy and run the application. After you click the Calculate button and return to Creator, here's how to display the log file. From the Server Navigator window, select Deployment Server and right-click. Choose View Server Log. Near the end of the file you should see output similar to the following.

```
[#|2004-07-16T12:06:31.093-0700|INFO|
sun-appserver-pe8.0.0_01|
javax.enterprise.system.container.web|_ThreadID=12;
|WebModule[/payment1]button clicked|#]
```

(The output from the server log file on your system may be slightly different.) Note that the output from the `log()` method shows you more than the text you called it with. The output includes date and time information, the thread ID of your application, and the web module name (project name).

9.10 Finish Debugging

To finish your debugging session, click Debug on the Creator menu bar and select Finish Sessions. A popup menu may appear with details about the debugging session. Click the checkbox if you want to suppress this popup menu in future calls.

TroubleShooting Tip

A good way to end a debugging session is to clear all breakpoints before you select Finish. In the Breakpoints display of the Debugger window, you can either disable your breakpoints or delete them.

9.11 Key Point Summary

- Defensive programming means that you plan ahead for debugging.
- An assertion is a boolean expression that is expected to be true at run time. If an assertion fails, the Java Virtual Machine throws an `AssertionError`.
- You can run and deploy programs with Creator in debug mode.
- Creator has debugging features with which you can set breakpoints, step through code, track variables, and set watches.
- The Creator Debugger window enables you to examine sessions, threads, the call stack, local variables, watches, classes, breakpoints, and properties.

- A breakpoint is a spot in your program at which the debugger stops the execution of your program.
- The Creator debugger can step you through your code one line at a time. You can also step in or out of a method or run your program to a selected line.
- Tracking allows you to follow the creation and initialization of a local variable in a method. Tracking is a handy way to see if a method is working correctly for a range of test values.
- Watches let you monitor key variables as they change values during the execution of a program. Creator lets you display watches as your program runs.
- The Call Stack shows you the order of method calls as your program runs, with the most recent method at the top. Call stacks are useful for determining when a method was called and which method threw an exception.
- The Creator debugger lets you select exception breakpoints from a wide variety of different Java packages.
- In debugging mode, you can set a breakpoint when an exception is caught, uncaught, or both.
- Creator lets you view the server log to which you can write from your code. Log files are useful to monitor program flow, show intermediate data, and determine whether an event occurred.
- The `log()` method is handy for displaying log information during debugging. This method can only be called from Creator's preconfigured managed bean files.

Index